If I'm a Christian, Why Be a Catholic?

The Biblical Roots of Catholic Faith

by
James E. Hanson, C.S.C.

PAULIST PRESS
New York/Mahwah

Acknowledgements

This book would never have been written had it not been for many people who contributed both their personal encouragement and their specialized talents. First I would like to thank Bro. Patrick Sopher, C.S.C., Provincial, Brothers of Holy Cross, South-West Province, and Bro. James Kell, C.S.C., Director of Personnel, for their fraternal support in giving me permission to spend a sabbatical year in Mexico researching and writing the original manuscript. Secondly I would like to thank Bro. Stephen Walsh, C.S.C., President of St. Edward's University, Anne Crane, Chair of Humanities, and Bro. Henry Altmiller, C.S.C., then Academic Dean, for their encouragement to spend 1981–82 in sabbatical travel and writing.

A special debt of gratitude is also owed to Grace Reardon, Bro. Gerald Mueller, C.S.C., and Martha Anne Zivley for their helpful editorial suggestions and proofreading of the original manuscript which was submitted to Paulist Press.

At Paulist Press, Fr. Joe Scott, C.S.P. and Donald Brophy have provided painstaking and consistent help in revising the original manuscript to free it of excessive theological jargon and develop an interesting and attractive format.

Finally, I owe a profound debt of gratitude to Joseph Sprug, Chief Librarian, Scarborough-Phillips Library, St. Edward's University, for his superb and careful preparation of the Index and the Index of Biblical Texts. To him and his staff, no words can adequately convey my appreciation.

Nihil Obstat: Rev. Richard Teall, C.S.C., Censor Librorum
Imprimi potest: Brother Patrick Sopher, C.S.C., Provincial Superior,
   Brothers of the Holy Cross
Imprimatur: Vincent M. Harris, D.D., Bishop of Austin, Texas,
   August 27, 1982
The Nihil Obstat and Imprimatur are official declarations that a book or pamphlet is free of doctrinal or moral error. No implication is contained therein that those who have granted the Nihil Obstat and Imprimatur agree with the contents, opinions or statements expressed.

Contents

Dedication

With sincere gratitude to God for the faith he has given me, and to those who helped him communicate that faith:

To my mother, who taught me how to pray to Jesus and Mary,

To my late father, who taught me how to question everything,

To the Brothers of Holy Cross, who educated me in theology and still school me in spirituality.

Introduction

This book is born of personal pain and pastoral concern for those who struggle to integrate their experience of being human, their experience of being Catholic, and their experience of reflecting on the Bible. I have frequently been asked by college students and older adults, "Brother, what can I read that isn't trite, boring, or frustratingly abstract to learn more about our Catholic faith? Why does my boyfriend tell me I have to leave the Catholic Church to become a Christian? Do you believe in these Holy Spirit meetings or are those who attend just religious fanatics? Why are people using bumper stickers to say that Jesus is coming soon?"

Another whole string of questions arises from friends who have more successfully integrated their humanity than their Catholic faith: "Isn't religion a personal matter—who needs the Church or the Bible? Why is the Church 'meddling' in politics? Why doesn't the Pope stay out of our sex lives?" Personally I have searched and found no biblically based statement of Catholic faith that is up-to-date, comprehensive, and sensitive to such legitimate questions from the people. This book seeks to fill that gap.

To be human is essentially to form judgments of truth and to choose to do what one thinks one ought to do. But to be human is much fuller in its lived experience than in its essential definition. To be human is to grow, to search, to discover, to share what one has found, and to invite criticism of what one has shared. To be human is to know the warmth of being hugged and the loneliness of being rejected. To be human is to be the offspring of a family, to have friends, enemies, and acquaintances from the village, town, or city. To be human is to hunger physically, to hunger intellectually, to hunger emotionally, to hunger spiritually, always to want more. It is

1

precisely into that human hunger that God speaks his word as "food for life."

Despite the distance of history and culture, the Bible is unembarrassedly full of human people just like ourselves. Whether it be Abraham's anxiety over being childless, Rebecca's intrigue to get the best for her favorite son, the group orgy around the golden calf, the disarming candor of Qoheleth as a mature scholar and retired teacher, Elizabeth's frank announcement of Mary's unexpected pregnancy, the special friendship of Jesus for John, or Paul's being carried up "to the third heaven"—these kinds of experiences live on in our human family today. Each chapter of the book presents human people in their historical reality.

To be Catholic today is to live in the pluralism of the post-Vatican II Church. For many the experience is as confusing as it is renewing. Gradually the dust is settling as the wheat is separated from the chaff while gently nurturing new shoots of life at the same time (Mt 13:25–30). This author is convinced that all truth is beautiful and that the revealed truth of Catholic faith is compellingly beautiful when it is properly understood. In John 10:14 Jesus called himself the good shepherd who knows his sheep and is known by them. When Pope Gregory the Great preached on that text, he wrote, "If someone does not love the truth, it is because he has not yet recognized it."[1]

Each Catholic brings personal associations derived from life experience and religious education about what is central to faith and what is contrary to faith. This book provides a journey through the primary sources of Scripture and official Catholic teaching. Reflection on these sources will both affirm one's personal perceptions when they are adequately informed and challenge them when they lack a knowledge of the sources of faith. My goal is to affirm legitimate pluralism within the Church and to challenge simultaneously contemporary currents which exceed the boundaries of justice, holiness, and mutually forgiving love so that the unity of truth and the unity of the Spirit can be even more deeply renewed (Mt 7:16).

For Catholics, personal Bible reading as recommended by
Vatican II and Bible study groups in the home has been both a
tremendous blessing to the faith of the Church and another
source of confusion to many. Catholic biblical scholars are
only just now publishing solid Scripture commentaries de-
signed for the laity which hungers to understand the inspired
texts. In the absence of balanced study aids, many have wound
up "demythologizing" the Bible until it is entirely empty of
miracle, historical fact, or transcendent truth. At the opposite
extreme others have been intellectually seduced by the decep-
tive clarity of twentieth century fundamentalism. The former
group tends to eliminate the formally supernatural from divine revelation and personal faith. The latter group tends to
deny the historically conditioned nature of the inspired texts
and to ignore the finite structures of human knowing through
which God speaks his word. Neither extreme is consistent
with Catholic faith. Chapter I relates the revelation of the Old
Testament patriarchs to Catholic teaching on the dynamics of
revelation, faith, tradition, and Scripture. The whole book
progresses historically. The Old Testament history is organized around an introduction by way of the patriarchs, and
then three chapters each devoted to an historical experience
of divine transformation: the exodus, the Babylonian captivity
and the Maccabean crisis. This section culminates with a
chapter on Old Testament wisdom which also explains why
Catholics use the longer list of inspired books in the Old
Testament.

Convinced that the unity of the Old and New Testaments
is found in the progressive revelation of God in Christ, I treat
the revelation of Christ as it developed historically in the
primitive Church. Chapter VI thus explains the oral preaching of Jesus as the risen Lord, Chapter VII treats the handing
on of the words and deeds of Jesus about the Kingdom of God,
and Chapter VIII is devoted to the spread of the Church and
the life and worship of its earliest members. In this way the
whole book progresses historically, showing how changing circumstances, human problems, sin, and grace have all shaped

the inspired and inerrant Scriptures from the six days of
creation in Genesis to the reign of Christ for a thousand years
in Revelation.

And yet the book tries to be much more than an introduction to the history of Palestine or a literary-critical analysis of
the Scriptures. First, it seeks to help the reader understand
the human context, then move to the Scripture, Church teaching, and liturgy as they emerge from and relate to the historical context. In this way, Scripture, Church teaching, liturgy,
and human experience are all seen in faith as "signs of Christ
among us," the eternal Word.[2] Second, the book is written as
an invitation to a deeper, more comprehensive Catholic Christian faith. As such it might most technically be labeled "an
evangelizing catechesis for adults." But since it is aimed at the
non-specialist in theology, technical jargon has been generally
relegated to the notes. In this way I have tried to make the
prose both clear and interesting. More theologically trained
readers can consult the notes to find the key sources for every
critical theological choice I have made.

If Catholics must begin evangelizing, as Pope Paul VI
taught, by evangelizing the Church,[3] this book is not intended
for Catholics only. Hopefully ecumenically-minded Protestant
and Orthodox Christians will find its scripturally based pre-
sentation a common source for continuing to seek unity with
one another. To them the book is offered as an invitation to
produce similar books written out of their own ecclesial traditions. That would help all of us stretch in new ecumenical
directions without diluting the faith we now possess.

Likewise the book is offered to the unchurched who are
seeking truth, meaning, hope, and the assurance that they are
loved. Before all else the Gospel offers that message of the
Father's love to everyone. I beg you not to substitute the
reading of this book for reading the Bible. And when you read
the Bible I encourage you to have the courage to pray to the
Holy Spirit for the light of understanding and a heart open to
what is true. In that way, may this book help you to find your
way into the family of the Church.

While I have tried to avoid a polemical tone and make

this book a joyful announcement of salvation, I am especially indebted to two contemporary adversaries of the Catholic Church without whose goading I would never have ventured into this project. I refer not to individuals alienated from the Church by misunderstanding and sin on both sides, but rather to the two primary opponents of faith in the twentieth century: *militant atheism* on the one hand, and *sects and cults* on the other. *Militant atheism* believes that the Catholic Church must be destroyed as an enemy of human progress. The first attempt to assassinate Pope John Paul II and the struggles of the Church for religious freedom in communist countries are ample evidence that such hostility is real and not imagined. At the opposite extreme the rise of popular "mysticism," the lack of spiritual dynamism in some local churches, the passion for instant religious experience, and the desire for quick answers to the complexity of modern life have all led to the rapid rise of new sects and cults. Many of these sects and cults are explicitly anti-ecumenical and professedly anti-Catholic. They actively try to proselytize Catholics out of their Church, thus further damaging the visible unity of the body of Christ and reducing the preaching of the word to a few texts of Scripture usually quoted out of context. Less educated Catholics are again being inundated with pamphlets blithely telling them that the Catholic Church is "the whore of Babylon," that "the Pope is the anti-Christ," that the sacraments are "man-made rituals," and that one can only "accept Jesus and be saved" by renouncing the Catholic Church.

Chapters II and VII amply show that the Catholic Church understands its mission of salvation to include human promotion for the progress and liberation of all peoples. Chapters IV and VIII show that the ministerial priesthood and the celebration of the sacraments are deeply rooted in Scripture and integrally related to the personal following of Jesus ever since Pentecost in 33 A.D.

Pope John Paul II has repeatedly affirmed that the Catholic Church has a special affection for the poor. In addition to motivating needed action on behalf of justice for the poor in the secular arena, this book hopes to be a useful resource for parish evangelists and catechists who work more in the formally religious spheres. I would especially like the book to be of service to those readers who are working with the Hispanic poor and daily face their religious questions and the terrible family problems caused by the rise of proselytism in their neighborhoods. The origin of this book is thus deeply indebted to the sufferings of the Hispanic poor who have done so much to reveal the marvelous power of God to me:

> God chose those whom the world considers absurd to shame the wise; he singled out the weak of this world to shame the strong. He chose the world's lowborn and despised, those who count for nothing, to reduce to nothing those who were something; so that mankind can do no boasting before God (1 Cor 1:27–29).[4]

Notes

1. The translation is my own. See Gregory the Great, Homily 14, 3–6; PL 76, 1129–30.

2. In this way I have tried to let this book develop the four kinds of signs of Christ as outlined by the *National Catechetical Directory: Sharing the Light of Faith*. The directory uses the more technical terms: biblical signs, ecclesial signs, liturgical signs, and natural signs. Since all of these are found in Scripture, I have not tried to follow any artificially rigid scheme of reflecting on them. I develop their implications for revelation and faith as they emerge in the historical development of the inspired text.

3. Pope Paul VI, "On Evangelization in the Modern World": Apostolic Exhortation, *Evangelii Nuntiandi*, December 8, 1975; Eng. trans. U.S. Catholic Conference, Washington, D.C., 1976, par. 15, p. 13.

4. The New American Bible is quoted throughout. I have taken the liberty to insert the more ancient personal name "Yahweh" for "the Lord" in Scriptures dating from the period of Abraham to the exile. In Luke 1:28 I have at times preferred "full of grace" to "highly favored one" simply to show the theological connection with later ecclesial tradition.

Chapter I

The Old Testament Patriarchs and Catholic Teaching on Divine Revelation

"My father was a wandering Aramean."
—Dt 26:5

The Old Testament

Why was the Old Testament written?

Catholic Bibles include forty-six books in the Old Testament. These writings took their present shape gradually from the time of Abraham (ca. 1850 B.C.) to the last book of the Old Testament, "The Wisdom of Solomon" (ca. 150 B.C.). The central event in the Old Testament is Israel's exodus from slavery in Egypt (ca. 1285 B.C.). The certainty that *God* had helped them escape, the feeling of exultation in their new freedom, and the promise that he would bring them back to the land of Abraham were the human circumstances in which the Holy Spirit inspired the people to write the song of Moses and Miriam (Ex 15:1–21). It is one of the oldest Hebrew poems in the Bible.

The Israelites knew, however, that the God of their exodus was also the God of their ancestors. Their patriarchs or tribal fathers had been guided by the same God (Ex 3:6) at least six hundred years earlier. As a result, the Israelites wanted to remember the earliest hints of God's special care for them. So they began to collect the earliest oral traditions and fragmentary bits of tribal literature. Genesis 12—50 is the result. It should be read as the prologue to the formation of the exodus tribes as God's covenant people.

The other books of the Old Testament look back to the Book of Exodus in the way we Christians look back to Jesus. The historical books, the prophets, and the wisdom books should be read as further development, renewal, reform, and prayerful reflection on what happened to Israel in the exodus. The lived experience of Abraham pre-dates the inspired meditations on God, creation, and the spread of sin which are revealed in Genesis 1—11. Genesis 12, then, not Genesis 1, is the place to begin to study the historical origins of Judaeo-Christian faith.[1]

Why do Christians read the Old Testament?

Christians have always read the Old Testament for at least four reasons: (1) to remember our spiritual past helps us renew our faith today; (2) to know the God of the Old Testament is to know the Father of Jesus; (3) to read the Old Testament is to continue the apostolic practice of the early Church; (4) to read the Old Testament is to imitate the authors of the New Testament.

(1) *To remember our spiritual past helps us renew our faith today.*

When we reflect on our own personal histories, we are frequently amazed that we had the strength to endure some suffering or the energy to pull off some success. We sense the hand of God in our lives and thank him for all he has done for us. The Book of Deuteronomy used this approach with the Jews. It asked them *to remember* what God had done for them. Six hundred years earlier they had been aliens or slaves at the time of Moses. When the inspired author was writing in 621 B.C., the same families were middle-class Jews living in the comfort of Jerusalem. In their prosperity they tended to forget who they really were. They owed gratitude to God and should be able to feel compassion for the poor in their midst since they too had once been desperately poor. Like them, we today can also *remember* that our father Abraham was nothing but a wandering Aramean who lived almost four thousand years ago. We too can marvel at all God has done for us and open ourselves to the sufferings of those around us.[2]

In our own century, the theologian Louis Boyer once wrote that every Christian must first become a spiritual semite.[3] There is a Jewish-Arab thread of culture in the faith of each Christian. To become a spiritual semite is not just longing for "the good old days." Rather it flows from our desire to follow Jesus. A convinced disciple wants to become very much like the Master. The only Jesus of Christian faith was born a Jew, preached in Jewish synagogues, and participated in Jewish temple liturgies. Jesus was circumcised because he was a physical descendant of Abraham (Gen 17:10).[4]

(2) *To know the God of the Old Testament is to know the Father of Jesus.*

Jesus owed his Jewish faith, morality, prayer, and messianic hopes to the tradition that began with Abraham. The God he dared to call Abba, Daddy, was from the *Old* Testament. The twenty-seven books of the New Testament were gradually written only after Jesus was risen—probably between 50 and 150 A.D. The only God and Father of Jesus is the one revealed in the Old Testament.[5] The only Father we have in heaven is the one who began to speak to us in the Old Testament.

(3) *To read the Old Testament is to continue the apostolic practice of the early Church.*

Even before the New Testament was written, the primitive Church felt the freedom of the Spirit to discard many of the laws of the old covenant of Moses (Acts 15:22–29). They did not, however, feel free to discard the Old Testament. When the Gnostic heretic Marcion suggested in the second century that the God of the Old Testament was a God of wrath and the God of the New Testament was a God of love, Catholic Christians rejected this false distinction.[6] For orthodox Christians there is one God, one gradual revelation, and a genuine continuity

between what we believe today and what God revealed to the
family of Abraham. We, like the primitive Church, consider
ourselves to be the spiritual descendants of Abraham.

(4) *To read the Old Testament is to imitate the authors of
the New Testament.*
Both the Gospels of Matthew and Luke turn the reader's
gaze back to Abraham. Matthew opens his infancy narrative
by referring to David and Abraham. "A family record of Jesus
Christ, the son of David, son of Abraham" (Mt 1:1). For Matthew, this family record is continued in the Church. At the
end of this Gospel the risen Christ divinely orders that baptism replace circumcision and that the new faith in him be
spread to all the nations of the earth (Mt 28:18–20).[7] In this
way Matthew understands the Christian Church as the spiritual continuation of the family of Abraham. In Luke's infancy
narrative Mary understands her pregnancy as the divine fulfillment of God's promise "to Abraham." Mary understands
herself as a daughter of Abraham whom "all generations" will
call "blessed" (Gen 15:5 and Lk 1:55). Such Scriptures show
how Matthew and Luke must have pored over the Old Testament to give substance to their proclamation that Jesus is its
perfect fulfillment. Their example invites us to mine the Old
Testament to continue to testify to Jesus in our own lives.

The Patriarchs: Abraham, Isaac, Jacob, and Joseph

What do we really know about Abraham and his family?

Historically Abraham lived sometime between 2000 and
1750 B.C. He and his extended family first appear in the Bible
in Genesis 12. Most biblical historians place Abraham about
1850 B.C. The episodes in the Abraham cycle correlate with
the archeological investigation of Middle Bronze Palestine.
Caravan routes, customs of hospitality, semitic names, laws

for business and commerce all betray historical memories—if not the scientific history we prefer today. In short, if Christians value Abraham and the other patriarchs because of faith, there is no reason to dismiss them as pure myth or legend.[8] In critical historical investigation, Abraham stands as the semitic nomad, that "wandering Aramean," with whom biblical history began.

How did God speak to Abraham?

Not only biblical history, but also biblical revelation began at the time of Abraham. Revelation is the gradual unveiling of God hidden in mystery; it is the divine communication of his will for all peoples; revelation finally is God's promises to his people that through him the forces of life in history will triumph over the forces of death. It is divine revelation which invites and makes possible the human response of faith. This revelation—present incipiently in all cultures—according to St. Paul (Rom 2:14–15) came to a new force and clarity in the life of Abraham. God said to Abraham that he should "leave" the land of his youth and go "to a land that I will show you."[9] By doing that God would bless "all the communities of the earth" through Abraham. Genesis says, "Abraham went . . ." (Gen 12:1–4).

When Abraham left the Tigris-Euphrates Valley to wander south into Palestine, the history of Judaeo-Christian revelation began. Scripture does not tell us *how* Abraham heard or knew that his God was telling him to move. It does not portray Abraham as the subject of mystical experiences. He does not receive visions or interior voices or unmistakable interior promptings of the divine Spirit like the prophets. There is an "ordinariness," a "this-worldliness" about Abraham and his wives and children and tents and cattle that makes him very human.

Contemporary research on Middle Bronze Mesopotamia reveals that Abraham's time was an historical period of great social turbulence.[10] It thus seems most likely to conjecture that Abraham "heard God speak" through "the signs of the times."[11] Somehow Abraham knew that God wanted him to move his wife and cattle toward the south. That's all he knew. They had to leave the intimacy of the extended family and the security of their own culture. Away from Abraham's father, Terah, they would have to risk the loneliness and danger of travel and future hardship.[12]

What did God reveal to Abraham?

From Abraham on, the human family knew with the certitude of faith that it was called to be a pilgrim people,[13] to journey with God through never-ending changes. As pilgrims with Abraham, the human family knows itself to be "called, blessed, and promised" a new historical future by God (Gen 12:2–3; 15:5–6). For Abraham's family, there was no concept of heaven, hell, purgatory, or eternal judgment by God. To be "blessed" by God was to be gifted with long life, children, cattle, and land. To be cursed was to suffer childlessness, attack from enemy tribes, famine, violent or premature death.[14]

Given these human expectations Abraham awaited a male heir from his wife to continue his line and fulfill God's promise of blessing. As Sarah's fertility cycle waned with the advance of old age, Abraham struggled with doubt and fear about their future.[15] In that state of anxiety, Abraham received a further revelation from God. God "cut a covenant" with Abraham and promised to protect Abraham and his descendants from all threat of destruction. As Abraham's covenant partner, God revealed himself to be a protector. "Fear not, Abram! I am your shield...." Then God said to Abraham, "Look up at the sky and count the stars, if you can. Just so ... shall your descendants be" (Gen 15:1–6).

How did God fulfill his promise of many descendants to Abraham?

From Genesis 15 on, an ever wider circle of communion in faith develops in the history of the Old Testament: clan life with Abraham and Isaac developed into the larger circle of the twelve distinct tribes of Jacob.[16] The tribe was a larger communion than the clan. At Mount Sinai with Moses, the twelve tribes agreed in solemn covenant to become one priestly people with Yahweh God as their king.[17] When David conquered Jerusalem, the chosen people became a nation-state (2 Sam 2:1–4; 5:1–5). Much of the rest of the history of the Old Testament is the struggle to adapt and renew that sense of peoplehood to new economic and political circumstances while remaining faithful to God and their sacred covenant with him. In the New Testament, the coming of the Spirit at Pentecost extended the communion of God with his chosen ones to all the peoples of the earth (Acts 2:5–6). When we are baptized into the new covenant in Jesus' blood, we too are spiritual heirs of Abraham. In this way God still commits himself to be our shield too.

Why did God ask Abraham to sacrifice his son Isaac (Gen 22:2)?

The faith of Abraham depicted in Genesis was not only obedient and patient; it was also driven to the most unthinkable limits of paradox. "Take your son, your only one, whom you love, and ... offer him as a holocaust ..." (Gen 22:2). To sacrifice is to offer to God what already belongs to God as its Creator. To sacrifice to God what one loves most is the deepest depth to which faith can go. It requires deep trust to believe that Yahweh will fill the sense of loss which is caused by a difficult personal sacrifice. Because Abraham was willing to give up Isaac, Isaac became God's own in a new sense. Abraham's family thus became "consecrated" or "holy" in a new way. God, however, did not allow their consecration to him to be destructive of their created humanity.[18] Rather we can conjecture that such an experience freed the family from the natural instincts of possessiveness and dependency. Furthermore God revealed himself as the "awesome one of Isaac" who will give his people everything twice: once by nature; once by grace (cf. Gen 31:42, 53).[19]

What else did God reveal through Isaac, Jacob, and Joseph?

Besides the account of Isaac's brush with sacrifice, Genesis recalls only his delightful romance with Rebekah (Gen 24). Nothing else remains of Isaac's early biography. Isaac's life thus reveals God's transforming presence in the human experiences of near-death (Gen 22:10) and the joy of male-female companionship. "In his love for her (Rebekah) Isaac found solace after the death of his mother Sarah" (Gen 24:67).

With Jacob the patriarchal faith loses its image of moral innocence. Our father in the faith, Jacob, is depicted as a "mama's boy" (Gen 25:27–28) conniving with his mother to cheat his blood brother (Gen 27). This is hardly a spiritually uplifting thought. However, through Jacob God revealed two very important truths about the way he works with his people. First, God confounds human expectations and social conventions in his choice of leaders; he picks the younger brothers over the older ones (Gen 25:19–20).[20] Second, God's action of forming a people centered in himself is not doomed to failure because its human leaders are weak or immoral. The God of Jacob triumphed in spite of Jacob and formed Israel (Gen 32:23–32). This revelation can still give hope to the modern family of Abraham when it is confused or appalled by the quality of its leadership.

Genesis reveals Joseph to be almost the reverse of his father Jacob. The patriarch Joseph was gifted with wisdom (Gen 37:5–11; 41:39), sufffered innocently (Gen 37:28) and forgave his betrayers (Gen 45:1–3; 50:15–21). Joseph thus combines practical administrative skill, prayerfulness, and high moral integrity (Gen 39:6–10). He is also the historical transition from the freedom of nomadic life to the disastrous effects of imperial politics and court intrigue (Gen 39:19–20; 41:40–41). In Genesis to leave the desert and live on a farm or enter a city is to live like Cain, not Abel (Gen 4:17). To live in a city is frequently to be robbed of the legitimate fruits of one's labor by a power elite. The changing fortunes of Joseph's life in Egypt hint at the themes of the abuse of power and the danger of monarchy. Centuries later the judges and prophets of Israel will remember what happened and warn the people against enslaving themselves in oppressive structures (1 Sam 8:10–18). With Joseph, however, the gentleness of kindly speech reassures his brothers of his wise use of Egyptian political power (Gen 50:21).

Relation of the Patriarchs to Catholic Faith

What do Catholics believe about the place of Abraham in God's plan for history?

In Catholic teaching the call of Abraham to become a great nation was part of God's preparation for the Gospel, the fullness of revelation.[21] Accordingly Catholic faith understands revelation not as the divine unveiling of strange secrets about the past or the future plan of God for history. That superstitious view of revelation borders on fortune telling. Catholic faith, therefore, understands revelation as God making known himself and the hidden purpose of his will. This revelation consists in the deeds and words of God in history. His deeds manifest who he is and confirm his will to save all people. His words clarify the meaning and proclaim the hope contained in his deeds. In Genesis 12 Abraham is God's first response to the spread of murder and social chaos in Genesis 3—11. God's words to Abraham about the "promised land" and "many descendants" point to the Christian Church as "the new Israel" and baptism as the sign of belonging to God which replaced circumcision. For Catholic faith, Abraham begins that history of divine revelation which was closed with the death of the New Testament apostles. "By this revelation . . . the deepest truth about God and the salvation of man is made clear to us in Christ . . . the Mediator and . . . the fullness of revelation."[22]

Why do Catholics believe in both Scripture and tradition?

The inspired words of Genesis and Deuteronomy which reveal God's deeds and words about Abraham took over a thousand years to assume their final shape in the Bible. Oral tradition (the action of the Holy Spirit in the community of faith) was handed on by various people and was gradually crystallized into the written words of the inspired Scriptures we now venerate. This pattern of oral tradition being codified into inspired written Scriptures recurs throughout the Old and New Testaments. The community judged, purified, and continually reshaped its inspired tradition before it became inspired Scripture. Thus because Scripture is a product of inspired oral tradition and God is the author of both, Catholic faith reveres both Sacred Scripture and sacred tradition. "For both of them, flowing from the same divine wellspring, in a certain way merge into a unity and tend toward the same end."[23]

For Catholics, in what sense are the inspired Scriptures free from error?

The inspired character of the Scriptures consists in their having God as their principal author who used men and women as "true authors." Since, for Catholics, the Scriptures are inspired by the Holy Spirit, "it follows that the books of Scripture must be acknowledged as teaching firmly, faithfully, and without error that truth which God wanted put into the sacred writings for the sake of our salvation."[24] Thus Catholics look to the Bible for inerrant truth about God and his will for all people, but not for inerrant truth about history, science, or other forms of secular knowledge.

Why don't Catholics take the Bible literally?

There are at least three reasons Catholics do not take the Bible literally.

(1) Internal evidence within the Bible does not allow it. For example, was the first male human created before everything else (Gen 2:7) or only after everything else (Gen 1:27)? Did John the Baptist recognize Jesus at his baptism (Mt 3:14) or fail to recognize Jesus during the baptism (Jn 1:31)? Evidence of such internal contradictions could be multiplied at length. Therefore, according to Catholic teaching, the interpreter of Scripture "should carefully investigate what meaning the sacred writers really intended, and what God wanted to be manifest by means of their words."[25]

(2) Trying to take the Bible literally confuses the concepts of divine inspiration and inerrancy with diabolical possession and interior slavery to a supernatural power. When God speaks his word, it humanizes those who hear it. They remain free. The inspired authors did not become puppets or gods. They remained humans with finite minds. Therefore the inspired authors expressed themselves in the historical circumstances, cultural styles, and customs of their own period. Thus the modern interpreter needs to determine the literary form of an inspired passage. By contrast, in authenticated cases of diabolical possession, people become puppets spouting obscenities and embarrassing those around them by public "revelation" of their most secret sins. Victims of diabolical possession do things they do not want to do. Inspired authors, on the other hand, actively cooperate with God, speaking his revelation in their personal uniqueness and cultural style. Because God created that uniqueness, he delights in its exercise.

(3) The claim to "take the Bible literally" is utterly novel. Neither Scripture, nor the Fathers of the Church in the early centuries, nor the Protestant Reformers in the sixteenth century ever suggest that a Christian should "take the Bible literally." This modern movement began as one American Protestant way of responding to Darwin and other attacks on the authority of the Bible in the nineteenth century. It received its most thorough development when conservative Presbyterian theologians began to speak of "the fundamentals" of Christianity at their seminary in Princeton, New

Jersey. Their theology was coupled with popular preaching that Jesus was returning soon and summarized in the *Scofield Reference Bible.*

Without literal interpretation, how do Catholics stand firmly on God's word?

When the word of God is heard either through sacred tradition orally or through Sacred Scripture interpreted according to the intention of its inspired author, then the Christian is obliged, according to Catholic teaching, to the obedience of faith. In this way Catholic teaching asks every Christian to continue the same response to revelation which Abraham gave in Genesis 12. He had no Scriptures, only his faith. Such a human response to revelation is, however, itself a divine gift of the Holy Spirit (Rom 16:26; cf. 1:5; 2 Cor 10:5–6). Such divine help gives "joy and ease to everyone in assenting to the truth and believing it."[26]

Why do Catholics still use Church authority to guide their interpretation of Scripture?

Catholic teaching notes a difference in the kinds of obedience to which different members of the Church are called by God. As the first Apostles in the New Testament "handed on" divine revelation in the infant Church (Acts 2:42) and the faithful "were taught" by the Apostles, so a distinction of roles continues in the Church today. The bishops as successors of the Apostles and the Pope as the successor of Peter have the responsibility of "handing on" revelation in the most formal sense. This is their ministry in the Church; they are not above the word of God, but are servants of the word of God. The general faithful "hold, practice, and profess" that word of God so that there results "a remarkable common effort . . . under the action of the one Holy Spirit."[27] For Catholics, sacred tradition, Sacred Scripture, and the teaching authority of the Church, by God's wise design, are so linked together "that one cannot stand without the others. . . . Working together under the one Holy Spirit, they all contribute to the salvation of souls."[28]

Do the Catholic bishops encourage individual Bible study?

Yes. Catholic teaching urges everyone to study the Scriptures and to pray over them. "For ignorance of the Scriptures is ignorance of Christ."[29] At Vatican II the bishops spoke of their hope for "a new surge of spiritual vitality from intensified veneration for God's word" (Is 40:8; cf. 1 Pet 1:23–25).[30]

What do Catholics think about those who believe in God, but not in the New Testament?

Historically neither Roman Catholics nor Christians in general are the only people who venerate the word of God spoken to Abraham. Through Abraham the three great monotheistic religions of Judaism, Christianity, and Islam share a common spiritual heritage. The Moslem peoples understand themselves to be the descendants of Abraham through his son Ishmael; the Jews are the most direct bloodline descendants through Isaac; we Christians are spiritual descendants through Christ (Gal 3:7).

Mindful of our common Abrahamic roots, Catholic faith looks upon the Moslems "with esteem." With them we adore God as Creator, Revealer, and Judge. With them we revere Jesus as a prophet (but they do not revere him as God). With them we venerate Mary and prize the moral life of prayer, almsgiving, and fasting.[31]

In the Jews Catholic faith finds its closest "spiritual bond" with a non-Christian religion. With the Jews we share a common call from Abraham, the revelation of God in the Old Testament, and the unity of Gentile and Jew in Christ (Eph 4:14–16). Likewise within the history of the Church we share with the Jews the Jewishness of Jesus, Mary, Joseph and the original Apostles and disciples. With Jews, Catholic Christians wish to pursue "biblical and theological studies and . . . brotherly dialogues." The Catholic Church "deplores . . . displays of anti-semitism directed against the Jews at any time and from any source."[32]

Finally Catholic faith, like Abraham, acknowledges that the God of Abraham can be partially known by human reason unaided by revelation.[33] Abraham, in gratitude for God's help to all the Palestinian peoples, did not hesitate to celebrate a communion meal of bread and wine with the pagan Arab priest, Melchizedek (Gen 14:17–20). Melchizedek, for his part, recognized that his God was the same as Abraham's God. Thus Melchizedek could lead them in a common prayer of blessing God. Likewise Catholic faith recognizes that elements of truth exist in all human minds which affirm the existence of God as the source and goal of created reality. All contemporary theists, who may lack the support of an authentic church home, but have reasoned their way to God, are modern "Melchizedeks." With them the Catholic Church wishes to bless and thank God for his goodness to all people.

Conclusion

How can we live the faith of the patriarchs today?

We can (1) open, (2) remember, (3) hand on, and (4) step out.

(1) *Open.* In our conversations with God we can stop telling him what we need or want. Instead we can let him tell us who he is. Like Abraham, we can use our daily anxieties to begin our prayer and ask God to manifest himself and his will to us as he did to Abraham. Doing this deepens our inward journey of faith and obedience to God. We can discover that God is our "awesome shield" as he was for the patriarchs.[34]

(2) *Remember.* We can reflect on our personal biographies in faith and thank God for who we are and for the various circumstances which have brought us to this time and this place. Accordingly we can find the interior freedom to let go and give our "beloved Isaacs" to God. Likewise we can remem-

ber the vivid humanity of many biblical characters and learn a deeper acceptance of the whole range of human feelings within ourselves. With Sarah, each of us can laugh in doubt at the divine promises to make us fruitful. With her we can laugh in joy when we discover those promises fulfilled "impossibly." With Jacob, each of us can wrestle with God until he subdues the conniving schemer in us and transforms us into members of Israel. With Joseph, each of us can forgive those who hurt us and use our careers to feed the poor and give wise counsel to those in power.

(3) *Hand On.* As Christians we can cherish, study, celebrate and share the heritage of faith which is ours from Abraham. Abraham's family today is handed on to future generations through oral tradition, Scripture, and the Church. We can study these as part of who we are and share our discoveries and delights with our children. Also we can learn a larger sense of who we are as Abraham's family by cultivating friendships with Jews, Moslems, and all who believe in God. To hand on that enlarged sense of the family of faith helps God broaden the communion he wants to create among all the peoples of the earth.

(4) *Step Out.* When Abraham heard God speak to him through the signs of the times, he uprooted his life and moved gropingly in that direction toward which he thought God was calling him. Abraham was neither a loner nor a capricious enthusiast; he lived a daily pilgrimage in faith as father of an extended clan. We too can discuss what God is doing in the social turbulence of today. In our families and communities we can discuss together: "Just where is God leading us for tomorrow or next year?" We too can decide to uproot ourselves from the familiar and the comfortable to try the novel and say "yes" to God in the mysterious. When we step out with the wisdom of a Joseph, such fidelity, obedience to God, and practical action transform the curse of sterility into the blessing of fruitfulness. To step out wisely in faith and act concretely allows us to believe that we are each contributing to God's plan to bring countless millions of people into that commu-

nion to which God is calling them. Then each of us can say with a new humility and a new pride, "My father was a wandering Aramean"; his name was Abraham.

Notes

1. Here we presume the general reliability of the four-source theory of the authorship of the Pentateuch. J-Source (the Yahwist) lived in the tenth century B.C. in Jerusalem and compiled his version of salvation history beginning with "a man" and "a woman" in the Garden of Bliss (Gen 2). This led into the sin of Adam ("mankind") and Eve ("life"); the history of the spread of this sin moves through Genesis 3—11. J's history of salvation begins in Genesis 12 with the call of Abraham and culminates in the coronation of David. Thus all of the past was seen as Yahweh's way of working to create the nation state of Israel. While Genesis 2—11 may preserve some ancient historical memories like the floods of the Tigris-Euphrates Valley (Gen 6:5—9:2) or the Babylonian skyscrapers like the tower of Babel (Gen 11:1-9), in general the characters of Genesis 2—11 are not historical. They are projections backward from the existing tribal life in the Middle East between 2000 and 1000 B.C. Thus, "Shem" is the eponymous ancestor of all "semites"; "Ham," the eponymous ancestor of all hamitic speaking Middle Easterners (the Egyptians, etc.). This "history" has no knowledge of contemporary events in the Far East, deep Africa, or the migrations of people through Polynesia to the Americas, etc. The characters in Genesis 2—11 should thus be read as universal types. They profoundly reveal the truth of the human condition as created by God and wounded by sin and the social evils which flow from sin. It is this truth which the inspired human author intends to reveal, and it is a distortion of Scripture to look for scientific history or biology or physics in the opening chapters of Genesis.

Genesis 1 was written by P-Source (the priests) and was originally probably a hymn sung in the temple in Jerusalem. Later it was carried into the Babylonian exile where the priests made this hymn the introduction to "the torah of Moses" (the Pentateuch). With no nation state and no temple, the priests reshaped the tradition to reveal God's goodness in all of creation, passing through a series of covenants leading up to Moses which definitely constituted Israel

—not as a political entity but as a holy priestly people set aside by God for torah observance and sabbath celebration.

The Book of Deuteronomy took its present shape during the religious reform and renewal movement authorized by King Josiah in 621 B.C. For all of these reasons Abraham, not Adam (mankind), is the historical point critically selected for beginning a reflection on the biblical origins of Catholic faith. For a more thorough explanation of the development of the four sources of the Pentateuch, see A. Weiser, *The Old Testament: Its Formation and Development*, Association Press, N.Y., 1968, pp. 99–142. See also Brevard G. Childs, *Introduction to the Old Testament as Scripture*, Fortress Press, Philadelphia, 1980, pp. 109–127.

2. In the New Testament the theme of remembering reaches its climax when Jesus institutes the Eucharist as a "remembrance" of his sacrifice of himself on the cross (Lk 22:19).

3. Louis Boyer, *Introduction to Spirituality*, Liturgical Press, Collegeville, Minn., 1962, p. 34.

4. Because the J-Source version of the covenant of Abraham in Genesis 15 does not mention the obligation of circumcision as a sign of the covenant—even though the practice is very ancient—the P-Source attribution in Genesis 17 of the origin of infant male Jewish circumcision to Abraham may be more honorific than historical.

5. This does not mean that Jesus did not deepen and further that revelation in his own life and preaching of God as Abba.

6. For Abraham, see Lk 1:55; Jn 8:33–37; Rom 1:13; 9:7; 11:1; 2 Cor 11:22; Gal 3:16; 3:29; Heb 2:16. For Isaac, Mt 1:2; Lk 3:34; Acts 7:8; 8:11; Lk 13:28; Rom 9:10; Gal 4:28; Heb 11:9, 17, 20; Jas 2:21. For Jacob, Mt 8:11; Jn 4:6; Rom 11:26. For Joseph, Acts 7:9–14; Heb 11:21–22. Jaroslav Pelikan, *The Christian Tradition: A History of the Development of the Catholic Tradition (100–600)*, The University of Chicago Press, 1971, pp. 68–81.

7. Jesus' command to baptize did not formally suppress circumcision. It cost the Jewish-Christian Church much controversy and finally took a solemn Church Council in Jerusalem to make circumcision optional for Gentile Christians (Acts 15:5–12).

8. John Bright, *A History of Israel*, Westminster Press, Philadelphia, 1952, pp. 61–78.

9. It is most unlikely that Abraham ever used the name "Yahweh" for God. If "Yahweh" existed as a clan-god name prior to Moses, it would have been used in the tribe of Midian. See H.H. Rowley, *The*

Midianite Hypothesis, "The Nature of God," in *The Faith of Israel,* The Westminster Press, Philadelphia, 1956, p. 54.

In Genesis J-Source uses the name Yahweh for God from the time of Enosh, the ancestor of Enoch (Gen 4:26). *The New American Bible* translates "Yahweh" as "the Lord," following the later Jewish custom of refraining from speaking the holy name out of profound reverence for its holiness. *The Jerusalem Bible* has restored the more ancient nomenclature. Here I quote the NAB and change "Lord" to "Yahweh."

10. Bright, pp. 42–45 and 78–86.

11. In John's Gospel these "signs" reveal the presence of God among us in Christ (Jn 2:11). They are not the same as the "signs" or demands for verifiable proof of messianic identity which Jesus condemned in the Pharisees (Mt 16:4). Likewise they are not the extraordinary or supernatural signs of God's will demanded by Gideon (Jgs 6:36–40). These "signs of the times" are recognized through communal reflection in faith on what God is currently doing in human history. Thus historical events become the infallible signs of God's will for us. Gerhard Friedrich, *Theological Dictionary of the New Testament,* Vol. VII, pp. 211–16.

12. Gerhard Von Rad, *Genesis: A Commentary,* trans. by John H. Marks, The Westminster Press, Philadelphia, 1961, p. 154.

13. "Dogmatic Constitution on the Church," par. 48 in Walter M. Abbott, S.J. (ed.), *The Documents of Vatican II,* Guild Press, N.Y., 1966, pp. 78–81.

14. John L. McKenzie, S.J., *Dictionary of the Bible,* "Blessing," pp. 96–97.

15. Since the long ages attributed to the patriarchal families in Genesis are a P-Source literary form, we cannot know historically how old Abraham was when he began to doubt the possibility of a male heir. Eugene H. Maly, "Introduction to the Pentateuch," par. 17, in *The Jewish Biblical Commentary,* Vol. I, p. 4.

16. The historical origin of the twelve tribes is much more complex than the simplified biblical portrait. See Bright, pp. 120–123.

17. See Ex 19:7-9; 24. This sense of "peoplehood" did not, however, eradicate a strong sense of tribal identity. Thus, when the people Israel conquered the land of the Canaanites, the country is parceled out to individual tribes. See Jgs 13—21.

18. Some commentators see in the sacrifice of Isaac an Israelite protest against the very common practice of Canaanite child sacrifice. See Eugene H. Maly, "Genesis," in *JBC,* Vol. I, par. 72, p. 23.

Such an exegesis seems strained and fails to recognize the importance of offering sacrifice for redemption in the Hebrew mind.

19. This interpretation of the sacrifice of Isaac comes from James Sanders. I first heard it in a colloquium at the Ecumenical Institute for Advanced Theological Studies in Jerusalem in 1973.

20. This is a favorite theme of J-Source. Since David was the youngest of his brothers, J looked for the pattern of a divine election in the earlier history of God's saving action.

21. "Dogmatic Decree on Divine Revelation," par. 3, in The Documents of Vatican II, p. 113.

22. *Ibid.*, par. 2, p. 112.

23. *Ibid.*, par. 9, p. 117.

24. *Ibid.*, par. 11, p. 119.

25. *Ibid.*, par. 12, p. 120.

26. *Ibid.*, par. 5. pp. 113–114.

27. *Ibid.*, par. 10, pp. 117–118.

28. *Ibid.*, par. 10, p. 118.

29. *Ibid.*, par. 25, p. 127, quoting St. Jerome, *Commentary on Isaiah*, Prol.: PL 24, 17.

30. *Ibid.*, par. 26, p. 128.

31. "Declaration on the Relationship of the Church to Non-Christian Religions," par. 3, in *The Documents of Vatican II*, p. 663.

32. *Ibid.*, par. 4, pp. 663–667.

33. "Divine Revelation," par. 6, p. 115.

34. For a clear contemporary explication of the theological problems associated with the theme of revelation, see Richard P. McBrien, *Catholicism*, Winston Press, Minn. 1980, Vol. I, Ch. VII, pp. 201ff.

Chapter II

The Exodus and Catholic Teaching on the People of God Today

"By the might of your arm ... O Yahweh ...
the people you had made your own passed over."
—Ex 15:16

The Exodus in History

**What happened between the time of Joseph
and the birth of Moses?**

Between the death of Joseph in the last chapter of Genesis and the Hebrew slave labor depicted in the first chapter of Exodus, a significant historical gap must be posited. Exodus 12:40 says that the patriarchal families had lived in Egypt for four hundred and thirty years. The inspired author does not indicate from which point of Hebrew-Egyptian contact he is deriving this figure, but it is historically plausible.[1]

To move from the patriarchal period to the exodus formation of the tribes as God's passover people constitutes a kind of quantum leap in the history of ancient Israel. Not only is there a big jump in time from the patriarchal families, but there is also a new depth and power in the revelation given to the twelve tribes through Moses. The Hebrews accepted that revelation in the context of painful oppression in Egypt. Through God's transcendent initiative in rescuing them and through their agreeing to become God's covenant people, the twelve Hebrew tribes were transformed into the one people Israel. If the exodus had not occurred, the Old Testament would never have been written.[2]

How do we know just when the Hebrews escaped from slavery?

Archeology discloses that Exodus 1 has its probable historical setting during the reigns of Pharaohs Seti I and Ramesses II. It is they who initiated the construction of the grain cities in Pithom and Ramesses mentioned in Exodus 1:11. Seti I began his reign ca. 1309 B.C. and was succeeded by his son, Ramesses II in 1290 B.C. Thus the slave labor of the Hebrews cannot be dated prior to 1309 B.C.[3]

At the opposite end of the history, the passover escape of the Hebrew slaves must have occurred prior to 1220 B.C. Archeology has discovered a stele recording a battle between the Egyptian military commander Marniptah and a group in the Sinai desert called "the Israelites." This battle would be equivalently dated 1220 B.C. in the Christian calendar. Since allowance must be made for a long period of desert wandering before the conquest of Canaan began about 1200 B.C., most historians date the exodus between 1290 and 1250 B.C. Here we follow John Bright and opt for 1285 B.C.[4]

Why were the Hebrews exploited by the Egyptians?

Either Seti I or Ramesses II feared the high birth rate of the Hebrews as a minority group in Egypt. They might join with one of Egypt's enemies and leave the country (cf. Ex 1:8-10). Pharaoh adopted a two-plank government plan to protect the ruling elite: forced labor to build the government grain cities (Ex 1:11-14) and selective birth control through murder of infant male Hebrews (Ex 1:15-22). When the Hebrews got "uppity" and "complained," Pharaoh escalated the oppression. He labeled the people "lazy," refused to let them offer a religious "sacrifice," and withdrew the government "straw" supply for making bricks. Those new measures caused the people to "scatter," thus weakening their resistance (Ex

5:6–9).[5] The Hebrew response to the experience of being tortured was as spontaneous as it was genuine. "They groaned," says Scripture, for the first time in the history of the people (Ex 2:23–24).

How did God liberate the people from slavery?

In the Book of Exodus God worked through five steps or historical moments: (1) groaning, (2) vision, (3) commitment (4) rescue, and (5) covenant. Through these five moments the Hebrew scattered slaves were transformed into the one chosen people of God. They became Israel.

What was accomplished by "groaning"?

The Old Testament admirably discriminates between *groaning, complaining,* and *sadness.* While *complaining* is a sinful act of the proud, and *sadness* the depression which results from personal guilt, *groaning* implies the depth of intercessory prayer.[6] The oppressed groan for the recognition of their human dignity; the tortured cry out for divine protection from the assaults of their enemies; the terrified beg that Yahweh rescue them from the jaws of death. Thus the inspired author writes, "As their cry for release went up to God, he heard their groaning and was mindful of his covenant with Abraham, Isaac, and Jacob. He saw the Israelites and knew . . ." (Ex 2:24–25). To *hear* and to *know* carry intimate personal connotations in the ancient semitic mind. It is almost equivalent to saying: "God empathized and suffered with them."[7]

How did God work through "vision"?

At this moment the God of Abraham acted in new and liberating ways. He revealed himself, called Moses by name (Ex 3:4), and commanded him: "Remove the sandals from your feet, for the place where you stand is holy ground" (Ex 3:5). An historical change can only occur when someone begins to act and succeeds in encouraging others to collaborate.

The experience of the awesomeness of God seems to have freed Moses from his fear of being killed in Egypt (Ex 14—15) and to explain his willingness to be alienated from his own culture (Ex 2:21–22). Moses, the murderer and coward, really struggled to believe that God could make him a recognized and respected leader. He told God that his own Hebrew people would consider him a religious fraud and the Egyptian power elite would find him an unimpressive stutterer (Ex 4:1–2, 10–11). In the experience of the burning bush, God began to transform Moses from a frightened coward to a courageous leader. God spoke to Moses his own ineffably holy name, Yahweh, and promised Moses the help of Aaron as a human collaborator (Ex 3:14–15; 4:14).

Fiery Yahweh, of the burning bush, whose presence fascinates and whose otherness threatens to consume, is not the reasonable God of some later philosophers nor the sentimental God of superficial piety. This is the transcendent God whose immensity confounds the human intellect and whose majesty chastens the human will into spontaneous acts of reverence for the holy one.[8]

What does Yahweh mean as a name for God?

Old Testament scholarship has commented at length on the origin and meaning of the divine name "Yahweh." Four characteristics of the divine name Yahweh have a general consensus. First, in Hebrew religion Yahweh was a *novel* name, a new revelation by God about God which seeks to convey a deeper concept of the divine reality.[9] Second, the name Yahweh was *personal.* It is not simply a designation of some theological abstraction. It is the unveiling of a new depth in the divine center of self-awareness in God. It is spoken to a human listener, Moses. This unveiling of a deeper personal divine center in God to Moses occurs whether Moses ever heard the word "Yahweh" before or not.[10] Only in the burning bush experience does the reality of God which the name tries to reveal become apparent to Moses.

Third, the name Yahweh is *efficacious*. It conveys the living presence of the invisible God and allows a deeper personal communion with him by way of human response. In this sense, it is the Old Testament example *par excellence* of the dynamic power of God's word. The fact that God speaks shows how he wants the reality of his personal mystery to have an impact on human life. Yahweh is not content to exist in divine isolation. He wants to share his person with us. He wants us to know that he exists for us. What precisely did God say to Moses and to us in the name Yahweh? The Hebrew text says that the name is a symbol for the phrase *eyeh asher eyeh*. Most Bibles still translate this, "I am who am" (Ex 3:14).

Most obviously this can imply that Yahweh is the God who has no creator; he is substantially different in power and dignity from all the other gods. That is why from the time of Moses, Yahweh alone could be adored (Ex 20:3). Historically, however, we must remember that Moses did not deny that the other gods existed. For him Yahweh meant that the people were being commanded to worship only one of the many available gods. His religion is technically called monolatry (one worship). It may have taken as long as five hundred years for this to develop into the explicit monotheism (only one God exists) that we find in the great prophets of Israel.

The divine name may also reveal God's being with respect to the future. It is possible to translate *eyeh asher eyeh* as meaning, "I will be who I will be." If this were the divine intent, then Yahweh would be revealing himself as leading us through a series of future historical dangers. He is the God of promise and of hope. He is not disclosing himself as existing in our very midst in the present, but as the God who will lead us through the most unimaginable changes in future history. Here not only does he transcend history, but he is the dynamism of historical change.

Finally, if the name Yahweh was novel, personal and future-oriented, it was also revealed as *traditional*. "Thus you shall say to the Israelites: Yahweh, the God of your fathers, the God of Abraham, the God of Isaac, the God of Jacob, has sent me to you" (Ex 3:15). If centuries of religious tradition frequently need a "dusting off" and renewing of the vibrancy of the original inspiration or values which gave rise to subsequent practices, likewise novelty thrives best, it seems, when grounded in the solidity of tradition. For Moses, the name Yahweh was not a "gimmick" or some superficial religious "attention getter." The name Yahweh said something true —something that had always been true, but had never been understood so profoundly or experienced so intimately before. God did not become Yahweh in the thirteenth century B.C.; he had always been Yahweh even though the patriarchs invoked him by other names: "Shield of Abraham," "Fear of Isaac," "Mighty One of Jacob." Underneath these familial titles, fiery Yahweh was preparing the community to know him and respond to him in a far more profound way.

The fiery God who spoke his ineffable name to Moses is thus neither apolitically transcendent nor an "opium" for the people. He is the transcendent initiator of liberating spiritual, economic and political change. His insistence that no idol be worshiped is a challenge to all subsequent generations that all ideologies be subordinated to adoration of the transcendent God. The vision of fiery Yahweh allows us to raise critical questions and to imagine how our future might be better. For Moses, the vision of Yahweh was a call to lead.

Why did Yahweh have to work through the commitment of Moses?

If Moses had not finally agreed to say "yes" to the divine desire to liberate the people, the passover transformation could not have occurred as it did. Someone had to hear Yahweh, as Yahweh had heard his people—someone had to lead. No sane Hebrew would have wanted to carry the divine impulse into history. The risks to life, family, and reputation were enormous. Reflecting on the interior struggle which Moses experienced in responding positively to Yahweh, one wonders how many men and women had already been called and had refused to hear or had forthrightly said, "No." On this point Scripture and history are silent and we are free to conjecture. What is beyond historical debate is that the divine initiative has as its term a human "yes" freely uttered: "I will serve; I will lead."

Exodus 4 recounts only the initial difficulty which Moses experienced in saying "yes" to Yahweh. That yes had to be repeated and deepened many times in subsequent years. Exodus 5:22—6:29 tells of the discouragement and powerlessness Moses felt when he first returned to Egypt and tried to lead. The ten plagues which followed supported and encouraged the yes of Moses. In the plagues, Moses found himself embroiled in a struggle far larger than his own making. God was using flood, pestilence, and untimely death to soften Pharaoh's heart. By contrast, the yes of Moses seemed quite powerless. Pharaoh's final capitulation to the exodus of the Hebrews was Yahweh's doing—it was not due to the persistence of Moses.

It was not as easy to continue that yes when Moses was afraid of being stoned by the people because of their thirst for water (Num 20:5). The Israelites have not been the only people who preferred slavery with fresh water to freedom with thirst. Moses resorted to prayer and to seeking divine guidance. The inspired text does not tell us why Moses struck the rock twice with his staff instead of once. Was it desperation, doubt, or anger with the people? Scripture only reveals that this time Moses had *not* said yes fully to Yahweh, so Moses would never see the earthly success of his efforts to lead (Num 20:12).

However the yes of Moses to Yahweh had sufficient integrity that the man who started out his adulthood as a murderer and a coward could later be called "the meekest man on the face of the earth" (Num 12:3). In terms of God's plan for salvation the yes of Moses was powerful enough to sustain the unity of the people while they wandered through the desert. Without Moses they would have groveled back to their former life of slavery. Understood in this way, the yes of Moses is a sobering reminder of the historical importance of personal fidelity to God's call.

On passover night, just how did Yahweh rescue the Israelites?

Exodus 3:18 suggests that the Hebrews told Pharaoh they would return to Egypt after holding a three-day celebration of religious sacrifice in the desert. When Pharaoh sensed that their voluntary return would be unlikely—if not ludicrous—he sent the Egyptian army in hot pursuit to bring the Hebrews back. Against Pharaoh's armed forces, the Hebrew slaves had not the least human defense. Left to their own devices they would have been killed or returned to slavery.

Biblical scholarship has recognized for the past hundred years or more that Exodus 14, the crossing of the Red Sea, is the work of at least two divergent inspired sources.[11] The older source presents Yahweh rescuing the Hebrews through a series of divinely coordinated events in nature. In Hebrew the Red Sea is called *Yam Suf.* Originally Yam Suf designated a swamp north of what we call today the Red Sea. The Hebrews passed through the marsh of Yam Suf when the water was at an unusually low ebb and hid all night behind a bank of fog (Ex 14:19–20). Pharaoh's chariots spent the night in the marsh waiting to continue the pursuit the following morning. At daybreak, thunder, lightning, and torrential rain overwhelmed them. "In the night watch just before the dawn Yahweh cast through the column of the fiery cloud a glance upon the Egyptian force that threw it into a panic. And he so clogged their chariot wheels that they could hardly drive" (Ex 14:24–25). This account ends, "When Israel saw the Egyptians lying dead on the seashore and beheld the great power that Yahweh had shown against the Egyptians, they feared Yahweh and believed in him and in his servant Moses" (Ex 14:31).

This account of the divine rescue allows us to see how Yahweh most likely acted in Israel's historical experience of being freed. To the eyes of Hebrew faith, it was quite clear. It was marvelous. It was "a miracle" of being saved from the Egyptians. The family of Abraham was finally free and Miriam could pick up her tambourine—upon seeing the wreckage of Pharaoh's army in Yam Suf—and lead the tribes in a tremendous song of rejoicing and exultation (Ex 15). Yahweh had won, and they had done nothing all night long but wait. The inspired poem of Exodus 15 is one of the oldest compositions in the Old Testament. It probably dates back to the time of the rescue. As such it shows us how the inspired Scriptures grew out of the concrete human history of Yahweh acting as Israel's deliverer.

If skeptics lived in the thirteenth century B.C., they would have seen nothing at Yam Suf on the holy night of passover but "a coincidence" or "a happy accident." The parallels for the contemporary community of faith are obvious. For those who have the interior eyes of faith to see, Yahweh is still rescuing the victims of oppression wherever human freedom has committed itself to cooperate with his saving action.

Those inspired verses of Exodus 14 which portray Moses as opening and closing the waters of Yam Suf by holding out his staff were composed by the temple priests (Ex 14:15, 17, 21). The priests stressed the mediatorial role of Moses. As Moses had mediated between God and the people, so did the priests in the liturgical life of the people from the time of Levi on (Gen 34). The priests saw no problem in intertwining the older narrative and the later liturgical one into one inspired composition.

How did the twelve tribes become the one covenant people, Israel?

Through the covenant of Moses Yahweh invited the tribes into a new relation with him and with each other. Because Yahweh desired an exclusive relationship with his people and because he wanted the tribes to deepen their bonds of unity with one another, he had to *invite* the people into covenant. He could not impose it as some cosmic fate, for then it would have ceased to be personal or human (Ex 19:2b–6).

The twelve tribes responded freely and affirmatively to the divine invitation: "The people all answered together, 'Everything Yahweh has said, we will do' " (Ex 19:8). Becoming the covenant people thus depended both on the divine initiative and on the human consent.

The remainder of Exodus 10 depicts the Israelites in a state of "being sanctified for holy war."[12] In the ancient patterns of Middle Eastern thought, this allowed the power of God to become especially manifest against his enemies. The account of the ritual preparation and of Yahweh's awesome theophany in Exodus 19 probably reflects subsequent liturgical customs practiced by the Israelites. It is quite possible that groups returned to Sinai periodically for covenant renewal festivals.

Exodus 20:1–17 reveals Yahweh's stipulations for becoming his people. He will be their God if they will live by his ten words. By living the ten words Yahweh will be worshiped as King. The first three commandments specify the minimal ways in which the tribes must dedicate themselves to the exclusive worship of Yahweh. They cannot be his people if they make light of his holy name or adore other gods as potential sources of help and protection. Every seventh day is to be given over to worship of Yahweh. The last seven commandments provide minimal guidelines for maintaining intertribal justice. The fourth commandment, "Honor your father and your mother . . ." (Ex 20:12), is the only positive law among those dealing with human relationships. Within the family, the minimal requirements of justice are to be exceeded by gratitude and reverence.

Yahweh's ten words are thus a revelation of divine wisdom about how to develop humanly as God's people. They are not ten arbitrary little rules to test people. As rooted in God's will and specially suited to the human condition they are absolute, not relative, in their eternal validity. However, the existence of hundreds of other case laws in the Books of Exodus and Leviticus is ample proof that the ten words needed to be rethought continually in terms of new situations. Ultimately, of course, the Jewish legal tradition failed to help the people abide in an authentic covenant relationship with God. Endless lists of laws and learned interpretations of the minute prescriptions of every law were powerless to reveal Yahweh as choosing them or as inviting them to live in interpersonal union with him. To make up for this deficiency, the New Testament will later insist on the necessity of the grace of sonship in Christ (Gal 3:4).

In Exodus 24, why does Moses sprinkle the people with blood?

To the Hebrew mind "life" was conveyed in the blood. To be sprinkled with the same blood which was poured over Yahweh's altar was to be made one with him through a liturgical rite. This constituted *sealing* the covenant. Now all the tribes had been fashioned into one people committed to living in fidelity to one God.

Being sealed as the people of God culminated in the sublime moment of a communion feast reserved to Moses and the seventy elders on Mount Sinai. They "beheld the God of Israel ... yet they could still eat and drink" (Ex 24:9–11). Such intimate communion with God was the fruit of agreeing to live a new life as God's people. Generally in the Old Testament, no one "can see the face of God and live" (Ex 33:20).

The covenant pattern of moving from divine invitation through the experience of word to the experience of communion repeats itself many times in the Old and New Testaments and is still operative in the life of the Church today. When the divine word is heard and freely accepted, we are *sealed* in union with God and his people through sacramental signs like baptism, Eucharist, and reconciliation.

How did God develop order among his people?

God's passover people may have been rightly called a "motley crew" (Ex 12:38) as they fled across Yam Suf on that holy night of their divine rescue. They did not, however, remain completely disorganized in their peoplehood. Scripture does not clearly state just when Moses designated Aaron to officiate over sacrifice, but both Exodus 29 and Leviticus 8 state that Moses consecrated Aaron, and depict Aaron officiating in the tent of meeting. Although both chapters are colored by the priestly practices developed six or seven hundred years later, there is no reason to doubt the unique liturgical role Aaron exercised in the desert.

The covenant people not only provided for designated liturgical ministers, they also came to recognize an inspired prophetic authority in temporal administration. According to Numbers 11, Moses found the demands of leadership too burdensome and prayed to God for relief (Num 11:14). Then by divine command Moses chose seventy "elders" who were "authorities" (Num 11:16) among the people. God shared with them the spirit of prophecy he had given to Moses (Num 11:25). Subsequently Moses had to teach Joshua that Eldad and Medad were validly "inspired" prophets because they were named by Moses and manifested the gift of prophecy even though they missed the communal commissioning at the tent (Num 11:26–30). The sign of prophecy may have been some type of ecstatic babbling which was common in prophetic circles of the ancient Middle East. Whatever sign was manifested, from that point on the covenant people were a prophetic people who looked to a special group of prophets for more direct guidance from Yahweh.

The development of priestly authority among the people did not go unchallenged. In Numbers 16 Korah, Dathan, and Abiram led two hundred and fifty Israelites in an attempted coup against Moses, saying, "Enough from you. The whole community, all of them are holy. Yahweh is in their midst. Why then should you set yourself over Yahweh's congregation?" (Num 16:4). After Moses' prophetic denunciation of their false charismatic claims to have the right to usurp divinely constituted priestly authority, they were swallowed alive by the nether world (Num 16:28–35).

The two hundred and fifty rebels who died had been holding censers. Moses ordered that these be melted into plates to cover the altar and be a sign to the people.

> ... no layman, no one who was not a descendant of Aaron, should approach the altar to offer incense before Yahweh, lest he meet the fate of Korah and his band (Num 17:5).

While the antiquity of that Scripture can be debated, its teaching on the nature of peoplehood in God is clear. There is a real distinction between priesthood and laity.

How did God want his people to treat the disadvantaged?

Leviticus 19:18 says: "You shall love your neighbor as yourself." Other verses in the chapter explicitly mention the "day laborer," the "deaf," the "blind," the "aged," and the resident "alien" (cf. Lev 19:13–14, 32–36). No one could live as a member of God's people and take advantage of those who were powerless in Israelite society.

Besides observing laws of fair treatment, the covenant people were to live in a continual effort to redistribute family property equitably. Every seventh year the land was to rest as a sabbath year. During this time the extended family, the slaves and the tenants were all to rest and to share equally the produce from previous years (Lev 25:6–7).

Every fiftieth year was to be a year of jubilee. It began with a trumpet blast throughout the land on the day of atonement. This sabbath of sabbath years was to facilitate redistribution of the land in favor of the poor. The right to private property was only relative—not absolute. Yahweh owned the land and those who had legal title were only his "tenants." No property could therefore be sold in perpetuity; the poor man always had the right to buy back his original holdings or get help from a relative to do that for him (cf. Lev 25:23–27). In that way every fifty years the gap that had grown between the rich and the poor would be equalized anew. Thus the economically poor were given a fresh start.

All these laws come from the holiness code in Leviticus 17—26. The holiness code is the oldest legal material in the Old Testament. Thus these Scriptures reveal the profound socio-economic consequences which were implied in becoming God's covenant people at Mount Sinai. If the unity among the tribes was spiritual in their exclusive worship of Yahweh, their unity with each other was eminently concrete in the

norms of covenant justice by which they were to develop
Israelite society around Yahweh as King.

Why did the Israelites begin to celebrate the passover with a meal?

All of the history of the exodus and the sense of religious
identity as God's people, chosen for covenant living, were
annually celebrated by the Israelites each spring at passover.
On the first day of the first month of Abib (Ex 12:1; 13:4) the
Israelites gathered by families to prepare the feast. As the
passover meal gradually developed, it included three principal
elements: the sacrifice of the lamb in thanksgiving for what
God had done in rescuing them, the eating of unleavened
bread and the offering of the first-born to God. One had to be a
member of the people to celebrate, but aliens could join in the
feast if they first submitted to the rite of initiation (Ex 12:18).
By celebrating in families, the elders educated their children
into the knowledge of what Yahweh had done for his people
and how blessed they were to be chosen for covenant living.
The passover supper thus became the central rite celebrating
the most important event in the history of the chosen people.

How do Christians share in a "new passover"?

The New Testament use of passover images and ideas is as
profound as it is vast. Jesus' last meal with the Apostles was a
passover during which he told them to continue "doing this"
(Lk 22:19). Subsequently the God of Israel rescued Jesus the
crucified "lamb" of God (Jn 1:29) from the jaws of death. Thus
Jesus had "passed over" from death to resurrection as Israel
had "passed over" from slavery to freedom for covenant peoplehood. As risen Lord, Jesus was a new type of consecrated
"first born" (Col 1:15–18). His most important "birth" had
been, however, from *death*—not from the womb. Thus the
central content of the Gospel frequently expressed itself as a
new passover.

The new passover of Christ gave birth to the new people of
God (1 Pet 2:9–10). Just as God had saved the Hebrews from

Pharaoh's efforts to scatter them, the crucified-risen Christ has rescued Christians from the isolation, loneliness, and social fragmentation caused by sin. Transformed from a series of individuals closed in on themselves and vulnerable to every form of manipulation, practicing Christians live as members of God's priestly, prophetic people. As such all the members know that they are "precious in God's eyes" and capable of offering "spiritual sacrifices acceptable to God through Christ" (1 Pet 2:4–5). In this way their whole view of human life and of their personal possibilities before God and society are transformed as they come to understand themselves as Church.

Relationship of the Exodus People of God to Catholic Faith

For Catholics, who belongs to the people of God today?

Catholic faith looks on all men and women of goodwill as having varying degrees of active participation in the people of God today. Unbelievers who profess no faith and still do not enjoy any explicit knowledge of God belong to the people of God in the least explicit and least conscious way. They are members of God's people because they "strive to live a good life thanks to his grace." Catholics interpret the moral goodness of such people as "a preparation for the Gospel."[13]

Catholics find themselves linked even more closely to all who consciously seek to do God's will and to all other Christians "though they do not profess the faith in its entirety or do not preserve the unity of communion with the successor of Peter."[14] Ultimately the Catholic Church understands the term "people of God" to include all those who search in history for "unity and peace."[15] Catholic teaching urges all Catholics to befriend and support all those who suffer "trial and tribulation" today as they struggle to achieve peace among persons and nations.[16]

If unbelievers are part of God's people, why become a baptized Christian?

Christian baptism into the Church of Jesus Christ contributes special blessings to the baptized person, and the Christian Church of the baptized is a source of special blessings for the world. Through the preaching of the word (cf. 1 Pet 1:23) and the life-giving water of baptism (cf. Rev 22:17), a Christian becomes a participant in the new covenant in Christ's blood (Jer 31:31–34; 1 Cor 11:25). This covenant belonging to the Church occurs by way of a *rebirth* from water and the Holy Spirit (cf. Jn 3:5–6). Faith in Jesus provides a new source of strength to struggle on behalf of truth, justice and love (cf. Rom 8:14–39). Membership in a Christian community deepens and educates that faith into mature commitment. The interior transformation worked by rebirth in water and the Holy Spirit allows one to live by a hope which nothing in this world can take away.

The worldwide community of baptized Christians is the Church of Jesus Christ on earth. Because the risen Jesus lives in the baptized in a special way (Mt 28:20), and because the baptized are called to be a new messianic people transforming hatred into peace, the Church of Christ is a special source of blessings for the world. Catholic faith calls the Church in this sense "a lasting and sure seed of unity, hope, and salvation for the whole human race." Because the visible members can manifest the invisible risen Jesus, the Church of Jesus Christ is called by Catholics "a visible sacrament of this saving unity."[17]

The Church effects this unity by striving to live it among its members as the new people of God, gathering regularly in local assemblies for prayer, sharing, and mutual help. These assemblies, when they are true to their mandate, strive to love selflessly as they know themselves to be loved unconditionally by Christ. Secondly, the Church functions as a sacrament of unity for the world by preaching the Gospel and by nurturing infant churches until they themselves can carry on the work

of establishing others. "In this way each human simultaneously prays and labors in order that the entire world may become
the people of God . . . and that in Christ, the head of all, there
may be rendered to the Creator and Lord of the universe all
honor and glory."[18]

If all Christians are "a visible sacrament of saving unity," why become a Roman Catholic?

Before Vatican II, Roman Catholics simply said that the
Roman Catholic Church was "the one true Church founded by
Christ." This ignored the fact that Roman Catholics share
many elements of faith with Orthodox and Protestant Christians. Therefore at Vatican II the bishops taught that *the
fullness* of the truth and the ordinary means of salvation are
found in the Roman Catholic Church, but that some of these
beliefs and means of salvation are found beyond the visible
Catholic Church. Such spiritual gifts beyond the visible Catholic Church are expressions of the Father's divine love for all
who are baptized in the name of the Father, and the Son, and
the Holy Spirit (Mt 28:20). Because love seeks a unity and
harmony as its goal, Catholics believe that Jesus wants all to
be one in both heartfelt love and the visible bonds of communion in the human society of the Church (cf. Jn 17:21).[19]

In this spirit of celebrating what all Christians have in
common, Catholics point to faith in the Holy Trinity, belief in
Jesus as Redeemer and Lord, the inspired character of the
Scriptures, the importance of preaching the word of God, and
the transforming power of justice and love as the personal
testimony of the members when they live as Christ calls them
to live. These elements of saving truth Roman Catholics share
with all who rightfully call themselves Christian. On the other
hand, Catholics find elements of saving truth and means of
salvation within their own Church which have fallen into
disuse among some of its separated brothers and sisters. Thus
Catholics acknowledge the presence of the risen Jesus in the
sacraments of healing and reconciliation. At such times the
Church gathers to celebrate the Spirit's power to forgive and

make whole. Likewise Catholics see the light of Christ radiating through Mary and the communion of saints in heaven, and so actively befriend them. The same faith believes that the risen Christ makes one the bride and groom who profess their marriage vows before a priest, so that marriage is numbered as one of the seven sacraments. Catholic faith believes that the invisible presence of the risen Christ is linked intimately to the visible offices of the ordained priesthood, the college of the bishops, and the chair of Peter in Rome. For Catholics, the Bishop of Rome, the Pope, is the sign of visible unity in the truth of faith and the love of the members for one another. The fullness of this visible unity allows the Church to be a more dynamic source of light and healing for the modern world. For this reason Roman Catholics want to learn from the special charisms of the separated brothers and sisters and to share with them the spiritual fullness which Catholics find within their own Church.

If Scripture calls the whole Church a "royal priesthood" (1 Pet 2:9), why do Catholics distinguish between the priesthood of baptism and the priesthood of ordination?

For Catholics the priesthood of all believers is exercised through participation in the sacraments and through living the virtues. It is culminated as the community symbolically lays itself on the altar with Christ in the eucharistic sacrifice. In this action people make themselves priestly victims of love with Christ as the Divine Victim offered once for all. Thus both through this act of offering and through Holy Communion all perform their proper part in this liturgical service. The life of priestly virtue which flows from participation in the Eucharist should be centered in self-sacrifice so that the priestly people will become a living holocaust of love for God and the whole world.

Catholics find the distinction between the priesthood of believers and the priesthood of the ordained to continue the distinction of roles within the people of God which is revealed in both the Old and New Testaments. In the Old Testament God reserved certain functions to the levite priests and to the family of Aaron. In the New Testament the Apostles brought about the eucharistic sacrifice and offered it to God in the name of the whole people (cf. 1 Cor 11). Catholic faith finds a divine order in this arrangement whereby the two forms of priesthood work together and the authority to "mold and rule the people" is reserved to the ministerial priesthood.[20]

Where is the prophetic element in the Catholic Church today?

Catholics believe that prophetic charisms are at work whenever Christian lives of faith and charity manifest that the people have heard Christ's word.[21] Likewise courageous denunciations of sin, injustice, and oppressive structures belong to the prophetic dimension of the people of God.[22] For Catholics the most powerful prophetic sign in the Church is the unity of unerring faith in the whole people when "from the bishops down to the last member of the laity," it shows universal agreement in matters of faith and morals.[23] When such agreement is not present, its members should seek forgiveness and reconciliation quickly (Jas 3:5). Catholic bishops are encouraged not to "extinguish the Spirit" (cf. Thes 5:12, 19–21)[24] and to recognize the Spirit working in the unique gifts of diverse human cultures.[25] The prophetic dimension ennobles the Church with courage, challenging calls, and transforming actions on behalf of justice and love. When the people of God today work for redistribution of land, capital, and the various means of production, Catholic faith believes that it is helping Jesus proclaim a year of jubilee for the poor (Lk 4:18–19).

How can we live as the people of God today?

(1) *Exit.* Yahweh still invites us to leave our egotistical prisons of individualism. He wants to help us escape from the fear, anger, or suspicion that bottles us up in powerlessness. Unlike our ancient Israelite ancestors, we today may not even

identify with the tribe or extended family. We may stand utterly alone. Like the Israelites, however, we can find a way out if we will have the courage to groan, admit to ourselves the hurt and pain and slavery, and cry out to God for a new freedom.

(2) *Unite.* Moses, the murderer and the coward, dared to share his vision of God and himself with others. His sharing allowed them to imagine new possibilities for their future. We too can withdraw into the personal deserts within us to allow God to speak a new word of vision and commitment. Like Moses we can say yes and play our unique role in God's rescuing action today. Thus we will help scattered individuals come together to reflect on what oppresses them, to worship God, and to act together to transform systems and structures which exploit and dehumanize us today.

(3) *Integrate.* By reflecting on the Scriptures about the exodus, the jubilee year (Lev 25 and Lk 4), and the Church as the new people of God (1 Pet 2:9), we can correct the excessive privatization which has colored modern Christianity. Personal faith, the liturgical worship of Jesus as our new passover, communal reflection on Scripture, and liberating action in the political and economic sphere all come together as indispensable dimensions of living as the people of God today. Such awareness does not undermine the separation of Church and state in democratic countries. Rather it forces us to acknowledge that there cannot be two faiths or two moralities: one for Sunday and the other for the rest of the week. To live as the people of God today is to make Yahweh the King and center of our whole lives (Ps 47).

Notes

1. John Bright, *A History of Israel,* Westminster Press, Philadelphia, 1952, p. 103.

2. Claus Westermann, *Handbook to the Old Testament,* Augsburg Publishing House, Minneapolis, 1967, pp. 13–18. For a brief overview of the literary composition of the Book of Exodus, see Martin Noth, *Exodus: A Commentary,* Westminster Press, Philadel-

phia, 1974, pp. 9–18. For the most up-to-date bibliography, history of critical scholarship and hermeneutical reflection on the theology of the Book of Exodus, see Brevard S. Childs, *Introduction to the Old Testament as Scripture,* Fortress Press, Philadelphia, 1980, pp. 161–179.

3. Bright, pp. 110–114.

4. *Ibid.,* p. 113.

5. I am indebted to Benjamin Bravo for this insight into the tactics of oppression. See Lic. Benjamín Bravo Pérez, *Preparación a los procesos de conversión: precatecumenado,* Lago Cardiel 23, Colonia Argentina Antigua, Mexico 17, D.F., 1978.

6. Eugene H. Maly, *Sin: Biblical Perspectives,* Pflaum/Standard, Dayton, 1973, pp. 17–22.

7. This is not the place to develop a complete theology of intercessory prayer. The position sketched here is consistent with that developed by Aquinas which stresses the immutability of God. The differences would be that we find God himself acting as the principal agent in certain *kairos* moments in history as a result of intercessory prayer. This is neither divine providence nor miracle according to classical understandings. It would be a new chapter on the relationship of prayer, grace and history.

8. Rudolf Otto, *The Idea of the Holy,* trans. by John W. Harvey, Oxford Univ. Press, N.Y., 1967, pp. 72–75.

9. See G.E. Mendenhall, "Covenant," in *Interpreter's Dictionary of the Bible,* Vol. I, pp. 714–22. For more background on the Israelite concept of God in the Book of Exodus, see Albrecht Alt, "The God of the Fathers," in *Essays on Old Testament History and Religion,* trans. by R.A. Wilson, Oxford, Basil Blackwell, 1966; Raymond Abba, "The Divine Name Yahweh," in *The Journal of Biblical Literature,* Vol. 80 (1961), pp. 320–28; Walter Eichrodt, *Theology of the Old Testament,* Vol. I, trans. by J.A. Baker, The Westminster Press, 1961; Philip J. Hyatt, "Was Yahweh Originally a Creator Deity?" in *Journal of Biblical Literature,* Vol. 86, (1967), pp. 369–77; G. Ernest Wright and Reginald H. Fuller, *The Book of the Acts of God,* Doubleday and Co., N.Y., 1960; G. Ernest Wright, *God Who Acts* in *Studies in Biblical Theology,* No. 8, SCM Press, 1962.

10. The Midianite or Kenite hypothesis was first proposed by Ghillany in 1862 using the pseudonym von der Alm. It was popularized by K. Budde in 1899. H.H. Rowley has written its most cogent modern defense in 1950. According to this "Midianite hypothesis" Moses learned the name Yahweh from his father-in-law, Jethro, who

was a priest of Midian. If true, hearing the linguistic sound was not the same as receiving the revelation of the divine being which occurred in the experience of the burning bush. In Exodus 18 Moses tells Jethro what Yahweh has done for the Israelites in their escape from Egypt. In verse 11 Jethro responds, "Now I know that Yahweh is a deity great beyond any other; for he took the occasion of their being dealt with insolently to deliver the people from the power of the Egyptians." Had Jethro discovered that Moses' God Yahweh was really powerful? Or had Jethro discovered that his own clan-God, Yahweh, had more power than he had formerly believed? Yahweh could do mighty deeds outside the people of Midian too. I am convinced that Jethro learned that his clan-god had universal power to rescue and save. See H.H. Rowley, F.B.A., *From Joseph to Joshua: Biblical Traditions in the Light of Archeology,* Oxford University Press, 1970, pp. 149–61.

11. James Plastaras, C.M.S., *The God of Exodus: The Theology of the Exodus Narratives,* Bruce Publishing Co., Milwaukee, 1966, pp. 165–201.

12. For a good brief explanation of the Israelite concept of holy war, see "war" in John L. McKenzie, S.J., *Dictionary of the Bible,* pp. 919–21.

13. "The Dogmatic Constitution on the Church," par. 16 in Walter M. Abbott, S.J. (ed.), *The Documents of Vatican II,* Guild Press, N.Y., 1966, p. 35.

14. *Ibid.,* par. 15, pp. 33–34.

15. *Ibid.,* par. 9, p. 26.

16. *Ibid.*

17. *Ibid.,* par. 9, p. 25.

18. *Ibid.,* par. 17, pp. 36–37.

19. *Ibid.,* par. 8, p. 23.

20. *Ibid.,* par. 10, p. 27.

21. *Ibid.,* par. 12, p. 29.

22. Pope Paul VI, Apostolic Exhortation, *On Evangelization in the Modern World,* Dec. 8, 1975, par. 30, p. 22.

23. "Dogmatic Constitution on the Church," in *The Documents of Vatican II,* par. 12, p. 29.

24. *Ibid.,* par. 12, p. 30.

25. *Ibid.,* par. 13, pp. 30–31.

Chapter III

The Babylonian Captivity and Catholic Teaching on the Four Fundamental Truths of Faith

*"I will make you a light to the nations
that my salvation may reach
to the ends of the earth."*
—Is 49:6

What is meant by the Babylonian captivity of Israel?

Between 587 and 538 B.C. the Old Testament Israelites ceased to exist as an independent nation. They were conquered by the neo-Babylonian empire and the upper classes were all deported to Babylon by 587 B.C. The royal family of David ceased to rule from Jerusalem, the temple of Solomon was destroyed, women were raped, children were eaten for food and prophets and priests were scattered or butchered. It was the greatest period of collective suffering in the Old Testament. Christians might best think of the Babylonian captivity as the communal crucifixion of Yahweh's chosen people. In 538 B.C. Cyrus the Persian conquered the Babylonians and allowed the Jews to come home. In that way Ezekiel's vision of the dry bones of Israel coming back to life was fulfilled (Ez 37) under the direction of Ezra and Nehemiah. They rebuilt Jerusalem, restored the temple, renewed the temple liturgy, and guided the Jews in seeking personal holiness through fidelity to the torah of Moses.

How can we best understand the complex history of the Babylonian captivity?

The captivity of Israel was the second great transformation in the identity and faith of the Jews. It stands as a midpoint between the exodus (ca. 1285 B.C.) and the Maccabean crisis (167 B.C.). The creative tensions of history within the Babylonian captivity can best be understood as consisting in four historical moments: (1) the rise of royal messianism, (2) the prophetic call to repentance, (3) the exile in Babylon, and (4) the emergence of post-exilic Judaism.

Between Moses and the Rise of Royal Messianism
The Period of the Charismatic Judges

What happened to Israel's leadership when Moses died?

After his death, Moses was succeeded by Joshua (Jos 1:1). By that time the Israelites had left the desert and gone east of the Jordan River. From there, by conquering Jericho, they entered Canaan about 1200 B.C. (Jos 1—4). The Books of Joshua and Judges recount the history of the next two hundred years of conquest. Some details in the two books cannot be mutually reconciled, but we know from archeology that every major village in Palestine was leveled during the twelfth century B.C. Thus Joshua and Judges are generally trustworthy although not scientifically precise.[1]

Life for Israel was complicated by a new external threat, the Philistines. This hostile tribe lived along the Mediterranean seacoast. For the twelve tribes, mutual defense, according to the Mosaic covenant, required that all the tribes support anyone who suffered attack. Infidelity to this military obligation of the Israelites added to the increasing social chaos. The ancient victory canticle of Deborah recalls that Reuben, Gilead, and Dan had given little or no support to the recent war (Jgs 5:15–17). Such experiences contributed to a general rise in social chaos. The need for a central government and a standing army had become apparent to many. Thus the Book of Judges closes with a pithy comment on the political failure of charismatic Israel: "In those days there was no king of Israel; everyone did what he thought best" (Jgs 21:25). The book had just finished the sad saga of infidelity, rape, war among the tribes, and kidnaping women during a liturgical feast (Jgs 19—21). The political structures of the desert were not serving in the agricultural life of the settled territories. Some new system was needed.[2]

1 Samuel recounts the complex and sordid rise of the kingship between ca. 1040 and 1000 B.C. The prophet Samuel was the last great representative of the old charismatic Israel. The sources in 1 Samuel are very confusing and represent both pro-kingship and anti-kingship views as coming from Samuel.[3] The prophetic response to the cry for stronger central government warned against the dangers of such a pagan institution. Their sons would be conscripted as soldiers and government engineers; their daughters would be forced to help beautify the royal wives and do their cooking; their money would be heavily taxed, and their property usurped by government decree (cf. 1 Sam 8:10–18). In spite of these warnings against their loss of freedom, the people persuaded Samuel to anoint Saul, and subsequently Samuel withdrew the divine charisma when Saul superseded the limits of his royal authority.[4]

The scriptural sources likewise do not agree on how David first came into Saul's court.[5] That Saul became jealous and murderously paranoid about David's military charisma is beyond conjecture (1 Sam 19—31). This eventually caused David and his band of six hundred outlaws to flee Saul and hide in the Negeb desert. There they acted as double agents supporting Israel, but feigning allegiance to Achish king of Gath and Ziklag (1 Sam 27). When Saul and his sons were killed by the Philistines in the battle of Mount Gilboa in Galilee (1 Sam 31),

the way was opened for David to be anointed king of Israel.
First the southern tribes anointed him at Hebron. As such he
became king of the Judahites (2 Sam 1:1–6). After an interlude
of trying to have Saul's son, Ishbaal, reign as king in the
north, he was killed by men of the north. David had them
executed and then allowed himself to be anointed by the
northern tribes (2 Sam 5:1–5).[6]

With all twelve tribes recognizing his royal charisma as
coming from Yahweh, David attacked the Jebusites and made
their neutral city, Jerusalem, the capital of the new state of
Israel. Not only was this site neutral for all the tribes, but the
city was militarily defensible, supplied with water, and geo-
graphically central to all the tribes. There David moved the
ark (2 Sam 6) and the tent of meeting; there he built a modest
palace for himself, his wives, concubines and royal children. In
Jerusalem, the exodus people of Yahweh became the ancient
nation of Israel (ca. 1000 B.C.). This unified Israel endured
only until the death of Solomon whose oppression of the people (1 Kgs 12:1–20) caused a political schism in 921 B.C. For
the next two hundred years the kingdom of Israel had its own
capital in Samaria in Galilee. The king of David's line in
Jerusalem was called the king of Judah. The development of a
unified Israel in 1000 B.C. had set the remote context for the
Babylonian captivity.

The Four Moments of the
Babylonian Captivity
The Rise of Royal Messianism

What is meant by the term "royal messianism"?

"Messiah" in Hebrew means "anointed"—with oil by the
prophet on one's coronation day as king. In the coronation rite
the prince was adopted by God as "the anointed son of Yahweh," the new king of Israel. In the period of the New Testament, "anointed one" was translated as *christos* and applied to
the risen Jesus by Greek-speaking Christians among the Gen-

tiles. Thus for Christian faith, Jesus, the Anointed One, Jesus the Messiah, and Jesus the Christ are equivalent titles. The risen Jesus, the legal son of Joseph, of the house of David reigns eternally as the anointed Son of God (Mt 1:1, 16, 20–24).

How did this new belief in messianism develop in Israel?

This new religious current began in David's reign as recounted in 2 Samuel 7. This Scripture recalls David's concern to build a temple in which to house the ark containing the tablets of the Mosaic covenant. This was a move away from the traditional practice of using a tent or tabernacle as the mobile sacred shrine. The tabernacle admirably symbolized that the transcendent Yahweh could not fit in a building like pagan idols. Yahweh manifested his presence through his holy *breath* or *wind* (the Hebrew *ruah* is also translated *spirit*). This divine presence filled the tent and engulfed it at the same time. Since the ark was Yahweh's special dwelling place in Israel, would its move into a stone temple be equivalent to "encapsulating" Yahweh? Would David be trying to create a state religion subservient to his royal whims? The historical context allows us to conjecture that questions like these prompted David to consult Nathan, a court prophet, to learn Yahweh's will in the matter (2 Sam 7:1–2).

At first Nathan concurred in the rectitude of David's desire to build a temple (2 Sam 1:3). What a shock for both Nathan and David when Yahweh spoke to Nathan that night in the commanding power of a prophetic dream. Yahweh revealed to Nathan that he was quite pleased with his "tent" and did not want David to build a house (temple) for the ark (2 Sam 7:5–7). Instead Yahweh was going to build a house for David. This "house of David" raised up by God was to consist in the bloodline descendants of David. Each new generation would produce a male heir who would inherit the throne of David. As an anointed or royal "messiah," each king was to be thought of as a "son" of God. God's promise to the house of David was absolute: "Your house and your kingdom shall endure forever" (cf. 2 Sam 7:11–14). This prophecy of Nathan to David is also called the Davidic covenant. With it a whole new thrust enters the religious life of Israel. Certainly the Christian fulfillment of the prophecy of Nathan far exceeded anything he or David expected in the tenth century B.C. Nathan, David, Solomon, and all Israel accepted it as God's covenant with David's family to ensure its military and political survival until the end of time. No one special messiah was named or prophesied. On the contrary, every king of David's line was to be anointed on his coronation day as a specially adopted "son of God" enjoying divine protection from his enemies (Ps 110:1–3).[7]

How was royal messianism later misinterpreted?

It was not the Davidic covenant itself, but the subsequent perversion of it, which constituted the first moment of the exile. According to Nathan's prophecy, Yahweh had entered into covenant with the house of David so that they would not fear his removing from them his divine charisma, as he had removed it from Saul (2 Sam 7:15). In this reassuring aspect of the covenant, Yahweh seems to have allowed for the human need to feel security. A sense of personal and political security allows governments to exercise authority with due regard for freedom and initiative from the grassroots. A threatened ruler frequently becomes like Saul—paranoid and murderously oppressive. Unfortunately the feeling of personal security could be debased into one of insufferable smugness. The promise of perpetual divine guidance for the royal family could be disfigured into a religious-political ideology that put the human king above the divine king, Yahweh. When this abuse of power occurred, the religious and political life of Israel would degenerate into various forms of egoism and oppression. Periodic repentance would occur, as we shall see, but there was always that "ace in the hole." In effect, the rulers said, "Yahweh has said that the people of Judah are not like other people; we are not vulnerable to the forces of human history. Yahweh has promised that we cannot be conquered." As an example, note the crass nationalistic expansionism in Psalm 89, especially verse 28: "I will make him ... highest of the kings of the earth."

The Prophetic Call to Repentance

What is the difference between a biblical prophet and a superstitious fortune teller?

The Hebrew word for prophet is *nabr*. It may mean one who is "called" by God or one who "bubbles over" with spiritual enthusiasm. To prophesy was to proclaim an oracle on the authority of the divine inspiration to speak. Israel's earliest prophets, like those of her pagan neighbors, were ecstatic. They danced, sang, and played musical instruments to the point of nude frenzy (cf. 1 Sam 19:18–24). These early ecstatics developed into the prophetic brotherhoods of the ninth century who were known by their distinctive garments of a simple animal skin and a leather belt.

With David and Nathan court prophecy developed to help the king discern the will of God in decisions of state. When this type of prophecy degenerated into telling the king whatever he wanted to hear (cf. 1 Kgs 22), God raised up the "classical" prophets beginning with Amos ca. 750 B.C. The prophetic books of the Old Testament come from these men and their associates. The prophetic call to repentance spanned the time from Amos in 750 B.C. to Jeremiah and Ezekiel in 587 B.C. Then prophecies of consolation and restoration of Jerusalem continued until divine providence allowed the Jewish high priests to replace the kings and prophets as the religious and political leaders of the people (ca. 520 B.C.).

In general biblical prophets invited the people to renew their observance of the covenant of Moses. They stressed adoration of God and justice to God's poor. When they spoke of the future, it was either as a divine promise of blessings to come or as a threat of divine judgment for breaking the covenant. Therefore a biblical prophet is as different from a fortune teller as "discernment" of God's will is from "divination" of the future by use of magical techniques. Fortune telling had been developed in Mesopotamia into an elaborate array of superstitious practices. Every type was forbidden in Israel under pain of death (Lev 19:31). Divination was revealed to be less powerful than prophecy in Numbers 23:23 and was associated with an evil spirit in Acts 16:16–19.

Had not God called the people to repentance prior to Amos?

Yes. At the time of David (1000 B.C.) this prophetic call may have begun with a gentle reminder to live in the vulnerability of communion with one another and with Yahweh like the first man and woman. Genesis 2 (the older of the two inspired scriptural accounts of creation), Genesis 3 (the fall), and Genesis 4—11 (the history of the spread of sin until Abraham) were given some early coherent shape by the tenth century B.C. prophets living in Jerusalem.

By demythologizing the fatalism in the old Babylonian creation epics, the inspired authors re-presented the creation of the universe as Yahweh's act of growing a garden and giving responsibility for its cultivation to the first man (in Hebrew, *ish,* "a man"). He gave *ish* a partner, so he would not be lonely—woman (*isha*) in Genesis 2:18. This account of creation pictures Yahweh as a potter who marvelously shapes and breathes life into his handiwork (Gen 2:6). Also Yahweh is portrayed as a gardener who cultivates beauty and fruitfulness for his people (Gen 2:7). Man and woman had been created for mutual vulnerability in nakedness of body and spirit. At the center of that vulnerability had been their mutual communion with Yahweh. This is why they got married (Gen 2:24–25).[8] In the beginning they had walked together with Yahweh in the garden in the cool breeze of each evening (Gen 3:7–8). Such was the intimacy of their communion.

What was meant by "Adam" and "Eve"?

The inspired author never gave symbolic names to the man and the woman until after their initial act of disobedience.[9] Prior to that they are almost unreal, representing what ought to be true even today, but is not now true of human communion. Once *isha* knows sexual hunger for her man and understands its ambiguous consequences in the pleasure of orgasm and in the pain of childbirth (Gen 3:16), her husband names her Life (Eve). The truth of that woman's experience of life would have been easy to verify among the women of David's Israel. Their husbands in patriarchal Israel were very much their "masters." According to ancient semitic thought patterns, male dominance was one of Yahweh's "curses." Just as snakes were cursed to crawl on their bellies (Gen 3:14), women, as a result of the fall, were cursed by the uncaring dominance of their sinful husbands (Gen 3:16). This male dominance disfigured that naked vulnerable mutual sharing centered in Yahweh for which they had been created. Now husbands were refusing to worship Yahweh and tried instead to play God in their own homes. The curse of male dominance still cries out to God for redemption.

Ish is only named in Genesis 5:1. This ancient list of ancestors was given its present position by a later priestly author. Therefore it would be difficult to conjecture just when the Israelites began to think of the first man as Adam (*adamah* means clay in Hebrew). As male, his work takes on other frustrations of the fruits of sin. "By the sweat of your face shall you get your bread" (Gen 3:19).

What is the main point of Genesis 2—11?

After showing how Yahweh created us for sharing his life, the author teaches that humanity alone spread sin (Gen 3—11). Then the history of salvation began (Gen 12) with Abraham until the choice of David as king of Israel. Yahweh had always worked in unexpected ways using the young and weak to confound the strong and powerful. Yahweh had always brought life to the people; human disobedience had always brought shame, fratricide, and death. Yahweh had created the original couple for vulnerability in communion with him. They had preferred the invulnerability of "the wisdom of the gods" (Gen 3:5-6). Which path of humanity would David and his family choose? That of vulnerability to communion—Yahweh's way? Or that of resentment, jealousy, intrigue, murder, and exploitation of the people in cities —Cain's way?

Interpreted in this light, Genesis 2—11 was originally intended as a kind of extended prophetic parable inviting the court of David to live its messianic covenant in the spirit of its gracious giver, Yahweh himself.[10] A superficial reading of the court history in 2 Samuel provides ample testimony that the royal house frequently preferred the murderous intrigues of Cain.

When did Yahweh raise up the major prophets?

When gentle parable failed, perhaps more direct denunciation would succeed. Thus in the ninth century B.C. the prophetic brotherhoods of Elijah, Elisha and their successors boldly called kings and people back to covenant living (1 Kgs 17—2 Kgs 10). Eventually, however, the prophets themselves became so assimilated into the values of court and Canaanite culture that they failed to serve a critical function and largely endorsed the wishes of the king and the people (cf. 1 Kgs 22).

Amos

Ca. 750 B.C. Yahweh inspired the "prophet" Amos to leave his sheep in the southern village of Tekoa and to prophesy in the northern sanctuary at Bethel. Amos refused to call himself a "prophet" because of the inauthenticity of the recognized prophets (Am 7:12-25).

By the time of Amos, it seems that an oral tradition had grown up among the people that "a day of Yahweh" was coming. We have no prior Scripture revealing this. This "day" would be Israel's final day of victory against her enemies; the house of David would reign at last in a definitive victory over the surrounding nations. Thus the "day of Yahweh" was being used as part of a self-serving religious ideology. Amos turned this oral tradition upside down and shocked the people by saying, "Woe to those who yearn for the day of Yahweh! What will this day mean for you? Darkness and not light!" (Am 5:18).

To the smug and oppressive Israelites living in the northern capital of Samaria, Amos pointed out the oppression in their midst. For robbing and extorting their wealth from the poor, their castles would be pillaged by an enemy invader (Am 3:9–11).

Trying desperately to shock the people into recognizing their moral, political and spiritual peril, one of his final oracles reads, "By the sword shall all sinners among my people die, those who say, 'Evil will not reach or overtake us.'" As we might expect, the prophecies of Amos did not receive a warm reception. Amaziah, the priest of Bethel, reported them to King Jeroboam II as "conspiracy" and banished Amos to the south, saying, "Off with you, visionary! Flee to the land of Judah! There earn your bread by prophesying, but never again prophesy in Bethel; for it is a king's sanctuary and a royal temple" (Am 7:12–13). Judged in terms of earthly success, Amos' prophetic mission was a complete failure; the people had not been liberated from their moral blindness.

Hosea

If threats of destruction would not rouse the people from their religious torpor, perhaps the tenderness of intimate love would have the desired effect. Not long after Amos, Yahweh raised up the prophet Hosea. Whether Gomer was Hosea's historical wife or an allegory symbolizing the community of Israel is debated in critical scholarship. However, it is clear that the relationship of Hosea, husband-prophet, and Gomer, unfaithful wife and whore, reveals a deeper understanding of the covenant relationship between Yahweh and Israel. It is no longer simply an "agreement"; it is an interpersonal union full of longing and appropriately portrayed in the sexual imagery of married love. Israel, the bride of Yahweh, has forsaken her husband in not living the covenant of Moses; Yahweh wants her back (cf. Hos 2:8–18).

Here fiery Yahweh of Mount Sinai, the covenant King, reveals a new depth of personal caring within himself as Israel's "husband." Maybe he can arouse her passion for divine love and her hunger for deeper intimacy with him. Maybe if she understands her covenant relationship in this new way as passionately loving—not as something merely cultic or economic or political—maybe then the purity of single-hearted adoration of God and the flowering of justice will take root in the lives of the people. But alas, Israel will not allow herself to be seduced by her only true lover, and she will fall to the Assyrian invasion in 722 or 721 B.C. Like prophetic threat, prophetic wooing had also failed to achieve historical success.

One thing is certain, however. After the time of Hosea, no one could rightly say that the God of the Old Testament was a God simply of wrath and fear. To choose to ignore Yahweh the lover is simply "Christian" propaganda.[11] The inspired texts do not permit such facile labels.

Isaiah

Meanwhile in the southern kingdom of Judah, Yahweh was trying to renew covenant communion through the prophet Isaiah. His vocation seems to have come from a profoundly moving religious vision experienced while praying before an altar in the temple ca. 742–41 B.C. In this privileged glimpse of God's glory, Isaiah heard the heavenly choir chanting: "Holy, holy, holy is Yahweh of hosts. . . . All the earth is filled with his glory" (Is 6:3). Isaiah would have a long and at times trying prophetic career. He would be inspired to try threats, silence, consolations, and even preaching in the nude as a prophetic sign of shame (Is 20:1–5). All of this was meant to help Judah live the covenants of Moses and David in the confusing political life of the eighth century B.C. Middle East.

The oracles of historical Isaiah are found in chapters 1—39 of Isaiah. The oracles found in chapters 40—65 represent the revelation given by God to subsequent prophets. They preferred anonymity and understood their oracles as furthering the prophetic mission of historical Isaiah. Thus all of these prophecies were collected into one book and called "Isaiah." The historical Isaiah gives the prophecy of Nathan (2 Sam 7) a new sense of promise and of historical specificity. Since this too is important for understanding the Babylonian exile, we will limit ourselves to considering this aspect of Isaiah's prophecies. For with Isaiah, Judah began to believe not only in a divinely protected house of David, but in the coming of a special Messiah.

In what circumstances did Isaiah prophesy the coming of the Messiah?

The political context into which Yahweh called Isaiah to prophesy was somewhat complicated. The kingdoms of the Middle East were frightened by the expansionist moves of Assyria (modern Iran). The Assyrian king, Tiglath Pileser III, seems to have been bent on making Damascus (Syria), Samaria (Israel), and Jerusalem (Judah) his imperial subjects (2 Kgs 16 and Is 7:1–9). King Pekah of Israel and King Rezin of Syria had formed a political alliance to try to protect themselves from their aggressive Assyrian neighbor. King Ahaz of Judah had signaled his pro-Assyrian leanings early in his reign (735–ca. 715 B.C.). This caused Pekah and Rezin to think that their best option was to overthrow Ahaz and to install an anti-Assyrian collaborator, "the son of Tabeel," as an illegal ascendant to David's throne (Is 7:6). Chapter 7 of Isaiah is probably set in 732 B.C., the year Assyria took Damascus. Prior to that event, Pekah and Rezin were besieging the city gates of Jerusalem trying to carry out their anti-Assyrian strategy. In the midst of all this, Yahweh told Isaiah to take his son and go to the city gates to counsel King Ahaz.

"Take care you remain tranquil and do not fear" (Is 7:4), Isaiah began. Then he prophesied the fall of Damascus and of

Samaria within sixty-five years, and urged a "faith" in Yahweh (Is 7:6–9). This *faith* invited a trust in God from Ahaz that would fear neither the Assyrian threat nor the anti-Assyrian league. Ahaz was to take "the long-term view" and choose to do nothing at this time. Any other option would entangle Judah in a breach of God's will.

Isaiah invited Ahaz to seek a prophetic sign to confirm that this "ridiculous sounding" prophecy was truly from Yahweh. Ahaz knew what he wanted to do already, so he feigned piety and said that he should not seek a sign from Yahweh. Isaiah saw through this ruse and called Ahaz's disinterest in knowing God's will "wearying" to Yahweh (Is 7:10–13). Then Isaiah gave the unwanted sign by proclaiming his famous oracle on the birth of Immanuel through the virgin (Is 7:14–17).

How did Isaiah understand the Immanuel prophecy which Yahweh had prompted him to utter?

Most likely Isaiah expected the wife of Ahaz to be "the virgin" (*almah* in Hebrew means "maiden") who would give birth to a new royal son. This son was born and named Hezekiah. He is remembered as one of the three "saintly" kings of Jerusalem. This royal son, Immanuel, would be the special instrument Yahweh would use to deliver Judah from its current threat of being conquered. Not only that, but this son would bring "everlasting peace" (Is 9:5–6).

How did Ahaz respond to this gift of divine guidance?

Ahaz responded with complete disregard to the oracles and by resorting to political opportunism. Sensing that Assyria had all the power, Ahaz sent word to Tiglath-Pileser that he would become a vassal of Assyria, push aside the altar of Yahweh in the Jerusalem temple, manipulate the liturgical practices of the priests, and offer money to the Assyrians in exchange for military aid from them against Pekah and Rezin (2 Kgs 16:7–18). Naturally Tiglath-Pileser accepted the terms, invaded Damascus to divert the invading army from Jerusalem's city gates, and accepted Ahaz as a religious-political vassal of the Assyrian empire. In Ahaz, fear of his enemies and oppression of Judah's religious faith had triumphed over trust in the covenant of David.

Isaiah's response was justifiable anger and a complete sense of futility in his prophetic ministry. "Call not alliance what this people calls alliance," cried Isaiah, referring to the treaty with Assyria (Is 8:15). It is likely that Isaiah went into seclusion for about seventeen years and did not prophesy again until Ahaz died ca. 715 B.C. (cf. Is 8:16–20).

Why do Christians apply the Immanuel prophecy to Jesus?

About eight hundred years later, St. Matthew provided us with the inspired interpretation of the Immanuel prophecies of Isaiah. Using the new Christian experience of the abiding divine presence of the risen Christ in the Church (Mt 28:20), Matthew can see how the "Immanuel" prophesied by Isaiah is fulfilled in the birth of Jesus through the Virgin Mary (Mt 1:18–25). Here, as we saw earlier, the divine fulfillment of the prophecy resembles, but far exceeds, the human expectations of the Old Testament prophet.

How was the Immanuel prophecy misinterpreted in Old Testament times?

Isaiah's Immanuel revelation gave Judah the habit of looking for someone, a special anointed one, who would bring a different kind of peace—a peace more authentic than that brought by Ahaz and more enduring than that achieved by short-lived kings. Because Immanuel failed to reign during Isaiah's lifetime, the messianic hope which Isaiah bequeathed to Judah was to be distorted as Jerusalem again retreated into religious smugness and considered herself militarily invincible.

The Deuteronomic Reform

The final important prophetic failure which led to the Babylonian exile was the Deuteronomic reform attempted during the reign of King Josiah ca. 621 B.C. The Book of Deuteronomy was probably composed at this time in the form of a series of inspired sermons put back into the mouth of Moses who had been dead for about six hundred years. It is the Book of Deuteronomy which most Old Testament scholars now consider to be "The Book of the Law" found in the temple during the reign of King Josiah (2 Kgs 22:8—23:25).[12] The whole effort was to renew the spirit of Moses in a very different historical context.

Josiah, as a reform king in the tradition of Hezekiah and the Deuteronomist, shows strong affinities with the prophet Hosea. The Deuteronomic temple sermons were a sublimely inspired effort to woo an economically comfortable people back to Yahweh and to a covenant life of justice and love. "Hear, O Israel! Yahweh is our God, Yahweh alone! Therefore, you shall love Yahweh your God, with all your heart, and with all your soul, and with all your strength" (Dt 6:4).

It is the Deuteronomist who gives the whole concept of *remembering the past* a new spiritual depth and power. If the people would only remember how good Yahweh had been to them, they would live by warm-hearted gratitude in personal fidelity to covenant communion with Yahweh and with one another. Therefore the inspired author invites the people to remember how Yahweh had cared for them in the desert when they had been nothing but homeless aliens. Now as middle-class citizens living in the capital, can they not bring a thanks-giving offering to the priest to recognize God's goodness in the fruits of the earth? If they remember their own lowly origins, should they not offer compassion to the foreigners and aliens who live among them? To confess their faith and love and gratitude, they should stand before the priest and say publicly and humbly, "My father was a wandering Aramaean" (cf. Dt 8, 9, and 26) and share their goods with the poor.

With his strong backing of the Deuteronomic reform, what were the people to think of King Josiah? Was he to be the promised "Immanuel" who would bring "the everlasting peace"? For a few years it all looked so hopeful, but then, tragically, Josiah was killed in the battle of Megiddo against Pharaoh Neco of Egypt ca. 604 B.C. (2 Kgs 23:28–30). The last of the "saint" kings was dead; the inspired Deuteronomic homilies had failed to take deep root in the hearts of the people, and the external threat of the encroaching neo-Babylonian empire was daily becoming more serious. As if recognizing the failure of the Deuteronomic reform movement, and yet confident that Yahweh would eventually succeed in luring the people back to covenant living, the Deuteronomist has Moses say, "A prophet like me will Yahweh your God raise up for you from among your own kinsmen; to him you shall listen" (Dt 18:15).

Jeremiah

If Christian faith recognizes Jesus as the definitive prophet of biblical revelation, certainly Jeremiah must rank as a close second in terms of fidelity to Yahweh in spite of his experience of human rejection. His early career continued the Deuteronomic reform. According to Jeremiah Yahweh found no social group in Judah open to his will.

The poor are found in public houses imprisoned in ignorance of "the way of Yahweh" (Jer 5:4–5). They live in dishonesty and "have set their faces harder than stone" (Jer 5:1–3; also chapter 9). Likewise the educated rich have become impervious to covenant faith and the necessity of just relationships. Yahweh finds their life full of "owning slaves" (Jer 34:10), "rebellion, idolatry, and adultery." "They denied Yahweh, saying, 'Not he—no evil shall befall us, neither sword nor famine shall we see'" (Jer 5:12).[13] And finally the liturgical life had degenerated into beautiful rites lacking the substance of covenant faith and morality. "What right has my beloved in my house, while she prepares her plots? Can vows and sacred meat turn away your misfortune from you? Will you still be jubilant when you hear the great invasion?" (Jer 11:15-16).

In what came to pass as Jeremiah's weeping for exiled Judah, are we not invited to find a revealed image of Yahweh weeping too?[14] The divine wrath which exiled Judah was not arbitrary or uncaring. It was painfully medicinal—painful for Judah, but also painful for God. Perhaps the horror of death, destruction, and social displacement would liberate the people from sinful egoism and religious hypocrisy in all its forms. For both Yahweh and the people, the cure would eventually compensate for the pain (Jer 13:15-17).

Exile in Babylon

When did God reveal that he was going to side with the enemies of his chosen people?

The third moment in the Babylonian captivity was begun when Jeremiah saw that the Deuteronomic reform was failing and received a word from Yahweh to preach his famous temple sermon (Jer 7 and 26). In effect God said, "Because you did not listen to me, I will do to this temple what I did to Shiloh. I will cast you away from me" (cf. Jer 7:11-15).

Shiloh had been the central liturgical sanctuary for the ark during the time of the judges and had been destroyed quite suddenly (Ps 78:60). For prophesying against the temple, the priests and the prophets wanted to put Jeremiah to death (Jer 26:11). To them Jeremiah's prophecy sounded like sacrilege or treason—not like anything they had come to expect as "holy" or "loyal" to God and the government. And yet in 597 B.C. King Jehoiakin and the first group of Judahites were exiled to Babylon (2 Kgs 24:8-17). Even this was not enough warning to bring the people to repentance.

In the final days of the long siege of Jerusalem by Babylon, King Zedekiah sent for Jeremiah to seek the word of Yahweh. Jeremiah encouraged the king to surrender to the enemy to avoid more suffering for the people. Zedekiah confessed privately that he would like to, but he was afraid that if he surrendered he would be mistreated by those who had already defected to the enemy. Jeremiah assured him that this would not happen, but the king was intransigent (Jer 38:14–24). Fear, not faith, continued to undermine the life of Judah.

After fourteen months of siege, the Babylonians breached the walls. The fleeing king was caught and forced to watch his sons murdered; then he was blinded and brought to Babylon. "Every large building was destroyed by fire" and all the liturgical vessels were carted away as "booty" with no concern for their sacred character (2 Kgs 25:13–17).

With no king, no palace, no temple, no prophet, no priest, no army, no wise man, where was Yahweh's promise to David that his royal house would rule forever? Jerusalem simply did not exist anymore. Perhaps the bitter pain of Israel in the early exile is nowhere expressed more honestly than in Psalm 137: "Happy the man who shall repay you—happy the man who shall seize and smash your little ones against the rock," cried the exiles to their captors.

If such feelings are not religiously uplifting, their frankness is utterly liberating. The smugness of Israelite invincibility has given way to the sting of anger and lashing out at her conquerors. Who of us would not feel the same hurt and resentment? The God of Moses and David, who had led Israel out of Egypt, had now led her into Babylon. Who was this God of gods? With no land, who were the people of Judah? As anger subsided into resignation, as egotism was ground into piety and pride was transformed into a deeper poverty of spirit, the house of David was liberated to hear Yahweh speak anew. A deeper revelation would answer these questions.

The Rise of Judaism

During the exile the oracles of Ezekiel and Deutero-Isaiah (chapters 40—55 of Isaiah) nurtured the faith of the messianic people. The prophecies of condemnation faded as Jerusalem was destroyed and those of consolation began. God would resurrect the skeleton of Israel (Ez 37) and do this by the power of his holiness (Ez 39:25–29). The land, the temple and the priesthood would all be restored as Israel became a holy people (Ez 40—48). In all of this, Ezekiel revealed the transcendent holiness of God as the cause of the restoration. A similar emphasis is given to God's utter holiness, personal uniqueness, and power over all creation by Deutero-Isaiah in Isaiah 40:25–29. It was probably during the exile that the Jews began to venerate the name of Yahweh as so sacred that it was too holy to be pronounced. Therefore they began to substitute *Adonai* (the Lord) for the personal name of God, Yahweh.

What effect did the exile have on the development of the Bible?

The exile provided the historical context for making Genesis 1:1—2:4a (the six days of creation) the introduction to the whole Bible. This beautiful hymn may have been sung in the Jerusalem temple and carried into exile or it may have been inspired during the exile. It revealed to the discouraged Jews that the one and only God had effortlessly created all things that the neighboring peoples worshiped as gods. In truth, everything God created was *good*, not evil, nor divine as the pagans tended to believe.

In this way Genesis 1 revealed the universe to be a kind of temple where the ordering power of God reigned. Each stanza (day) shows how God progressively brought more order out of the original chaos and nothingness. Such a meditation must have stirred the hope of the exiles that God could also reharmonize the social chaos in which they found themselves. By the power of his word he would be able to bring them home.

Moreover the hymn revealed that human beings were the pinnacle of God's creation. Made male and female in God's own image (Gen 1:21), they were given "dominion" (Gen 1:28) over plants and animals, and invited to remember that God "rested" on the seventh day, "blessed" it, and made it "holy" (Gen 2:1–3). In this way Ezekiel, Deutero-Isaiah, and Genesis 1

brought the exiled Jews to faith in a monotheistic God. There
simply was no other god; there was no limit to God's power for
doing good.

Besides the unique power of the one God for doing good, what else was revealed to the Jews during the exile?

Among the prophecies of consolation, the servant songs of
Deutero-Isaiah were revealed during the exile (see Is 42:1–4;
49:1–7; 50:4–11). While there is great scholarly debate over the
identity of the "servant of the Lord" in these Scriptures, most
exegetes admit that the fourth servant song has an intensely
personal character while the first three poems envision Israel
more as a communal "servant of the Lord."[15] As God's "servant people" the smug messianic house of David had been
transformed into the "little poor ones" of God. They remembered their God and cried out in their pain, expecting that he
would restore them. The prayer life of the exilic psalms reflects this new faith that God hears the cry of the poor (cf. Ps
69:34–37).

How did the Jews return home?

In 538 B.C. the prayer of the poor ones of God was answered. Cyrus the Great overthrew the neo-Babylonian empire and gave Persia command of the whole Middle East.
Under the Persians, the exiled Jews could return to Palestine
as a district of the newly enlarged Persian empire.

The Jews brought back with them the new saving light of
monotheism, a deeper prayer life and the first five books of
the Old Testament codified for the first time into a single
"Book of the Torah of Moses."[16] They returned ready to make
themselves pious servants of torah observance (Neh 9—10).
They agreed, under the inspiring leadership of Ezra, not to
marry Samaritans and to keep themselves undefiled by ab-
staining from Gentile ways (Neh 10:31). Suffering had made
the Jews vulnerable to the communion for which God had
created them. They hoped to find perfect fidelity to that com-

munion in conscientious observance of the torah. Their time of pruning had ceased.

Relation of the Captivity Revelation to Catholic Faith

What are the four fundamental truths of Catholic faith?

The most basic truth of faith is the revelation of God as the Creator of the universe. The second most basic truth is the goodness of all that God created and the special place of man and woman in creation as the image of God. The third most basic truth of faith is the nature of original sin. In this doctrine we learn the moral condition of the human family before God and our need for Christ as the price of our redemption. The fourth most basic truth of faith is the morally responsible life of servant love by which we live in accord with God's will for us. For by servant love which God works in us by his grace (1 Jn 4:2–21), we are judged worthy of entering into eternal life (cf. Mt 25:31–46).

Catholic faith has only formulated its beliefs in these areas when the pastoral leadership of the Church has judged it necessary to dispel confusion in the minds of the members. Thus the officially defined teachings do not pretend to exhaust the meaning of the mysteries of faith they teach. They only seek to clarify specific points or to reject specific errors. Because of this limited function, Catholic dogmas (the most solemn teachings defined by Church Councils or Popes) seek to lead members of the Church back to a more faithful reflection on Sacred Scripture. Full assent to dogmas never properly substitutes for primary allegiance to the Scriptures.

What do Catholics believe about God as Creator?

In the modern period, the concept of the monotheistic God of Genesis 1 has been subject to a variety of philosophical attacks or subtle distortions. Rationalism, pantheism, and materialism have all distanced themselves from the God of revelation. To help Catholics remain faithful to the God of Moses and Jesus, the bishops at Vatican I gave formal teachings on God and his providence. The one God created the world out of nothing by his goodness and power—not because he needed the universe to complete anything lacking in himself. He created the spiritual realm of angels, the bodily realm of plants and animals, and human creatures with both spirit and body.[17]

What do Catholics believe about human nature?

In the twentieth century a whole variety of philosophies and religious cults offer distorted views of human nature. Some exaggerate the physical aspect and reduce human beings simply to links in the food chain. Others exaggerate man's natural potential for spiritual or divine self-realization apart from grace. Catholic faith knows the profound unity of body and soul in human nature and recognizes that we are wounded by sin and experience rebellious stirrings in our bodies.

The bishops at Vatican II (1965) taught that the human person is the "crown" of physical creation and yet can probe his interior nature to find that God "who probes the heart" awaits within. By turning within, each person can come to recognize that we are not just bodies, but also spirits which are "immortal."[18] We each have a soul that cannot die because it cannot decompose. In these terms Catholic faith develops the view of the human person revealed in Genesis 2 as "clay" which is "breathing" and has the mysterious power of "naming" all the rest of creation.

What do Catholics believe about original sin?

Catholic faith developed a major clarification of its understanding of original sin in the sixteenth century Reformation controversies with Martin Luther. Eventually the bishops at the Council of Trent insisted that the following points were central to Catholic faith on original sin: Adam "lost the holiness and justice in which he had been constituted," and "the whole Adam, body and soul, was changed for the worse through the offense of his sin." That sin, consisting in "the death of the soul," plus the other effects of suffering and physical death, was transmitted to mankind "by propagation, not by imitation." Original sin can be *remitted* only by Christ (1 Cor 1:30) whose merits can be applied through the sacrament of baptism to adults and children alike (Gal 3:27). The grace of Christ received in baptism "remits all guilt" of original sin and does not simply justify the guilty sinner in the eyes of God. It is not guilt, but "concupiscence" or "the inclination to sin" which remains after baptism. "This same holy Synod declares that it is not its intention to include in this decree dealing with original sin the Blessed and Immaculate Virgin Mary, Mother of God."[19]

Why do Catholics say they believe that the Bible is inerrant and that they can accept that the theory of biological evolution might be true?

In 1943 Pope Pius XII wrote the encyclical *Divino Afflante Spiritu* which told Catholic Scripture scholars to study the ancient literary forms and languages used in the Sacred Scriptures. Using this critical method, scholars have determined that the inspired author of Genesis 1 intended to teach the power of God, the goodness of creation, the dignity of male and female humans, and the importance of worship on the seventh day. The literary form is a song or a poem. Each day is a "stanza"; therefore the inspired author intended to teach nothing about how many days or millions of years it took God to create the universe. In 1950 the same Pope taught that Catholics could accept scientific theories of evolution as long as they did not deny that God creates in human beings an immortal soul.

**How can Catholics remain faithful to the teachings
of the Council of Trent on original sin being inherited
from Adam if they now accept the theory of evolution?**

Where Trent spoke of "Adam" in an historical sense,
Catholic theology would now say that the historical existence
of Adam was "presumed" in that definition and "not formally
taught." Trent intended to define the nature of original sin.

**If there was no historical Adam, then how do
Catholics explain the history and communication of
original sin?**

In 1950 when Pius XII taught the acceptability of evolution in his encyclical *Humani Generis,* he also taught that
polygenism is contrary to Sacred Scripture and cannot be true.
Polygenism is the theory of evolutionists that scientific data
indicates that there were many first couples. For the Pope,
Romans 5:12–19 indicates that we should hold that there was
a sin committed by one Adam which is transmitted to all
"through generation."[20]

In 1966 Pope Paul VI addressed a group of theologians at
a symposium on original sin and again asked them to exclude
polygenism from the Catholic theology of original sin. After
their discussion, the theologians ultimately replied that the
scientific data did not allow that intellectual option. Technically that is where the faith of the Church now stands on
polygenism and original sin.[21]

From its theological heritage in St. Thomas Aquinas,
Catholic faith knows that all truth is one.[22] Because God is the
author of both revelation and creation, the discoveries of science cannot ultimately contradict the truths revealed in the
Bible. Therefore, if the polygenism advocated by the evolutionists must ultimately be admitted as true, then theology needs
to find a new way to explain the fundamental unity of human-
kind both in original justice and in the death of the soul
communicated in original sin. Creative theological work has

already occurred in this area, but a new consensus does not yet exist in the faith of the Church.

Should this lack of clarity disturb the interior certitude of Catholic faith about original sin?

No. Since it took about seven hundred years for the Old Testament community to move from the monolatry of Moses to the monotheism of the exilic prophets, one need not be dismayed if it takes some time to clarify the faith of the Church on the nature of original sin. Its effects are obvious, so that its existence need not be doubted. The precise way it is communicated remains open to study. Two hundred years ago all Catholics would have thought that God created the world in six literal days. No one would have suspected the immensity of God revealed as creatively working for billions of years in cosmic evolution.[23] Likewise they read Genesis 1 so superficially that they lost sight of its spiritual depth as revealing truths of salvation, not the facts of science. We can expect the same type of growth in faith from future reflection on polygenism and original sin.

What do Catholics believe about the nature of "servant love"?

In Isaiah 53:12 the suffering servant was revealed to "take away the sins" of the many. John 1:29 proclaims Jesus as that suffering and victorious "lamb" who "takes away the sins of the world." Jesus taught on earth that love of God and love of neighbor summed up the whole law and the prophets (Mk 12:30–31). Paul taught the early Christians that simply to live by faith in Jesus was not enough—we are called also to share in his sufferings (Phil 1:29).

The life of servant love is not the effort to "save oneself" through good works. Rather the life of servant love begins by letting God first love us (1 Jn 4:10). As divine love takes root in our hearts, we are interiorly strengthened to love God by keeping the commandments (1 Jn 2:4; 3:24; 2 Jn 6) and to express that love in concrete acts of mercy toward our brothers and sisters in the human family. Matthew's Gospel says that we will be judged according to the quality of mercy by which we lived. Every human being is to be loved as the presence of Christ in our midst (Mt 25:31–46).

Thus Catholic faith sees Christ invisibly at work in the hearts of all those who live by servant love since acts of self-sacrificial love cannot arise from human nature unaided. Confident that the Kingdom of God on earth involves freedom both from sin and from external slaveries, the Catholic bishops at Vatican II called on all individuals to preserve the human freedom to live by love. Thus Catholics are obliged to work for the elimination of "crippling destitution" and "ivory tower isolation."[24]

Are individual Catholics free to follow the dictates of their conscience?

Yes. While teachers of Catholic faith must clearly reject falsehood in order to be faithful servants of Jesus the truth (Jn 14:6), neither Catholic teachers nor anyone else can rightfully dictate the prudential judgments made by an informed conscience. Catholic faith recognizes that respect for the dignity of the human person (Gen 1:27) consists in being "immune from coercion on the part of individuals or social groups and of any kind of human power."[25] Thus Catholic pastors care to serve the education of informed consciences and not to dictate the decisions of conscience which each person must make. In this way the servant Church strives to imitate its servant Lord. At Vatican II, the bishops explained how freedom of conscience is fully consistent with the faith of the Apostles.[26]

Conclusion

How can we live today the faith revealed during the captivity?

(1) *Be peacemakers.* Those Scriptures which relate to the rise of messianism invite us to take the risk to allow new

people to lead us in new ways. God can still make the nobodies and outlaws of today into the King Davids of tomorrow. Like ancient Israel we can learn to go beyond the morality of "each doing what he thinks best" and develop a new social order which values justice and peace. Just as David united the twelve independent tribes into a nation state, we can work for greater cooperation between persons and nations at every level of society.

(2) *Be self-critical.* The Old Testament prophets still call us to let go of our modern idols. They remind us to laugh when we hear "I'm OK, you're OK." No. We are all "the image of God" *and* "a faithless band." We are all prone to excessive trust in wealth, power, beauty, reputation, weapons, human skill, pleasure, political systems, or belonging to the "right" nation, race, or religion. Healthy self-esteem, yes! Self-justifying smugness, never!

(3) *Let God be God.* The Scriptures of the exile remind us that God draws with broken lines. None of us can fully know the infinity of his being nor fully understand the meaning of his promises to us. Such Scriptures invite us to look up into the immensity of the sky and hear the Holy One say, "To whom can you liken me as an equal?" (Is 40:25).

(4) *Let go of bitterness.* The Scriptures of post-exilic Judaism invite us to use personal prayer to face our hurts and transform our anger into the humble gratitude of servant love. They encourage us to strive for a purity of heart which will distance us from the values of unbelievers. When we feel lost, hopeless, or rejected, they reassure us that God will bring us home—if we but give access to him in our hearts. He invites us to belong to the family of faith and to be part of that servant light to all the nations on earth.

Notes

1. John Bright, *A History of Israel,* The Westminster Press, Philadelphia, 1952, pp. 123–27.

2. *Ibid.,* pp. 164–66.

3. See 1 Samuel 8 and 12 for an anti-kingship passage. Most

exegetes believe the pro-kingship passages are older since they would have been necessary to facilitate the rise of Saul. The anti-kingship passages would then be a subsequent prophetic protest.

4. Was Saul anointed at Gilgal (1 Sam 11:15) or at the high place of Samuel in the land of Zuph (1 Sam 10:1)? Was Saul rejected by Samuel because as king he usurped the cultic office of Samuel (1 Sam 13:2-14) or because he mitigated the traditional ban of holy war and took enemy prisoners rather than slaughtering them all (1 Sam 15:4-35)? In all of this various ancient traditions have been conflated and we cannot recover the historical facts with certitude. See rather Weiser, *The Old Testament: Its Formation and Development*, Association Press, N.Y., 1968, pp. 162-64.

5. Was David first introduced to Saul as the "skilled harpist," and subsequently made his "armor bearer" (1 Sam 16:14-23) or did Saul first notice David after he slew Goliath (1 Sam 17:55-58)? Again the text is not internally consistent. For more background on the historical problems see Brevard S. Childs, *Introduction to the Old Testament as Scripture*, Fortress Press, Philadelphia, 1968.

6. For a fuller treatment see John Bright, pp. 171-79.

7. The rise of messianism in Israel is not easy to reconstruct historically. For a survey of the biblical data see "Messianism" in J. B. Bauer (ed.), *Sacramentum Verbi: An Encyclopedia of Biblical Theology*, Vol. 2, pp. 575-82.

8. Von Rad suggests that the exclamation "This one at last is bone of my bones and flesh of my flesh" comes from an ancient marriage rite. Interestingly enough the form is matriarchal. From Abraham on, Hebrew boys never left their fathers' tents to marry their wives; rather Hebrew girls left their fathers' tents to enter the family tents of their husbands. Such a matriarchal feature may indicate the extreme antiquity of the verse. See Gerhard Von Rad, *Genesis: A Commentary*, Westminster Press, Philadelphia, 1961, p. 83.

9. Gen 3:20 and 5:1 in *ibid.*, pp. 93, 68-69.

10. I find this much more plausible than B. Anderson's suggestion that the J-source theology of history was a kind of crass glorification of the new state of Israel under David. See *Understanding the Old Testament*, Prentice-Hall, Englewood Cliffs, N.J., 1975, pp. 198-199.

11. The history of trying to convince Christians to exclude the Old Testament from inspired Scripture began in the second century

with the Christian Gnostic heretic Marcion. Modern Christians are usually not that bold. They just repeat that the God of the Old Testament is a "God of wrath" and that the God of the New Testament is a "God of love." Both statements need to be qualified. See Jaroslav Pelikan, *The Christian Tradition: A History of the Development of Doctrine*, Vol. 1, and *The Emergence of the Catholic Tradition (100–600)*, The University of Chicago Press, 1971, pp. 71–80.

12. A. Weiser, p. 13.

13. I am indebted to James A. Sanders for this interpretation presented in a colloquium at the Ecumenical Institute for Advanced Theological Studies, Jerusalem, 1973.

14. It is historically plausible that Jeremiah uttered his laments as he was rotting in a damp cistern accused of treason. If so, it makes his despair all the more intelligible and poignant (cf. Jer 38:1–13).

15. For more background on the servant songs, see Johannes Lindblom, Acta Universitatis Lundensis, "The Servant Song in Deutero-Isaiah," Lunds Universitets Arsskirft: Lund, 1952; John L. McKenzie, *The Anchor Bible Second Isaiah*. Doubleday Co. Inc., Garden City, N.Y.; Christopher R. North, *The Suffering Servant in Deutero-Isaiah: An Historical and Critical Study*. Oxford University Press, London, 1948; *idem, Isaiah 40–55*, SCM Press, London, 1959; W. Zimmerli and J. Jeremias, "The Servant of God" in *Studies in Biblical Theology*, No. 20, Alec R. Allenson, Inc., Naperville, Ill., 1957.

16. For a discussion of canonicity and communal faith identity see James A. Sanders, *Torah and Canon*, Fortress Press, Philadelphia, 1972.

17. J. Neuner, S.J. and J. Dupuis, S.J. (eds.), *The Christian Faith in the Doctrinal Documents of the Catholic Church*. Christian Classics, Westminster, Md., 1975, #412, p. 119.

18. "Pastoral Constitution on the Church in the Modern World," par. 14 in Walter M. Abbott, S.J. (ed.), *The Documents of Vatican II*, Guild Press, N.Y., 1966, p. 212.

19. J. Neuner, # 508–13, pp. 130–32.

20. *Ibid.*, #419–20, p. 121.

21. For a fuller treatment of the contemporary theology of original sin and the implications of evolution and polygenism, see Anon., "New Thinking on Original Sin," in *Herder Correspondence*, Vol. 4 (1967); Pope Paul VI, "Original Sin and Modern Science: Address of Pope Paul VI to Participants in a Symposium on Original Sin," in

The Pope Speaks, Vol. 11 (July 11, 1966), pp. 329–35; Maurice Flick, S. J., "Original Sin and Evolution: Towards a Possible Solution" in *The Tablet,* Sept. 12, 1966, pp. 1039–41.

22. "Declaration on Christian Education," par. 10 in *The Documents of Vatican II,* p. 648.

23. It is this kind of experience which led Pope Paul VI to teach in *Mysterium Ecclesiae* that the Church deepens its understanding of revelation through progress in the secular sciences. Quoted in Appendix of Richard P. McBrien, *Catholicism,* Vol. II, Winston Press, Minneapolis, 1980, p. xviii.

24. "Pastoral Constitution on the Church in the Modern World," par. 30, in *The Documents of Vatican II,* p. 220.

25. "Decree on Religious Freedom," par. 2, in *The Documents of Vatican II,* pp. 678–79.

26. *Ibid.,* par. 11, pp. 691–92.

Chapter IV

The Maccabean Crisis and Catholic Teaching on Priests, Popes, and Saints

"I saw One like a son of man coming on the clouds of heaven ... his kingship shall not be destroyed."
—Dan 7:13–14

What is meant by the Maccabean crisis?

In the second century before Christ a Jewish family, the Maccabees, led a guerrilla uprising against the Greeks who were trying to get religious and political control of the Jews. The critical year in the crisis was 167 B.C. The Jews entered this period with a special emphasis on the supreme authority of their high priests. They emerged from this period with new beliefs in the afterlife, heaven, hell, judgment day, and the communion of saints. The Maccabean crisis gave rise to new Scriptures which are very important for understanding Judaism at the time of Jesus. Historically the new elements of biblical faith which developed in the Maccabean period can perhaps best be understood as developing through four moments: (1) the rise of the Jewish high priests, (2) the success of the Jews in repelling the Greeks, (3) the development of pious visionary groups among the Jews, (4) the revelation of *heaven* as God's ultimate fulfillment of history.

The Rise of the Jewish High Priests

How did high priests become the Jewish leaders instead of kings and prophets?

When the Jews returned from the exile, the prophetic movement enjoyed only brief flashes of inspired renewal. Haggai (ca. 520 B.C.) rebuked the people for their slowness in rebuilding the temple.[1] Zechariah (ca. 520 B.C.) told the Jews that their just Savior would come "meek and riding on an ass" (Zec 9:9–10).[2] Later Malachi (ca. 445 B.C.) warned the people to prepare for the day of the Lord and to expect the return of Elijah, the prophet who had been assumed into heaven about six hundred years earlier (cf. 2 Kgs 2:9–12; Mal 3:23–24). On this startling note the canonical shape of classical prophecy ended in Judaism.[3]

The priest, Joshua, was the first to be anointed a high priest (ca. 520 B.C.). The precise circumstances are shrouded in historical guesses drawn from fragmentary records. We do know that Joshua, the priest, originally sat beside Zerubbabel, the post-exilic Jewish king, as the two "sons of oil" (Zec 4:11–14). The prophets Haggai (2:20–23) and Zechariah (6:11) both expressed high hopes for Zerubbabel's political success as the restorer of the messianic line of David. Their prophecies were bold and politically inflammatory. Soon afterward, Zerubbabel simply disappeared in mystery. We do not know what became of him. John Bright hypothesizes that Zerubbabel may have been deposed by the Persians due to his revolutionary Jewish tendencies.[4] Whatever happened, Joshua, as high priest, reigned over Jerusalem solely, without prophet or king to direct him.

Since Joshua was already a priest, when had the Jewish priesthood begun?

Roland de Vaux is probably right in his historical reconstruction of the origins of the priestly tribe of Levi.[5] If Genesis 34:30 preserves an historical memory—as is likely—then Levi was originally a non-priestly tribe in the line of Jacob which lived with Simeon and Judah in the south. In pre-Mosaic times this tribe had already specialized in liturgical rites at various local sanctuaries. The high proportion of Egyptian names in the lists of early Levites shows that they were with Moses in Egypt; he too was a Levite and set his fellow Levites aside for liturgical duties involving the tent of meeting and the ark during the period of wandering in the desert (cf. Num 26:57–58).

Originally, however, the sacrificial rites had not even been performed by designated levites. In the Abrahamic period, there simply was no levitical tribe. Ritual sacrifice had been performed by the father of the family (Gen 22; 31:54; 46:1). The only priests of that period in Palestine were pagan (Gen 14:18; 41:45).

In Israel the priesthood developed, not as a personal anointing with the charisma of Yahweh, but as an "office."[6] According to the oldest texts priests were appointed by men without any divine intervention. Micah, for example, in the period of the judges, "consecrated one of his sons, who became his priest" (Jgs 17:5). Micah later consecrated a young Levite as a priest for his private sanctuary to whom he said, "Be father and priest to me, and I will give you ten silver shekels a year, a set of garments, and your food" (Jgs 17:10).

According to the Bible, what is a priest?

The oldest technical term in Scripture for dedicating or consecrating a priest is "filling his hand." This may have meant that the hands of the newly designated priest were filled with the animal elements to be offered in sacrifice (Lev 8:27–28; Ex 29:24–25). Perhaps "filling his hand" originally referred to the priest's salary (Jgs 17:10; 18:4) or to the priest's right to share in the revenues of the local shrine (1 Sam 2:13). "Consequently priests in ancient Israel were not 'ordained' . . . but . . . 'sanctified.' " This means that "the priest no longer belonged to the profane world, but . . . was 'set apart' for the service of God."[7] Thus in the exilic period, the chronicler wrote that "Aaron was set apart to be consecrated as most

holy, he and his sons forever, to offer sacrifice before the Lord,
to minister to him, and to bless his name forever" (1 Chr
23:13).

What is meant by Jewish priests in the line of Zadok?

At the beginning of the Davidic kingship (ca. 1000 B.C.)
the priestly tribe of Levi underwent another historical modifi-
cation. In the final years of Saul's reign when his paranoia
had driven him to try to kill David, David had fled to the
priests at Nob to seek an oracle from Yahweh. When Saul
learned that the priests had ministered thus to his hated son-
in-law, he had eighty-five of them slain at Nob (1 Sam 22:18).
Only one priest, Abiathar, had escaped the massacre and fled
to David for safety (1 Sam 23:6–9; 30:7). As the grandson of
Ahitub, Abiathar was in the family line of Eli, the priest who
had formerly been the guardian of the prestigious sanctuary
of the ark at Shiloh. After the conquest of Jerusalem, David
entrusted Abiathar with the care of the ark (2 Sam 15:24–29),
but also appointed another priest, Zadok, to officiate over the
new liturgical activities in Jerusalem.

The Bible gives no genealogy for Zadok, but Aelred Cody
is probably right in suggesting that Zadok had originally been
a Jebusite pagan priest whom David incorporated into Yah-
wism to unify the remaining Jebusites with the intruding
Israelites in David's new national capital of Jerusalem. If
Solomon's mother was one of David's Jebusite concubines (cf. 2
Sam 5:13–14), that would explain why Zadok eventually supported Solomon, the half-Jebusite as David's successor, while
Abiathar would have preferred Adonijah, whose name indicates that he was a pure-blooded Israelite.[8]

Whatever Zadok's origins, the Scriptures of the Davidic
period mention Zadok with Abiathar every time. Zadok, however, is always listed *first*, showing that he had been given a
higher position (2 Sam 17:15; 19:12; 8:17; 20:25). Although
Abiathar had never been disloyal to David, when he sided

with Adonijah's effort to claim the throne (1 Kgs 1:7—2:22), Solomon, the royal victor, banished Abiathar to Anatoth (1 Kgs 2:26–27). That left only the sons of Zadok to serve as priests in the Jerusalem temple (1 Kgs 2:35).

While the exile in Babylon might well have destroyed the influence of the Zadokite priests, paradoxically their importance was further heightened. Ezekiel 44:15–31 explains in some detail how the Zadokites were to enjoy hierarchical supremacy over the other Levites in the post-exilic community.

What was meant by the priesthood of Aaron?

Critical scholarship now agrees that this religious idea developed during the Babylonian exile or later. Originally Moses' brother Aaron had been called "the levite" (Ex 4:14–16) during the wandering in the desert. It is clear that he had a position of leadership next in authority to that of Moses (Ex 7:1ff; 8:1; 17:8–10; 18:12; 19:24; 24:1, 9). However these traditions never called Aaron "a priest." In fact Aaron's identity as a designated Levite was tarnished by his making the golden calf (Ex 32; Dt 9.20) and joining his sister Miriam in a rebellion against Moses (Num 12). Those Scriptures which depict Aaron as a fully vested high priest date from the exilic and post-exilic periods when the descendants of rival priestly families were vying for superior positions in community leadership. Each family was trying to trace its genealogy back to Aaron to prove the greater antiquity of its priestly claims to officiate over the temple worship.

Wasn't the development of a high priest a pagan corruption of Jewish faith?

No. The concept of a hierarchical priesthood was not novel in post-exilic Judaism, but the term "high priest" was probably never used until the Greek influences on Jewish thought in the third century B.C.[9] In pre-exilic Israel the leader of the priests was called "*the* priest [*kohen*] (1 Kgs 4:2; 2 Kgs 11:9f; 12:8f; 16:10f; Is 8.2). The title "head priest" occurs once in 2 Kings 25:18 and its parallel in Jeremiah 52:14. His assistant was called the "second kohen" (2 Kgs 23:4; Jer 52:24). He seems to have been responsible for policing the temple sanctuary and was called "the superintendent of the temple" in Jeremiah 29:24–29. Beneath him three senior officials of the temple called "keepers of the threshold" (2 Chr 34:9) held the third rank of priestly hierarchical authority (cf. 2 Kgs 12:10; 22:4). Under this group of five leaders came "the elders of the priests" (2 Kgs 19:2; Is 37:2; Jer 19:1). They were probably the heads of priestly families and formed a parallel body to the laymen titled the "elders of the people" (Ex 3:18; Jos 9:11; Jgs 11:5; Dt 19:12; 21:3). The chronicler also mentions a lesser clergy consisting of twenty-four classes of levitical singers (1 Chr 25) and several classes of door-keepers (1 Chr 26:1–19).

From this sketch of the hierarchical organization of the pre-exilic priesthood, it is easier to understand why the people accepted the novel development of a *high priest* who later came to exercise even civil authority in post-exilic Judaism. From the Greeks, the Jews would have learned that a high priest (*archieros*) "denotes a man whom the king appointed as head of the state religion in a particular district or town" (cf. 1 Mac 10:20).[10] Almost six hundred years after the first Jewish high priest had been thus "anointed," the New Testament author of Hebrews applied the title "high priest forever in the line of Melchizedek" to the risen Christ (cf. Heb 4:10). About eighteen hundred years of levitical and Zadokite priestly sacrifice thus lay behind the New Testament faith in Jesus as the eternal high priest.

What did a priest do in the Old Testament period?

While liturgical customs evolved a great deal from the time of Moses to the time of Jesus, a priest had four principal functions.

(1) A priest was a "guardian" (*sadin*) of a local shrine in the period prior to Solomon. Priests protected the sanctuary from desecration and took charge of maintenance and donations (Num 1:53; 3:23–32). Each priest was succeeded by his sons (1 Sam 1—2; 2 Kgs 23:8).

(2) They acted as counselors in times of difficult decisions. They helped people know Yahweh's will for them in the early period by casting lots, little sticks called urim and thummim, kept in a pouch. The primary priestly vestment was the ephod. The most ancient style was probably a loin cloth like that of the Egyptian priests (cf. 1 Sam 2:18; 22:18; 2 Sam 6:14, 20). Later the ephod became the gorgeous linen robe embroidered with gold and purple and the pouch became the "breastpiece of decision" studded with beautiful jewels to represent the twelve tribes of Israel as the priest went into the holy presence of God (cf. Ex 28:6–30). Casting lots gave way to more prudent forms of giving wise advice.

(3) A more enduring function of the priests was giving instruction to the people on the Torah (Dt 31:20). To give teaching, the priests relied on the divine knowledge (*da-ath*). This was the sacred teaching on what was "clean or unclean" in the sight of God. *Da-ath* was not a product of direct inspiration like the oracles of the prophets, but was sacred knowledge that had been handed down to the priests since ancient times. After the exile the priests shared their teaching role with the lay scribes who could preach and teach in the synagogues.

(4) The most unique function of the priests was to offer sacrifice. The offering of animal and vegetable sacrifices had been one of the primary duties of the priests since the most ancient period (cf. Jgs 6:25–26; 13:16–33; 1 Sam 1:3–4, 21; 2:19; Lev 21:6). While at times the priests had exclusive charge of offering a sacrifice, others could be appointed to slaughter the victims (Ex 24:3–8). The priest's unique role involved the use of the blood of the sacrificial victim. This blood was believed to be the holiest part of the victim, the "seat of life" (Lev 17:11, 14). Therefore only a priest could present this sacred blood to God and lay that part of the sacrifice which belonged to God

on the altar. Throughout the whole Old Testament the priests thus became more and more exclusively the only "ministers of the altar" (Lev 1:14–15; 5:8; 2 Kgs 23:9; 1 Sam 2:28; Dt 33:10; Num 17:5; 1 Chr 23:13; 2 Chr 26:16–18).

What kind of sacrifices did the priests offer?

Amidst the rich complexity of different types of sacrifices the *holocaust* and the *communion sacrifice* were the most important. In the holocaust the entire sacrificial victim was burnt on the altar of Yahweh (Jgs 6:26, 28; 1 Sam 6:14; 7:9; 10:8; 13:9; 2 Sam 6:17f; 1 Kgs 3:4; 9:25; 18:38; Lev 3). Less total in nature was the communion sacrifice which was a joyous sacrifice in which the priest and the one (or the group) offering the victim ate a part afterward. The blood, the most sacred seat of Yahweh's gift of life, was poured out at the altar and the fat, the second-most-sacred part, was burnt on the altar (Jgs 20:26; 21:4; 1 Sam 2:15–6; 2 Sam 6:17–18; 24:25; 1 Kgs 3:15; 9:25; 2 Kgs 16:13).[11]

What was the spiritual meaning of offering God a sacrifice?

Three ideas run through the Old Testament theology of sacrifice: (1) a gift to God recognizing the divine superiority over human beings, (2) the smoke of an incense offering or the fire of a holocaust rising up to God and creating or expressing communion with God, and (3) a means of propitiation or expiation. In the early Old Testament propitiation tried to soothe the anger of Yahweh. In the later Old Testament propitiation was understood more sublimely as a sacrificial praise of thanksgiving to God. Expiation sacrifices were directed toward persons and objects which needed to be put in a right relation with God.[12] To offer God a sacrificial victim is to reverence God as the giver of all gifts. Thus David prayed in 1 Chronicles, "Everything is from you [God], and we only give you what we have received from you" (1 Chr 29:14).

Doesn't the Old Testament condemn the offering of sacrifices by priests?

In *specific* contexts, yes (cf. Mal 2:1–9). When priests allowed religion to degenerate into external rites lacking sincerity of heart, or used their office to exploit the poor, the prophets and wise men properly condemned such abuses. However priestly sacrifice, as *a divine institution,* was *never* condemned just as prophecy was never condemned because there were false prophets, nor were wisdom schools closed because some of the "wise" were in reality fools. The human side of all of Israel's religious institutions was always morally ambiguous. No matter what God ever did, men and women were free to take what was holy and to distort it.

How long did the leadership of the Jewish high priests last?

From the time of Joshua (520 B.C.), a line of high priests continued to govern—with a few upsets in the Maccabean crisis—until 70 A.D. At that time the Romans destroyed the second temple and the Jews were scattered to neighboring countries where rabbis of the Pharisee party handed on the faith through synagogue worship and torah study. Jewish sacrifice became exclusively moral or mystical—it was no longer part of the liturgy.

The Success of the Jews in Repelling the Greeks

How did the Greeks come to replace the Persians as rulers of the Jews?

Of the one hundred and ninety years between Darius I (522–486 B.C.) and Darius III (336–331 B.C.) we know surprisingly little about Jewish life and faith under Persian rule. One gets the impression that the Jews were allowed freedom in religious practices and received some state support for the temple's material needs. The Jews seem to have accepted their lot as part of the Persian empire with little trouble. For them it was a time neither of the national splendor of Solomon, nor of the acute suffering of the exile. That phase of relative peace and stability was destined to end when Alexander the Great conquered most of the known world (336–323 B.C.). Alexander's great dream was to spread the enlightenment of Greek culture to the "barbarian" world. This process was called "Hellenization" or making the world Greek. To Alexander and his countrymen it seemed the ideal way to make the world one. When Alexander died prematurely in 323 B.C., his empire was divided between the Ptolemies based in Egypt and the Seleucids based in Syrian Antioch. Thus between 323 and 64 B.C. the Jews were wedged between the two rival Greek powers who both wanted control over Palestine for the tax revenues it would provide.

How did the Jews respond to the new influence of the Greeks?

Between 301 and 198 B.C. the Jews were ruled by the Ptolemies in Egypt. A gradual, gentle, and acceptable level of Hellenization followed. A Greek-speaking Jewish colony was established in Alexandria—presumably by Jews seeking better economic opportunities in the capital. To serve their religious life, the torah was translated into Greek. This became what was later known as the Septuagint (Greek) Bible which was distinguished from the Massoretic (Hebrew) Bible and later the Vulgate (Latin) Bible translated by St. Jerome in the fourth century A.D. The Old Testament Book of Ecclesiastes (or Qoheleth) was probably written during this century and reflects a knowledge of Stoic and Epicurean Greek philosophy. The Greeks themselves established Greek-speaking colonies in Palestine at Sebaste (Samaria), Philadelphia (Amman), Ptolemais (Acre), Philoteria (south of the Sea of Galilee), and Scythopolis (Beth-shan). Thus between contact with Jewish relatives in Alexandria and Greek neighbors in Palestine some Hellenization of Jewish life was inevitable.

Why did the Greeks become more oppressive of the Jews?

Between 200 and 190 B.C. two key events caused a major shift in Jewish-Greek relations. First Antiochus III (222–187 B.C.) wrested Palestine from the control of the Egyptian Ptolemies and made the Jews part of the Seleucid empire based in Antioch. Second, Antiochus, at the urging of Hannibal, declared war on Europe in 192 B.C. The whole thing was a military disaster for Antiochus whose son was taken hostage by the Romans in 190 B.C. From that time on the Seleucids owed huge debts to Rome for war damages. Hence they were always looking for new sources of income—usually acquired by robbing the temples of their subject peoples.

How did the Greeks interfere in the life and faith of the Jews between 185 and 164 B.C.?

Antiochus III was succeeded by Seleucus IV (185–175 B.C.) Under his rule the money in the temple was taken. This money was a "care fund for widows and orphans" and also funds deposited there for safekeeping by private individuals (cf. 2 Mac 3:7–11). The holy high priest Onias III went to Antioch to protest in 175 B.C. While he was there, Seleucus was assassinated and his brother, who had been the hostage in Rome, came to power as Antiochus IV. Besieged by enemies on all sides, he decided to intensify the process of Hellenization.

Antiochus IV found an important Jewish collaborator in Joshua, the brother of Onias III, who bribed Antiochus to make him the high priest. Joshua, who used the Greek form of his name, Jason, then actively Hellenized Jerusalem.

A gymnasium was built where Greek sports were played in the nude and Jewish males had their circumcisions surgi-

cally disguised in order to look like their Gentile competitors
in the games (1 Mac 1:13–15). To join the sports club was to
become an Antiochene (2 Mac 4:9) which would have involved
political loyalty to Antiochus IV and worship of the Greek
gods Hercules or Hermes (2 Mac 4:18–20) the divine patrons of
athletics.

Three years later Menelaus outbribed Jason to get the
office of high priest (2 Mac 4:25–26). Then he started stealing
liturgical vessels. That same year the legitimate high priest,
Onias III, was assassinated while still in Antioch (2 Mac
4:33–38). In 169 B.C. Antiochus and Menelaus again plun-
dered the temple and even plucked the gold leaf from the
facade (1 Mac 1:17–24; 2 Mac 5:15–21). To worsen matters
Antiochus placed a Greek commissioner in Jerusalem to further Hellenize the people. That caused popular riots to break
out in the streets.

Therefore, to restore law and order in 167 B.C., Antiochus
sent Apollonius to Jerusalem to quell the disturbances (1 Mac
1:29–35; 2 Mac 5:23–26). Apollonius pretended to come in
peace and then mercilessly butchered many unsuspecting people in the streets of Jerusalem (2 Mac 6:18—7:42).[13] Then
Apollonius built a Greek military citadel, the Acra, and in-
stalled a Seleucid military garrison. The Acra constituted a
hated symbol of foreign domination, a colony of Hellenized
pagans and apostate Jews, which was trying to turn David's
city and God's holy temple into a Greek "polis" (1 Mac 3:45;
4:46; 6:21–14; 11:21). Economic, political, religious, and cultural oppression all emanated from the hated Acra. Religiously
the strategy was to combine Yahweh with the Greek god Zeus
and teach the people that this god was manifesting his will
through Antiochus IV. He took the title "Epiphanes" which
means "manifestation of god."[14]

At this time, Antiochus forbade all practices of Judaism—
reading the torah, the rite of circumcision, and the eating of
kosher foods—under penalty of death (1 Mac 1:41–67). The
ultimate blasphemy occurred when, on December 6, 167 B.C.,
a statue of the Greek pagan god, Zeus Olympios, was placed in

the sanctuary of God's holy temple (1 Mac 1:54). This was, for pious Jews, the "abomination of desolation" (Dn 9:27; 11:31; 12:11). For them, the choice had become appallingly clear: Hellenize or die.

What caused the Maccabean resistance?

The strong faith of most of the Jews caused them to fight or flee rather than to assimilate the Greek religion. The Book of Daniel began to be composed to reassure the people that God would intervene and that their blood would not be shed in vain. Likewise through "zeal for the law" (1 Mac 2:25) guerrilla war broke out in the village of Modein when Mattathias leaped up on the altar and slaughtered a would-be Jewish turncoat who was going to perform a pagan rite. Immediately afterward Mattathias and his five sons (John, Simon, Judas, Eleazar, and Jonathan) fled to the hills, summoning all pious Jews to join them in a resistance movement to preserve the ancient Mosaic covenant (1 Mac 2:12; 4; Dn 11:34). Mattathias died of old age in 166 B.C. He was succeeded by his son Judas who was called "Maccabeus." (Maccabeus may mean either "hammer-headed" or "Yahweh's Designate."[15] Antiochus IV could not respond adequately because he was already campaigning against the Parthians (1 Mac 3:27–37).

By December 164 B.C., exactly three years after its desecration, the temple was cleansed, a pure Jewish liturgy restored, and faithful priests reinstated. The Feast of Hanukkah (Dedication) was added to the Jewish list of high holy days to commemorate the successful purification of the temple.

Further problems with the Greeks would subsequently flare up and more internal Jewish corruption would develop. Greek dominance would yield to the equally strong Roman occupation when Pompey captured Jerusalem in the summer of 63 B.C. But in December 164 B.C. the crisis was over. God reigned anew and more and more pious Jews were convinced that God's ultimate day of definitive victory for them was only a short time away.

The Development of Jewish Visionary Groups

Who were the Jewish visionary groups?

The same kind of pious Jews that were inspired to write the Book of Daniel were part of a larger religious movement within Judaism. The movement began at the time of the Maccabees with historical roots back in Ezekiel and Third Isaiah (Is 56—66). These Jews were devoutly trying to understand the "secret" of God's plan to bring about the victory of the everlasting *peace* which he had promised them through Isaiah. They pored over the Scriptures, fasted, prayed, and huddled in groups straining to know the higher wisdom of God's mysterious ways with all the nations on earth. While suffering much persecution, they were convinced that the blood of the Jewish martyrs would not be shed in vain. If God would only reveal his secret in a vision, then they would understand enough to endure faithfully. Their focus on *revelation* has caused biblical scholars to label this movement the rise of "apocalyptic" groups. *Apokalypsis* in Greek means "revelation" in the sense of *unveiling* some hidden truth, especially about God. This movement gave rise to two inspired books of the Bible, Old Testament Daniel, and New Testament Revelation (Apocalypse). Numerous other apocalyptic Scriptures were composed like the Book of Jubilees, the Assumption of Moses, The Apocalypse of Abraham, and the Dead Sea Scroll, The War of the Sons of Light Against the Sons of Darkness.[16] Neither the Jews nor the Catholic Christians recognized any of those writings as divinely inspired. The apocalyptic movement died out after three hundred years—about 100 A.D.[17]

Why are apocalyptic Scriptures so difficult to understand?

D.S. Russell has found four characteristics of apocalyptic writings that help us interpret them according to the intentions of their authors: (1) esoteric in character, (2) literary in form, (3) symbolic in language, (4) pseudonymous in authorship. Failure to understand these characteristics makes apocalyptic Scriptures almost impossible for later people to understand.

Esoteric

By "esoteric in character" Russell means that the apocalyptic books "claim to be revelations or disclosures of divine secrets made known to certain illustrious individuals of the past."[18] These revelations were believed to have been "hidden" and then "uncovered" centuries later for the encouragement of the just. The esoteric revelation may disclose God's "plan" for all human history or give "secret" information about the spiritual world. There were probably three lines of esoteric knowledge in Jewish apocalyptic: the secrets of Noah, the secrets of Enoch, and the secrets of Daniel. Historical investigations can find no evidence that any one of them was more than an ancient legendary figure.

Ezekiel 14:14, 20 associates a legendary Daniel with Job and Noah. They have the "power" to intercede with God for others. Ezekiel 28:3 refers to Daniel's "wisdom" and knowledge of "secrets." Ezekiel is probably referring to the Daniel of ancient Syrian legend who is mentioned in the fourteenth century B.C. Ras Shamra tablets discovered at Ugarit in Syria. In the legend of Aqhat, Daniel is a just man who cares for the widows and orphans in distress.[19]

The second century B.C. author of the Book of Daniel shows a thorough knowledge of Ezekiel (cf. Ez 31 and Dn 4:10–12, 20) and probably intended to continue revealing the esoteric secrets of this ancient Daniel. For that reason the word "secret" (or "mystery" in Greek) occurs nine times in the Aramaic section of Daniel (Dn 2:18, 19, 27, 28, 29, 30, 47; 4:4, 6). The Book of Daniel was thus offered to the pious Jews as a new "interpretation" to give them spiritual "wisdom" to live through the "abomination of desolation" with a deeper faith.[20] Unlike the more ancient prophetic oracles, these revelations were always portrayed as the "opening of ancient scrolls" or literary.

Symbolic

In addition to being esoteric and literary the apocalyptic writings were heavily "symbolic in language." These symbols were drawn from both earlier sections of the Old Testament and from ancient mythology. These symbols could be mythological creatures or mystical numbers like seven, seventy, twelve, and forty. Mythical monsters or dragons are found in the ancient Babylonian myth where the hero god, Marduk, slays the female dragon, Tiamat, to create the universe. *Tehom* (Hebrew for chaos or abyss) shows the contact of Genesis 1:1–2 with the myth of Tiamat. In other scriptures the mythical dragon of Babylon became Rahab the snake, the female dragon Leviathan, or the male dragon Behemoth, referred to by Job and Ezekiel (Jb 7:12; 9:13; 26:12; Ez 29:3; 32:2). The inspired author of Daniel furthered this symbolic tradition of doing heroic combat with a symbolic monster in his horrifying experience of "the monstrous visions of the night" recounted in Daniel 7. A winged lion, a three-tusked bear, a winged leopard, and a ten-horned beast with iron teeth symbolized the oppresive evil which had been inflicted on the Jews by the Babylonians (the lion), the Medes (the bear), the Persians (the leopard), and the Greeks (the arrogant surrealistic beast).[21] One could not find a more powerful metaphor to reveal the collective depth of Jewish suffering experienced between 587 B.C. (the exile) and 167 B.C. (the prohibition of Jewish religion and the desecration of the temple by Antiochus IV). Because the inspired author spoke in such veiled symbols, the Book of Daniel has nurtured the hopes of other oppressed peoples dehumanized by the monstrous political powers of succeeding centuries. Thus the use of symbolic language allows apocalyptic writings to function not as historical memory, so much as inspiration for future hope.

Pseudonymous

The tradition of adopting a pseudonym and portraying the revealed secrets as the vision of some ancient holy one was found also among the Egyptians and the Greeks of the same period. The Jews, however, did not simply copy a literary fashion from their contemporary pagan neighbors. Likewise the inspired authors among the Jews did not try to "trick" their fellow Jews by artificially adopting the name of an ancient seer as the author of their apocalyptic composition. Nor were such apocalyptists "deluded" in believing themselves to be furthering the ancient esoteric traditions with new revelation. To understand the semitic mindset of the inspired apocalyptists with respect to their practice of pseudonymity, it is necessary to reconstruct the situation in which a pious Jew longed to understand how God would fulfill his promises of messianic peace for his chosen people. The anonymous inspired authors poured over the torah and the prophets. They prayed to the holy ones like Daniel and Enoch to help them understand the secret and mysterious ways of God with men. In contemplative ecstasy and vision God spoke his word to them—perhaps through the images of a Noah or an Enoch or a Daniel—and revealed the immensity of his divine glory and the assurance of his power to lift the just out of their current experience of being persecuted by the great world powers. After the vision had passed, the inspired authors must have asked themselves whether they had merely "imagined" what they had seen? Was it simply their own openness to God that had won for them such an overwhelming insight into the immensity of God's secret plan to transform the universe into his Kingdom of peace? No. The sincerity of their piety and the intensity of their experience precluded such superficial explanations. Certainly they had "seen" God. Knowing themselves to be sinful men, they could only attribute the gift of the vision to the prayers of the ancient holy ones like Daniel which had won for them such revelations of new hope in the power of God to triumph over the current evils which appeared to be cosmic in breadth. Thus these pious Jews interpreted their own religious experience as the legitimate continuation of the ancient justice of such legendary figures as Noah, Enoch, and Daniel. It is easy for us to see that they had their facts wrong. There never was an Enoch, a Noah, or a Daniel, but there really was a line of ancient holy ones lost to us in the mists of history.[22]

Later apocalyptists may have imitated pseudonymity as a literary device. The origins of pseudonymity, however, lie buried in the sublimity of contemplative prayer. Thus the genuine apocalyptists lived by that faith which knew God in the personal experience of authentic mystical phenomena associated with the higher states of contemplation: visions, auditions, and raptures. God spoke to them in this depth of personal interiority—from that inner depth emerged their apocalyptic scrolls (cf. Dn 7—8).

What truths of faith did God reveal in the Book of Daniel?

(1) Be faithful to God in times of persecution. This is the central truth revealed in Daniel 1—6 culminating in the famous story of Daniel in the lion's den. These stories are "haggadah" or stories told to reveal a moral. They may be based on historical memories, but the facts are sometimes confused. The religious truth is that second century B.C. Jews could remember the heroism of the Jewish saints of old and keep the torah—no matter what the personal cost.

(2) Expect a divine revolution. Daniel 7 is the heart of the book. There the anonymous author resolves the horrifying dreams of the night by receiving an inspired vision. The Jews are called "the son of man" whom God will raise up into an everlasting kingship of peace (Dn 7:14) Where human efforts might fail, the miraculous power of God could transform the entire universe. This is a new invitation to believe in the power and goodness of God in spite of all the suffering and injustice on earth.

(3) The just will be victorious and the wicked will be requited. Daniel 12:2 is a new revelation that the day of the Lord will involve a bodily resurrection of all who have lived. The blood of the just will not have been shed in vain. They, like the wise, will shine like stars forever sharing in the eternal glory of God.

(4) God may reveal his breathtaking glory through angelic messengers. Contact with the Persians allowed the Jews to learn that the heavenly court of angels could be used by God to establish deeper bonds of communion between the citizens of heaven and earth. Therefore in Daniel the names of the angels Gabriel (Dn 9:21) and Michael (Dn 12:1) are revealed for the first time in Scripture. (The only other angel named in the Old Testament is Raphael in the wisdom book, Tobit.)

(5) It is possible to hope in the very midst of suffering. The first four truths revealed in the Book of Daniel all combine to teach the community of faith how to praise God and expect much when, from a merely human point of view, there is no rational basis for hope. This divine invitation to hope remains forever central to living by faith.

Life in Heaven

If Daniel 12:2 expected a final resurrection of the dead at the end of time, it said nothing about being with God in heaven when one died. Most Jews, in fact, had not believed in either going to heaven or rising from the dead. The Maccabean Scriptures gave new revelation about the communion of saints.

What did Maccabees reveal about the value of martyrdom?

One of the most touching stories in the Old Testament is the account of a Jewish mother watching her seven sons butchered at the hands of the Greeks (2 Mac 7:1–19). Their deaths are interpreted as their "witness" to their faith in God. (Martyr in Greek means witness.) At the end the mother proclaims that it was God who gave them life as his gift and it is God who will give it back to them "because you now disregard yourselves for the sake of his law" (2 Mac 7:23). From that time on, Jewish martyrs began to be especially revered.

What was revealed to Judas Maccabeus about the prayers of the saints in heaven?

According to a "dream" of Judas Maccabeus, which the inspired author calls "a kind of vision worthy of belief" (2 Mac 15:11), the saintly high priest Onias III, who had been recently assassinated in Antioch, "was praying for the whole Jewish community with outstretched arms" (2 Mac 15:12). Onias then pointed to another saint and said, "This is God's prophet Jeremiah, who loves his brethren and fervently prays for his people and their holy city" (2 Mac 15:14).

What did Maccabees reveal about the value of sacrificial prayer for those who had died in sin?

When Judas Maccabeus discovered that some of his slain soldiers had been wearing pagan amulets around their necks to protect them during battle, he sent money to the priests in the Jerusalem temple to have them offer "an expiatory sacrifice" for the soldiers who had died in sin, so that they too could share in the resurrection of the just (2 Mac 12:38–46).

Relation of the Maccabean Revelation to Catholic Faith

From Daniel and Maccabees Catholic faith has developed four principal beliefs (1) the hierarchical priesthood, (2) the papacy, (3) devotion to the saints, (4) prayer for the dead.

The Hierarchical Priesthood

Why do Catholics believe that their ordained ministers are priests when the New Testament never calls them priests?

(1) Jesus prophesied the destruction of the Jerusalem temple (Mk 13:1–4), and thus the end of the Jewish priesthood of Aaron and Zadok. Jesus himself acted as a priest at the Last Supper by the ritual act of offering his own body and blood. He

told the Twelve to do the same "as a remembrance of me" in "the new covenant of my blood" (Lk 22:19–20). About 85 A.D. the Epistle to the Hebrews revealed Jesus as the risen "eternal high priest" according to the priesthood of Melchizedek (Heb 6:20). It came directly from God and was open to Gentiles (Gen 14:18ff).

(2) The Christian community of the New Testament thought of itself as "a temple" of living stones whose members were instructed: "Offer your bodies as a living sacrifice holy and acceptable to God, your spiritual worship" (Rom 12.1). Christ was the chief living cornerstone of this new temple of sacrifice, and all the baptized constituted a universal lay priesthood (1 Pet 2:1–10).

(3) While no uniform vocabulary existed for the office of the Apostles and their successors (cf. Eph 4:11; Acts 6:6), Paul thought of his apostolic ministry as his "priestly" service of the Gospel of God, so that the offering of the Gentiles may be acceptable, sanctified by the Holy Spirit. The offering over which Paul presided as a priestly minister was both the holiness of life of the baptized and the cultic act of celebrating the Eucharist as a participation in Christ's death (cf. 1 Cor 9: 13ff; 10:14–22; 11:17–34; Gal 3:13, Rom 3:24ff; 8:3).

(4) The hierarchical authority of the ordained ministers was given early emphasis in the pastoral Epistles of Timothy and Titus. The standardization of the Church vocabulary is first attested in the letters of St. Ignatius, bishop of Antioch (d. ca. 117 A.D.). Because Gnostic Christians were mixing pagan moral teaching into their eucharistic gatherings, he enjoined the Catholic Christians to obey their bishop as representing God the Father and their presbyters as the council of God and the college of the Apostles. They should respect their deacons as they would Jesus Christ. From that time on the tripartite hierarchy has developed as an integral dimension of God's gift of the Church. St. Ignatius taught that apart from the bishop, presbyters, and the deacons, "there is nothing that can be called a Church."[23] Thus Catholic faith understands that "where two or three are gathered in the name of Jesus, he is truly in their midst" (Mt 18:20), but if they do not live in the

communion of obedience with their local bishop, they are not fully living by the mind of Christ to have his followers united as one in heart and listening to the teachings of the Apostles (Acts 2:42).

(5) The oldest written reference to the bishop as a *priest* comes from *The Apostolic Tradition* of Hippolytus of Rome (d. 235 A.D.). The prayer which was to be used for consecrating a new bishop speaks of the bishop as God's "high priest."

During this time the Church frequently celebrated Mass over the tombs of the martyrs in the Roman catacombs. The testimony of their blood shed for love of Christ also provided the occasion for the Spirit to teach the Church how sacrifice and the priestly offering of Christ as the saving victim were at the heart of Catholic faith. No one objected to equating the "overseer" (bishop) with a Christian high priest or thinking of the "elder" (presbyter) as a ministerial priest until fourteen hundred years later at the time of the Protestant Reformation.

If Matthew 23:9 says "Call no man your father," why do Catholics call a priest "Father"?

Matthew used a form of deliberate exaggeration to teach the unique fatherhood of God. Literal adherence to his teaching would not allow any children to call their male parent "Daddy." The Catholic custom of calling the priest "Father" may be as old as St. Paul: "Granted you have ten thousand guardians in Christ, you have only one father. It was I who begot you in Christ Jesus through my preaching of the Gospel" (1 Cor 4:15).

If Hebrews 9:26–28 says that Jesus was sacrificed once for all, why do Catholics offer the sacrifice of the Eucharist every day?

The inspired author of Hebrews is probably thinking of the body of Jesus as a Jewish "holocaust" which was destroyed by his atoning death on the cross. The Christian sacrificial meal of thanksgiving was not a "holocaust" but a repeatable "communion sacrifice" which shared in the acceptability to God of Christ's one perfect sacrifice. We know from 1 Corinthians 11 that the earliest Apostles understood the celebration of the Eucharist as the people's participation in the death of Christ.

The Papacy

Why do Catholics believe that the Pope in Rome is the successor of Peter the Apostle?

(1) All New Testament scholars agree that Peter was first among the Apostles. His name appears first in every list of the Twelve. Mark's Gospel credits Peter with being first in faith (Mk 8:29) in spite of Peter's many blunders and infidelities. Written in 85 A.D., probably in Antioch, Matthew 16:18 depicts Peter as having the power to "bind and loose" with the "keys of the Kingdom." Peter is called the "rock" on which the Church is founded. Historical Peter had been dead since his martyrdom in Rome in 64 A.D. Thus a growing tradition of interpreting his office as the head Christian rabbi was early at work in the New Testament Church. By 90 A.D. the local church of John also recognized the headship of the office of Peter (cf. Jn 21). Since Peter had presided over the church at Rome, his successor bishops thought of themselves as sharing in some vague way in his "primacy" over their fellow bishops in the other local churches. Thus in 90 A.D. Pope Clement wrote a letter to the church at Corinth exhorting them not to fire a local presbyter because he was a morally upright man—even though they might not find him terribly stimulating.[24] Theological reflection on the papacy did not really occur until the time of Pope Leo the Great (d. 461). When the Church had come out of hiding, the first Ecumenical Council had listed the bishop of Rome as having first place and the bishop of Constantinople as having second place among the five apostolic bishoprics or patriarchal sees of the early Church (325 A.D.). That sense of papal primacy grew until the schism of 1054

A.D. when the Catholic and Orthodox Churches fell into disunion. Between 476 A.D. and 1870 the Popes had varying degrees of secular power in Europe.

What do Catholics mean when they say the Pope is infallible?

In the wake of nineteenth century liberalism and anticlericalism many local bishops of Europe found it difficult to maintain their freedom to teach the apostolic faith as they knew it. They looked to Rome to help and defend them. Simultaneously Pope Pius IX wanted the primacy and autonomy of Peter's chair reaffirmed in the wake of its weakened secular influence. Therefore the Catholic bishops at Vatican I in 1870 defined that the *ex cathedra* definitions (formal teachings) of the Roman Pontiff were "irreformable." His teachings did not need the subsequent approval of the local bishops to be binding on all local churches. In that restricted sense Catholic faith believes that the *ex cathedra* teachings of the bishop of Rome are "infallible."[25]

Only two such infallible teachings have been defined by a Pope: that the Virgin Mary was conceived without sin (believed by the people since the fourth century, but only defined by a Pope in 1854) and that the Virgin Mary was bodily assumed into heaven (also believed since the early centuries, but only defined by a Pope in 1950). In both cases the Popes had consulted bishops all over the world to see if these truths about Mary had been planted in the hearts of the Catholic faithful by the action of the Holy Spirit in the Church.

In 1965 the bishops at Vatican II sought to balance the emphasis on papacy at Vatican I with restoration of the ancient sense of "collegiality." Therefore they taught that the Pope governs the Church through the college of bishops while retaining his authority of office to govern the universal Church without their approval or consent. Now synods of bishops, diocesan synods of priests, parish councils of pastors and laity, and married permanent deacons all share in the governance and teaching office of the Pope.[26]

Devotion to the Saints

Why do Catholics pray to the saints?

Catholic faith can be understood as having a twin emphasis on Eucharist and martyrdom. St. Stephen in Acts 7 was the first Christian to witness to the resurrection of Jesus as the living Lord with the testimony of a martyr's blood. Revelation 7:9 envisions a huge crowd of holy ones in heaven "which no one could count" from all the nations on earth. James 5:17 speaks of the special efficacy of the prayers of holy people like Elijah. Catholic faith sees in each saint a unique experience of the light of Christ which radiates through the communion of saints. Friendship with the saints is thus friendship with Christ. The first life of a saint was written by Athanasius in the fourth century. At the request of the hermits, with whom he was hiding while being persecuted for teaching the equality of Christ with God the Father, Athanasius wrote the *Life of St. Anthony* (251–356). We have written testimony that Christians reverenced the relics of the saints at least since the death of Polycarp (d. ca. 156).[27] Polycarp had heard the Gospel from John the Evangelist. Faith in the resurrection allowed the Catholic Christians to see the day of the martyr's death as his "birthday" into heaven. Thus the custom of celebrating a saint's feast day on the day he died entered the liturgical life of the Church quite early.

Prayer for the Dead

Why do Catholics pray for the souls in purgatory?

The custom of praying for the dead who died in sin dates back to the Jews at the time of the Maccabees as we saw above (2 Mac 12:39–49). The rabbinical school of Shammai later taught that Gehenna could be a temporary refining by fire. Jesus seems to have continued the school of Shammai's teaching that those who are not spotlessly pure can escape hell (Mt 8:12; Lk 12:20; 16:22; Jn 9:4; 11:9). Some Christians in the second century thought that all people just "slept in death" until the return of Christ for a thousand years (the millennium). Others in the second and third century offered prayers and works for the dead. Origen, Tertullian and others counseled prayer for the dead. Augustine interpreted 1 Corinthians 3:12–15 as the *ignis purgatorius* or cleansing fire a soul could experience after death to be purified of lesser sins. 1 John 5:14–19 had taught that all wrongdoing is sin, but that not all sin is "deadly" or mortal. The "everyday" or venial sins could be the object of Christian prayer.

While popular piety has thought of purgatory as a place, Catholic teaching, in deference to the Orthodox, has never defined the existence of purgatory as a place. When prayer for the dead was abused by selling indulgences in the sixteenth century, Protestant and Catholic reformers insisted that superstition be eliminated from the life of the Church. Protestants ceased the sutom of praying for the dead. The Council of Trent insisted that superstitious excesses be eliminated by Catholics but that charity demanded that Christians pray for the dead through offering the Eucharist and other prayers and good works.[28] That pious custom has continued until today. A Catholic may believe that the "cleansing fire" which a soul encounters on the day of death is God himself whom Scripture calls a "consuming fire" (Heb 12:29).

Conclusion

How can we live the faith revealed in Daniel and 1 and 2 Maccabees today?

(1) *Expect victory.* The Scriptures of late Judaism point us more toward the future day of the Lord. As Christians we know that Christ will return as the risen Son of Man (Mk 14:62) "to bring all in heaven and on earth into one under his headship" (Eph 1:10). No one knows the day or the hour (Mt 25:13), but we do know that we are being prepared for a time when "he shall wipe away every tear . . . and there will be no more death . . . or pain" (Rev 21:1).[29] Therefore we can contin-

ue to insist on religious freedom for all and the rights of minorities to preserve their language, customs and cultures. Knowing that Christ has assured the ultimate victory, we can encourage others to let go of apathy and discouragement in resisting oppression.

(2) *Offer sacrifice.* The priestly and Maccabean Scriptures invite us to live by self-sacrificial love. Fruitful participation in the Eucharist is increased if we do not merely hear the word and receive Communion. We can actively offer up our bodies, our whole lives, on the altar symbolically with the sacrificial gifts of bread and wine. We can cooperate with priests and bishops. We can use our talents to enhance the liturgical worship in our local churches. We can encourage our sons and brothers to respond to Christ's call to serve his Church as priests.

(3) *Behold the glory of God.* The book of Daniel invites us to meditate on the majesty of God and the beauty of his angels and saints. It reveals the possibility that each one of us can become a contemplative receiving overwhelming graces in prayer as we live in the midst of immense earthly confusion.

Notes

1. See John Bright, *A History of Israel,* The Westminster Press, Philadelphia, 1952, pp. 341–351.

2. Arthur Weiser, *The Old Testament: Its Formation and Development,* Association Press, N.Y. 1968, pp. 272–273.

3. On the notion of "canonical shape" as important to exegesis, see Brevard S. Childs *Introduction to the Old Testament as Scripture,* Fortress Press, Philadelphia, 1980, pp. 77–81. The notion of canonical shape of a given book is a healthy correction to exegesis which segments verses according to source criticism and fails to see the unity at work in the final inspired redaction of any given book of the Bible. However, *canonical shape* relates Scripture more to theological investigation than to Church. It is only exegesis and theology which investigate and debate the canonical shape of a given book. Catholic faith knows the fuller life of the Church in prayer and official pastoral teaching also to be key hermeneutical elements in appropriating the meaning of any revealed text. While Childs is sensitively

ecumenical, he leaves us with the text of Scripture in isolation from the Church.

4. John Bright, p. 355.

5. Roland de Vaux, *Ancient Israel*, Vol. 2, *Religious Institutions*, McGraw-Hill, New York, 1966, pp. 270f. See also Aelred Cody, O.S.B., *A History of the Old Testament Priesthood*, Pontifical Biblical Institute, 1969, pp. 33ff.

6. De Vaux, p. 346.

7. *Ibid.*, pp. 347–48.

8. Cody, pp. 88–92.

9. The term high priest found in four pre-exilic Scriptures was probably the result of post-exilic reactions (cf. 2 Kgs 12:11; 22:48; 23:4).

10. De Vaux, p. 398.

11. *Ibid.*, pp. 427–28.

12. Robert J. Daly, *Christian Sacrifice: The Judeo-Christian Background Before Origen*, The Catholic University of America Press, Washington, D.C., 1978, pp. 42–45.

13. Bright, p. 406.

14. *Ibid.*, p. 408.

15. This etymology is found in note *b* on the text of 1 Maccabees 2:6 in the unabridged *The Jerusalem Bible*.

16. D.S. Russell, *The Method and Message of Jewish Apocalyptic*, SCM Press Ltd., London, 1964, pp. 15–16.

17. *Ibid.*, p. 35.

18. *Ibid.*, p.107.

19. *Ibid.*, p. 115.

20. The word "interpretation" occurs thirty times in the Book of Daniel, *ibid.*, p. 117.

21. *Ibid.*, pp. 122–127.

22. This statement is based on extrapolation from contemporary experience that some men and women simply live with great integrity throughout their entire lives. Secondly, the Yahwist portrays the primaeval history as rooted in the descendants of Cain and Abel. Abel is a theological metaphor for the history of the just and pious.

23. See St. Ignatius of Antioch, Epistle to the Ephesians, par. 2 and Epistle to the Trallians, par. 3 in *The Fathers of the Church: A New Translation. The Apostolic Fathers*, Christian Heritage, Inc., 1948, Washington, D.C., pp. 88, 102–103.

24. Pope Clement I, "Letter to the Corinthians," in J. Neuner, S.J. and J. Dupuis, S.J. (ed.), *The Christian Faith* in the Doctrinal

Documents of the Catholic Church, Christian Classics, Westminster, Md., 1975, #1701, p. 463.

25. See J. Neuner, #839, p. 227.

26. See Walter Abbott (ed.) *The Documents of Vatican II, passim.*

27. The Catholic Church wanted to "have fellowship with the holy flesh" (relics) of Polycarp who had been burned. The Jews had the Romans remove the body and refuse to give it to the Christians on the pretext that they might begin to worship Polycarp in the place of the crucified one. The author explains: "For we worship him as the son of God, while we love the martyrs as disciples and imitators of the Lord, for their insuperable affection for their own King and Teacher." See "The Martyrdom of Polycarp," Ch. 17 in *The Fathers of the Church: A New Translation, The Apostolic Fathers,* Christian Heritage, Inc., 1948, p. 160.

28. J. Neuner, # 2310, pp. 626–27.

29. Walter Schmithals aptly compares ancient apocalyptic with modern Marxism. See Walter Schmithals, *The Apocalyptic Movement,* Abingdon, N.Y., 1975, pp. 236ff.

Chapter V

Biblical Wisdom, the "Catholic Bible," and Mary's Immaculate Conception

"The fear of the Lord is the beginning of wisdom."
—*Ps 111:10*

The Nature of Biblical Wisdom

How does Old Testament wisdom differ from philosophy?

As distinguished from the reasoned systematic view of the world and man which is the conscious aim of philosophy, wisdom may be defined as the direct practical insight into the meaning and purpose of things that comes to "shrewd, penetrating, and observant minds, from their own experience of life, and their daily commerce with the world." It is the fruit not so much of speculation as of native sagacity and wit. . . . In spite of this distinction the two are closely allied. The knowledge of life reached by wisdom is the raw material out of which philosophical systems are evolved. And in its bolder flights wisdom moves in the atmosphere of philosophy.[1]

Where do we find the wisdom Scriptures of the Old Testament?

Within the Old Testament, the wisdom books constituted the fourth category. The Jews called them "the writings" to

distinguish them from the torah, the prophets, and the historical books. The wisdom books thus include: Job, Psalms, Proverbs, Ecclesiastes, Song of Songs, Wisdom of Solomon, and
Sirach. Current scholarship is also inclined to see books like
Ruth, Tobit, Judith, and Esther as wisdom books rather than
historical narratives.

Where did Old Testament wisdom originate?

Contrary to the view of some nineteenth century scholarship which held Old Testament wisdom to be a late borrowing
from Greek philosophy, Hebrew wisdom is now universally
acknowledged to be very ancient. Its historical roots lie in the
pagan cultures of Abraham's Babylon and Joseph's Egypt.
Archeology has revealed that there were flourishing wisdom
schools in both places, and comparative studies have shown
that Proverbs, Job, Psalms, Song of Songs, and Ecclesiastes all
have striking parallels in Egypt or Babylon.[2]

What ideas did the Hebrew sages borrow from their pagan neighbors?

Hebrew wisdom, like its Egyptian and Babylonian fore-
runners, was predominantly practical. A thorough study of
the parallels is beyond the scope of this work. For the sake of
concreteness, we can mention the dependence of Old Testament Proverbs on the Egyptian collection entitled "The Instruction of the Vizier Ptah-Hotep" which purports to come
from the Fifth Dynasty (ca. 2450 B.C.). From the Babylonian
side we find interesting similarities between "A Pessimistic
Dialogue between Master and Servant" and Old Testament
Ecclesiastes.

Rhys Davids aptly summarizes the major themes of Egyptian wisdom: "... diligence, courtesy, faithfulness to trusts,
humility, self-restraint, purity, loyalty to friends, love of wife
and family, kindness to dependents ... temperance, modesty
of speech, a gracious demeanor ... consideration for the poor
and aged, reverence toward parents ... chaste and loving

worship, prayer, praise and sacrifice."³ All of these are included in the Old Testament.

How did the Old Testament sages transform the pagan wisdom they borrowed?

The pivotal idea around which this transformation occurred was "the fear of the Lord." This concept envisioned a moral and spiritual conversion with profound intellectual consequences. It makes Hebrew wisdom utterly *theocentric*. As such it is a legitimate contribution to the faith community of Moses. This point is never made more clearly than in Psalm 14, "The fool says in his heart, 'There is no God.' Such are corrupt; they do abominable deeds" (Ps 14:1). By contrast the inspired sage of Proverbs reminds us, "The fear of the Lord is the beginning of knowledge; wisdom and instruction fools despise" (Prv 1:7).

If it is true that the intellect informs the will so that one must know the good before one can choose to live wisely by the good, the opposite is also true. One must have some deep longing of the will for what is good in order to begin to search for what is true. The Hebrew sages emphasized this second aspect and thus gave primacy to the moral dimension of the quest for wisdom. The good fruits of choosing wisely to live a moral life are delightfully sketched in Psalm 34. By living the torah, the soul is refreshed, the heart is rejoiced, the eye is enlightened, and the fear of the Lord is pure, enduring forever (Ps 34:8–10). Here we learn that the sobriety of a God-centered life according to the commandments is humanly fulfilling. Such a personal morality provides a living center and divine strength for the wise person throughout the confounding turns of history and personal fortune.

Two examples can clarify how the Jews revealed God as the unique source of wisdom. In Egyptian wisdom we find counsels on respecting the *ka*. This was a kind of guardian spirit which functioned as a causal principle in human affairs. At times reference to the *ka* seems to border on immanentism (the divine force is an aspect of the universe, not a free gift), determinism, or fatalism.

> As for the great man when he is at meals, his purposes conform to the dictates of his *ka*. . . . The great man gives to *the man whom he can reach,* [but] it is the *ka* that lengthens out his arms.[4]

The Hebrew sages suppressed any concept of a determining immanent force in human affairs. The Creator God who hears prayers and rewards and punishes according to justice and mercy was inserted in place of any other concept of the supernatural.

In all of semitic pagan wisdom there was a crude mixture of science, philosophy, and occult practices of superstition. The following selection from an Akkadian sage shows how this functioned in the wisdom circles of the ancient world.

> My affliction increases, right I cannot find. I implored the god but he did not turn his countenance; I prayed to my goddess, but she did not raise her head. The diviner through divination did not discern the situation. Through incense offerings the great interpreter did not explain my right. I turned to the necromancer, but he did not enlighten me. The conjurer through magic did not dispel the wrath against me.[5]

From the covenant of Moses, the Hebrew sages knew that they had no right to try to manipulate God or human affairs through occult arts. The only truly wise response to human suffering could be intensified prayer, fasting, sackcloth, ashes and the prudential use of human freedom to make wise decisions in accord with God's revealed will in the covenant. They therefore suppressed all references to the use of magic and occult arts to seek divine wisdom.[6]

If pagan wisdom could be superstitious, why did the Jews study it?

Because of the possible occult associations with wisdom a "wise" or "gifted" person (in Greek a *magos*) could be very evil. For this reason, the witch of Endor could be called a "gifted" woman and yet be guilty of practicing arts abominable to Yahweh (2 Sam 14:2). In the New Testament Simon Magus clearly reveals that in these occult practices the fear of the Lord was displaced by the personal quest for spiritual power (Acts 8:19). Because of these negative connotations to being a *magos,* St. Matthew's boldness startles us when he writes that three *magi* had divined the birth of Christ through astrology. Every other biblical and Christian testimony condemned the wise magos as an evildoer. In this sense Matthew 2:1–12 culminates the scriptural transformation of the pagan magical element in the wisdom circles. The story of the three *magi* coming to adore Christ, the star of justice, was a sobering reminder that, in the midst of superstition and illusion, pagan sages too could find the ultimate truth.

The History of Biblical Wisdom

The wisdom books give us almost no internal clues for dating the materials except linguistic ones.[7] In general all of semitic wisdom developed through three stages: practical, speculative, and paradoxical. The most ancient method for learning wisdom was to memorize proverbs. In Egypt, the wisdom school was called "the house of life."

Practical Wisdom

How did the wisdom schools understand wisdom as practical?

Throughout the Middle East the primary emphasis of the sages was on the divine gift of practical skills. Thus in the Old Testament Yahweh says to Moses in his directions for building the temple, "I have also endowed all the experts with the necessary skill to make all the things I have ordered you to make" (Ex 31:6). The context includes the skills of weaving, carpentry, brass work, sewing, stone cutting, embroidery and the pressing of oil. Strategic military advice for General Joab is the skill of the wise woman of Abel Beth-maacah (2 Sam 20:16). Seamanship is the practical gift which God takes away in Psalm 107:27. The ideal wife combines all the practical skills of household management with the wisdom of personal insight (Prv 31:10–31). Outstanding administrators manifest the practical skill of sound judgment in government—Joseph (Gen 41:33), Joshua (Dt 34:9), and Solomon (1 Kgs 3:12).

Speculative Wisdom

What is meant by speculative wisdom?

Practical wisdom had held that the good flourish in this life and the wicked suffer (cf. Ps 37:34–40). This neat theory, however, did not square with human experience. Therefore speculative wisdom developed a more philosophical or theological emphasis and posed questions about human happiness, suffering, and the very nature of wisdom itself.

Innocent people suffered and wicked people prospered. Why? Even today all the poverty and suffering on our planet cannot be facilely blamed on the "laziness" of the poor while ignoring the machinations of the powerful who exploit them. Honest men have been shot for telling the truth; innocent men and women alike have been physically brutalized or killed while trying to resist the violence of an attacker's disordered sexuality. Such things should not happen, but they do.

What is more, the biblical notion that sin causes sickness must be qualified by its correlative truth: mental and physical illness cause dehumanizing destructive behavior. Genetics, psychology and medicine all have something to teach about human motivation and moral responsibility. An alcoholic is not a sinner needing special repentance, but a sick person needing healing. By contrast the social drunkard who drives recklessly needs to ask forgiveness for the perverse use of his freedom. Could it be that some "hidden sin" lurked in the conscience of the apparently innocent sufferer? Eliphaz and the other friends of Job represented the moralistic theory of human suffering espoused by speculative wisdom (cf. Jb 4). All who suffered had committed some hidden sin.

Paradoxical Wisdom

What is paradoxical wisdom?

A paradox is a truth that defies the expectations of common sense. Jesus used paradoxical sayings to explain the nature of his Kingdom: "He who seeks his life will lose it" (Mt 10:39). In the same way some Old Testament sages denied the common sense proverbs of their forefathers. They dared to teach that innocent people do suffer. For this reason they are also classified as "left-wing" or "heterodox" Jewish wisdom authors. Job, Qoheleth, and Agur ben Jakeh are the three known representatives of the inspired paradoxical wisdom in the Old Testament.

Job

How does the Book of Job reconcile the suffering of the innocent with the goodness of God?

After Job's tortured effort to understand the suffering of the innocent and why the all-powerful good God allows such evil, God speaks to Job in chapters 38—42. God asks Job to reflect on the magnitude of the universe and of human achievements; then he asks him to reflect on the immensity of cosmic evil as symbolized in the sea monsters Leviathan and Behemoth. The whole dialogue relentlessly presses Job to come to the realization, "Am I, God, not greater than all of these?"

In this experience of coming to personal insight into the nature of God and the human race, Job's struggle ends. He has come to the intellectual humility of a paradoxical wisdom which knows no answer to all of life's questions, but knows how to surrender to the faith certitude of the Lord's infinite transcendence. The God of Israel has become the Lord of Job's intellect. The fruit of the search is that Job knew God, the complexity of creation, and his human finitude in a whole new way:

> I had heard of you by word of mouth,
>   but now my eye has seen you.
> Therefore I disown what I have said,
>   and repent in dust and ashes (Jb 42:5–6).

In "seeing with the eye" of his intellect, Job has appropriated the *ineffability* of God for the human intellect: God is too awesome to be expressed in human words. Job's repentance freed him from the illusion of being able to comprehend all of reality with his human mind. To stop trying to equal God intellectually did not imply that the wise sage should give up searching. That would be intellectual sloth. "The adornment of simpletons is folly, but shrewd men gain the crown of knowledge" (Prv 14:18). The fruit of paradoxical wisdom seems to have been, therefore, an intellectual humility (Prv 22:4) which avoided the false trap of being anti-intellectual.

Qoheleth

Who was Qoheleth?

Qoheleth, author of Ecclesiastes (the teacher), was the second most developed example of paradoxical wisdom in the Old Testament. Thus Qoheleth is like Job but with his own special flavor. For Qoheleth, all life is a vicious circle. "Vanity of vanities! All things are vanity" (Eccl 1:2). This was original-ly Qoheleth's opening and closing refrain. So shocking was it to pious ears that the rabbis almost excluded it from the Hebrew Scriptures. When they finally decided the book was inspired, they forbade Jews to read it until they were thirty years old.

Robert Gordis is probably right in suggesting that Qoheleth was a mature sage who had searched widely for the meaning of wisdom and the answer to human suffering. From his vantage point of many years of faithful search, he was trying to teach the young merchant class that to live wisely is to live in the present moment.[8] To live in the present moment meant to take time from the hectic affairs of business to enjoy family, food, and wine. Qoheleth is not counseling hedonism, but the prudent use of the divine blessings which life offers (Eccl 9:9–10; 11:9–10). They should be savored in one's prime before entering into the pain of old age and the darkness of death (Eccl 12:1–8).

Why were the wisdom books so popular in mature Judaism?

The helpfulness of the sages in the human quest for happiness may do much to explain their increasing prominence in post-exilic Judaism. Qoheleth (Eccl 7:23–25), Job (42:1) and Agur ben Jakeh (Prv 30:2–3) all recognized that simplistic answers to human suffering and the meaning of wisdom were stupid. Likewise they recognized that they had no better answers to explain "why." Job and Qoheleth furnished the community of faith with a paradoxical "spirituality" for dealing with suffering in the concrete ways human beings live. Their paradoxical wisdom served well at a time when Jesus had not yet revealed the transforming power of the cross.

The Beauty of Transcendent Wisdom

When the Hebrew sages began to meditate humbly on the very nature of wisdom itself, they knew through their faith that they could not attribute the source of wisdom to some god like their pagan neighbors. Who or what caused wisdom to dwell in the hearts of some? From whence came the beauty and harmony in all of creation? Gradually they came to know wisdom as an eternal, compellingly beautiful dimension or aura of God himself. Their descriptions of this eternal person of wisdom provide us with some of the most sublime Scriptures of the Old Testament. By the time of Christ Lady Wisdom had been revealed as (1) personal and eternal, (2) life-giving like a woman, (3) dwelling in Jerusalem, (4) a spotless image of God's power.

Wisdom as Personal and Eternal

Where does the Old Testament reveal wisdom as "begotten of God"?

In Proverbs 8:22–36 the Scriptures describe Wisdom as the "first-born" of God's ways, created before all else. Eternal Wisdom helped God as "his craftsman." This eternal personal Wisdom "plays before him" and "plays on the surface of the earth" as a kind of mediating principle between the uncreated God and the created universe. Personal Wisdom is described in the same passage as giving delight to God and finding delight in those people who choose to live wisely. The inspired sage has evidently entered into a whole experience of sublime contemplative wonder as God revealed that Wisdom is not some "thing" but ultimately some "One."

Wisdom as Giving Life Like a Woman

Where is wisdom revealed as life-giving like a woman?

The Hebrew word for wisdom (*chokmah*) is feminine. This linguistic association and the ancient fascination with the power of a woman's body to bring forth new human life (Prv 30:19) are probably two of the factors which caused the Hebrew sages to conceive of the person of eternal wisdom as feminine. Thus Proverbs 7:4 advises, "Say to Wisdom, 'You are my sister!' Call Understanding, 'Friend.'" To find her is to find life (Prv 3:18; 8:35).

Wisdom Dwells in Jerusalem

How can Wisdom live in a special place on earth?

The Jewish sage Judah ben Sirach developed this aspect of Wisdom and revealed her as fixing her abode in "the holy tent" of Zion (cf. Sir 24:1–12). The Book of Sirach (also called Ecclesiasticus or "The Church Book" because of its popularity in the Church) was written in Hebrew sometime between 200 and 175 B.C. Thus not too many years before the birth of Christ, God revealed that eternal Wisdom was "dynamic" and "incarnational'"—it wanted to live in his chosen people. This incarnational dynamism makes the person of eternal Wisdom very similar to that of the "living Word" in the earlier prophets. Sirach 24 calls to mind Isaiah 55, "So shall my word be that goes forth from my mouth; it shall not return to me void, but shall do my will, achieving the end for which I sent it (Is 55:11). John's Gospel completed this theme when it proclaimed that in the birth of the infant Jesus "the Word who was God ... became flesh and made his dwelling [literally, *tented*] among us" (Jn 1:1, 14).

Sirach envisioned the "tent" of God's personal Wisdom to be the Jerusalem temple in which God's special presence had deigned to dwell (1 Kgs 8:10–13). For Jesus, the "tent" was his human body. The "tent" of the divine Word-made-flesh was the womb of Mary. Her "yes" to God was the indispensable offer of her human creativity to the divine creativity of the Holy Spirit. "I am the servant of the Lord. Let it be done to me as you say" (Lk 1:38). Mary's "yes" to being the dwelling place of incarnate divine wisdom is the historical completion of the incarnational dynamism which Sirach revealed.

Wisdom as the Spotless Mirror of God's Power

What does the image of "the spotless mirror" intend to reveal about Wisdom?

About 100 B.C. an anonymous Jew living in Alexandria, Egypt wrote The Wisdom of Solomon in a Greek that imitated the style of Hebrew poetry. He revealed Wisdom to be not only eternal and feminine, but "mobile, penetrating, pure," and "a pure effusion of the glory of the Almighty," who is "fairer than the sun and surpasses every constellation of the stars" (cf. Wis 7:24—8:1). Here God has revealed that he is the infinity of personal light. This light radiates the beauty of infinite Wisdom. She was with God in the beginning (Wis 9:9). She may thus be loved as God himself ought to be loved. Conversely her feminine beauty reveals God to the sage as infinitely lovable. As a spotless mirror she is a transparent medium revealing God as breathtakingly beautiful.

While it is likely that this Alexandrian Jew had been exposed to Plato and Plotinus, the horizon of his Jewish faith transformed any hint of an inner divine necessity to create the universe into a "metaphysics" that foreshadowed the Christian Trinity.[9] Wisdom shares eternally in the glory of God, but is not God. Because of this union between Wisdom and God, the sage could fall in love with the beauty of Wisdom, "who is spotlessly pure, an image of God," and not involve himself in the false worship of the beautiful (Wis 13:1-9).

Do we know anything about the author of The Wisdom of Solomon?

The careful reader glimpses the sage's own intimate union in love with the Wisdom of Israel's God.[10] The sage had "yearned" for her (Wis 8:8) and "determined to take her to live with me" (Wis 8:9). Only the divine femininity radiating from the darkness of ineffable transcendence could explain this sage's masculine passion for the One who is utterly spiritual. "Her I loved and sought after from my youth; I sought to take her for my bride and was enamored of her beauty. She adds to nobility the splendor of companionship with God" (Wis 8:1–2). He must have been a man in whom the grace of Hebrew faith combined with the Greek love for contemplation of the eternal. His experience invites us to continue to integrate the light of secular truth with the higher light of personal faith.

How did the New Testament develop the theme of Wisdom's beauty who gives us God's new life?

In the New Testament eternal Wisdom incarnated itself as male in Jesus, the crucified "wisdom of God" (1 Cor 2:24), through the woman whom God's angel had greeted as "full of grace" and "in the presence of the Lord" (Lk 1:28). From that time on, Christian faith contemplated her womanhood as transparently pure and saw in her "perduring fecundity" the "aura of the might of God." According to Luke's canticle, Mary testified to this unique dignity in herself when she proclaimed, "All ages to come shall call me blessed" (Lk 1:48). As God's chosen woman and the bearer of his eternal Wisdom, this historical woman continues to radiate the "glory" which was with God in the beginning. In her womanhood, Mary adds the "splendor of companionship" to the "nobility" of adoring Israel's God. For this reason John's Gospel reports Jesus crucified as giving this "woman" to those descendants of Abraham who stand faithfully at the foot of the cross. The Church, symbolized in the person of John the Evangelist, is ordered to recognize this "woman" as its spiritual "mother" (Jn 19:26–27).

The Relation of the Wisdom Writings to Catholic Faith

Catholic faith is rooted in the wisdom Scriptures in at least four principal ways: (1) its understanding of the mutual exchange between Church and secular culture, (2) its openness to world religions, (3) its belief in the immaculate conception of the Blessed Virgin Mary, and (4) its belief that the deutero-canonical books of the Old Testament are as equally inspired by God as the proto-canonical books.

The Catholic Church and Secular Culture

Is the Catholic attitude toward secular wisdom faithful to the Scriptures?

Yes. Just as the Israelite sages of old were open to learning from their pagan neighbors, so Catholics remember that God created everything in the universe as *good* (Gen 1). Therefore many of the Church Fathers of the early centuries borrowed heavily from Platonic philosophy to enrich the Church's understanding of God and his will for us as revealed in Scripture. In a similar spirit of secular search the Benedictine monks developed new technologies in agriculture and land reclamation. At times the evangelization of new cultures was carried out in the spirit of "building on the natural religiosity existing in a pagan culture" so as not to make faith in Jesus unnecessarily rending.[11]

How do Catholics today regard modern science and secular humanism?

After two centuries of fear and hostility, official Catholic teaching today respects science and secular humanism, but interprets them in the light of faith as a "mixed blessing" for the modern world. On the positive side, secular investigation has developed the critical thinking abilities of humanity and "purified" the Church of its tendency to ignore natural causes and explanations. This critical search has led many people today to raise the most fundamental questions about human nature, evil, death or technological progress. To hunger to know is good.[12] Better medicine and more food is good.

On the other hand official Catholic teaching points out that secular inquiry has *jeopardized* modern society by ignoring or excluding faith in Christ whose Spirit offers us "the light and the strength to measure up to [our] supreme destiny."[13] Thus, while helpful in its questioning, secular humanism creates a spiritual-psychological kind of prison or "no exit" from which the Church seeks to free human minds through the proclamation of the Gospel. Even when people oppose or persecute it, the Church recognizes that it profits from such antagonism.[14] In this spirit Catholic faith dialogues with secular culture to challenge what dehumanizes and to invite search into a deeper truth so that the human family may be more personalized according to the divine wisdom of its Creator.[15]

World Religions

How do Catholics regard the non-Christian religions?

Just as the Hebrew sages were willing to learn from the imperfect religions of ancient Egypt and Babylon, so Catholic faith "rejects nothing which is 'true and holy' in world religions."[16] Like the ancient sages, Catholic faith also rejects the superstitious and magical in favor of the responsible and the prudent. World religions may have a ray of divine truth whose fullness is Christ as known in the Church. It would be proud and foolish to be unwilling to learn from the world religions. St. Thomas Aquinas taught that "prudence" was the opposite of foolishness in practical decisions. For him prudence is the guardian of love.[17] With respect to world religions, Catholic faith strives for that practical wisdom which lives the truth in love (cf. Eph 4:15).

The Immaculate Conception of the Virgin Mary

Since the Bible never teaches that Mary was conceived without original sin, why do Catholics believe she was?

The place of the incarnation was, as we saw before, the womb of the Virgin Mary. This extraordinary happening has captivated the contemplative gaze of Catholic Christians since the Gospels of Luke and John. Gradually the Church sensed its evangelical freedom to see in Mary, "full of grace," "the spotless mirror of the power of God." As Catholic faith deepened, the grace of Christ was accepted as having the power to transform a human person from the very moment of one's conception. Gradually the Holy Spirit developed this faith-awareness in Catholics to the point of communal certitude.

Certainly this dogma goes beyond anything explicitly taught in the Bible, and just as certainly this dogma is the flowering of the feminine dimension of revealed wisdom which has its roots in Sacred Scripture. When Catholic faith could say with certitude that Mary really did radiate "the spotless glory of God" in every moment of her human life, it could simultaneously increase its hope in this awesome power of God to forgive and heal the tarnished glory in our souls wounded by sin. In this way reflection on Mary's immaculate conception helps the Catholic Christian live wisely in the "fear of the Lord,'" who "has done such wondrous deeds."

After consulting the Catholic bishops of the world to see whether this belief in the immaculate conception lived in the hearts of the laity, Pope Pius IX on December 8, 1854 solemnly proclaimed this belief as a dogma of faith. For Catholics a dogma is a belief "revealed by God and, therefore, firmly and constantly to be believed by all the faithful." Therefore we believe that "from the first moment of her conception, . . . in view of the merits of Christ Jesus, Mary was preserved immune from all stain of original sin."[18]

This beautiful effect of the grace of Christ is especially celebrated by U.S. Catholics whose national shrine is the Basilica of the Immaculate Conception in Washington, D.C. The feast of her immaculate conception is celebrated each year on December 8. Not only is Mary the patroness of the United States, but since she evangelized the "Indians" of the new world with her appearance in Mexico City in 1532 as Our Lady of Guadalupe, Catholics of both North and South America regard the immaculate Virgin with special affection and personal gratitude.

The "Catholic Bible"

What is meant by the long and short canon of Sacred Scripture?

"Canon" means "the list" of books which Jews and Christians consider to be inspired. The Jews used the term "pollutes the hands" because the holiness of an inspired writing would reveal the unworthiness of the reader by comparison with the glory of God. The long canon is included in the Greek Septuagint Old Testament which is considered normative by Catholics. The short canon is found in the Hebrew Masoretic Old Testament and is followed by Jews and Protestants. Christians believe that an inspired book has God as its principal author who guided the human authors with the special assistance of the Holy Spirit to reveal what he wanted taught in the Scriptures.

What are the disputed books of the Old Testament which are found only in the long canon?

These books include Tobit, Judith, The Wisdom of Solomon, Sirach, Baruch, and 1 and 2 Maccabees. Jews and Protestants do not consider these books inspired and call them "the apocrypha," a term which Catholics apply to non-inspired books like Enoch. Protestants label Enoch and similar books "the pseudepigrapha." In addition some short additions to Esther and Daniel are found in Catholic Bibles. Catholics call the additional books "deutero-canonical" (second or long canon). Therefore Catholic Bibles include forty-five books in the Old Testament while Protestant Bibles have thirty-nine.

Should Protestants or Catholics or Jews be blamed for this difference?

No one should be "blamed." To understand this discrepancy "wisely," sectarian bias needs to be eliminated from consideration at the outset. Protestants did not throw out Sacred Scriptures in the sixteenth century to justify their "novel heresies," nor did Catholics make up Sacred Scriptures to support their "papist superstitions." A more balanced reading of history can contribute to mutual understanding on this point of divergence.

How did the long canon develop historically?

It took from 1850 (Abraham) to 538 B.C. (return from the Babylonian exile) for the first five books of the Bible to be written, shaped into the book of the torah, and revered as "inspired" by the Jewish community of faith. By 323 B.C. prophetic activity had ceased and the *nevi'im* or "prophets" became a second unit of Scriptures recognized by the Jewish community of faith as inspired by God. The Scriptures which they called the "former prophets" were actually the early historical books: Joshua, Judges, 1 and 2 Samuel, and 1 and 2 Kings. The canon of the prophets was closed around 200 B.C.

The third category of Scriptures was the *ketuv'im* or "writings," which today we call the wisdom books. This cluster of scrolls continued to grow, and there was no Jewish consensus about which of these writings were inspired at the time when the Church came into existence in 33 A.D. Some books were universally revered, like Psalms and Proverbs. Others were debated, like Ecclesiastes and The Wisdom of Solomon. The New Testament authors certainly revered the wisdom books as worthy of being cited in their own inspired writings.[19]

The fluidity of the Old Testament canon was further reinforced by the translation of the Hebrew scrolls into Greek for Jews living in Alexandria, Egypt. This process had begun in the third century B.C. By the first century A.D. it seems that all of the Old Testament books in the "Catholic" Bible were being read by the Alexandrian Jews in Egypt. This version of Scripture came to be known as the Greek Septuagint Bible.

How did the short canon develop historically?

Between 33 and 100 A.D. Judaism suffered a new state of religious and political crisis. Numerous Jews were becoming followers of the "new way" and proclaiming their faith in the crucified Jesus as the risen Messiah. They went to Jewish synagogue on Saturdays and Christian Eucharist on Sundays. In 70 A.D. the Romans destroyed the Jerusalem temple and forced Judaism to regroup its religious leadership elsewhere. Under the inspiring and learned direction of Rabbi Johanan ben Zakai, a center of Jewish scribal learning emerged which did much to save Judaism from extinction through the piety of the Pharisee party. This center was located in the Palestinian seacoast town of Jamnia (Jabneh). About 85 A.D. rabbinical authorities excluded Christians from synagogue worship because of their radically novel religious doctrines. Between 90 and 100 A.D. the most learned and holy of the Palestinian rabbis studied and debated which of the "writings" should be considered as inspired and thus retained in the Bible and which should be excluded. By 100 A.D. the Jamnia rabbis had produced the list of inspired books to be used in the Hebrew Bible of the Masoretic text. Unfortunately we have no full history of the debates, nor the criteria these rabbis used.

Is the long (Greek) canon or the short (Hebrew) canon older?

Commenting on the divergence between the Greek canon and the Hebrew canon, J.C. Turro aptly writes:

> All too commonly it is assumed that great differences of opinion divided Palestinian Jews from those of the dispersion and that the differences sprang from divergent theories of interpretation prevalent in Alexandria and Jerusalem. This is a purely gratuitous inference. . . . If they used the deutero-canonical books in the diaspora, it was because they had received them from Palestine. . . . LXX [the Septuagint] reflects an older tradition than the Hebrew Bible.[20]

How did Catholics and Protestants develop divergent traditions about which canon to use in the Church?

The Church used the long canon for the first three hundred years of its existence without anyone questioning the propriety of this practice. In the fourth century St. Jerome and others adverted to the discrepancy between the Greek and the Hebrew canon with some concern. Jerome, living in Bethlehem and using the help of Jewish rabbis to translate the Greek Bible into the Latin Vulgate, included all the books in the Vulgate but labeled the proto-canonical books "canonical" and the deutero-canonical books "ecclesiastical." In this choice of terms, Jerome's respect for Hebrew culture seems to have clouded the clarity of his theological judgment. While Jamnia could rightfully demand the obediential assent of Jews to its decision to exclude certain books from use, Christians owed obediential assent to the apostolic tradition. The Christian apostolic tradition knew and used only the longer, but still fluid, canon of the Old Testament. We have extant only Christian Bibles from Alexandria, so we cannot know for sure what was the Jewish custom there with respect to the canon. Thus Jerome's choice of the term "ecclesiastical" was too ambiguous. It could imply "not inspired."

The inspired character of the deutero-canonical books was debated occasionally in the theological lecture halls of the Middle Ages, but it never became a burning issue. This changed considerably in the emotionally charged atmosphere of the sixteenth century Reformation. Protestant Reformers were very concerned to remove all "human accretions" from Church life. Luther denied the interpretative role of the Catholic magisterium in the Church's reading of Scripture. Scholarly theological opinion replaced episcopal authority as the pastoral guide for reading the Bible. At first such scholarly opinion labeled the deutero-canonical books as "apocrypha" and printed them in between the two Testaments. Finally in spite of the fact that a British law of 1615 forbade their suppression, the deutero-canonical books ceased being always printed in the King James Bible after 1611. Their exclusion made the Bibles cheaper and more portable.

Given this Protestant challenge to apostolic tradition, the Catholic bishops in 1546 at the fourth session of the Council of Trent deemed it necessary to solemnly define the inspired character of the forty-five books of the Old Testament and the twenty-seven books of the New Testament. "Following the example of the orthodox Fathers, it receives and reiterates with the same sense of loyalty and reverence all the books of the Old and New Testaments, for God alone is the author of both."[21]

How do Catholics today view the Protestant tradition of preferring the shorter canon of the Old Testament?

In the less polemical atmosphere of current Christian ecumenism, Catholic faith today can be more open to its "separated brethren" who are reluctant to assent to the inspired character of the deutero-canonical books. The "Decree on Ecumenism" of Vatican II (1964) encourages all members of the Church to preserve freedom and variety in the spiritual life and liturgical customs "and even in the theological elaborations of revealed truth." Charity that promotes such variety gives a richer expression to the catholicity and apostolicity of the Church.[22]

How can we promote variety with charity in the matter of the two canons of the Old Testament?

Catholic Bibles should label the deutero-canonical Scriptures very clearly to respect the variety in the ancient sources and educate Catholics into this history of the canon. Protestants, for their part, could reflect on their own tradition of distinguishing between "apocrypha" and "pseudepigrapha." Does not this Protestant practice suggest a faith awareness of a similarity between the canonical Scriptures and those labeled apocryphal? Perhaps the Spirit will eventually furnish searching Christians with some new categories which can distinguish between "canonical" and "deutero-canonical" as "inspired" but in different ways, so that they are simultaneously subsumed into the deeper unity of one divine authorship.

Do all Christians accept the same canon of the New Testament?

Yes. Happily there has been unity of opinion among all Christians on the inspired nature of the twenty-seven books of the New Testament since the fourth century A.D. After a long struggle, Hebrews, Revelation, 2 Peter, 2 John, 3 John, James and Jude were all recognized with the twenty other books by the Catholic bishops in the Synods of Hippo (393 A.D.) and Carthage (397 A.D.).

Conclusion

How can we live today the faith revealed in the wisdom books?

(1) *Relate the secular and the sacred.* In this way the light of faith uses the findings of secular research and the inventions of human art to deepen its grateful praise of God. The smallest atom is no longer simply a puzzle to be solved, but an invitation to acknowledge its mysterious Creator. The most abstract philosophy does not leave us with simply clearer ideas, but invites us to adore the infinite simplicity of God who is the ultimate author of all philosophy. The breathtakingly beautiful invites us to savor the beauty of God who inspires artists. Thus, for "those who fear the Lord," every created object of human reflection becomes a revelation of eternal Wisdom and an invitation to fall in love with God.

(2) *Choose life.* The gentleness and receptivity of God's Wisdom gives us the fullness of life. A wise life-style is physically and mentally healthful. A wise life-style learns to balance work and play, family and career, future goals and present opportunities. The wise will of the life-giving God is preferred over the foolishness of personal whims. Jesus said that he came to give us more abundant life—both in this world and in the next. He called the Eucharist our "bread of life" (cf. Jn 6).

(3) *Give birth.* The wisdom Scriptures repeatedly teach that the path of foolishness leads to death. Life, on the contrary, grows through birth. We give birth to babies, to life-plans, to ideas, inventions, and cures. The path of creativity, not of death and destruction, is God's way. The birth of Christ ushered Wisdom into space and time. The immaculate woman who gave him birth lives in heaven as the "Seat of Wisdom." She knows the confusion and fear involved in giving birth; she wants to befriend each of us as we strive to make our lives a fruitful process of giving birth. O Immaculate Virgin Mary, pray for each of us; pray for our planet. Walk with us into the dawn of the third millennium of your Son's reign over us.

Notes

1. T.W. Rhys Davids, "Wisdom," *Encyclopedia of Religion and Ethics,* Vol. 12, p. 742. For more background on the wisdom Scriptures, see Evode Beaucamp. O.F.M., *Man's Destiny in the Books of Wisdom,* Alba House, Staten Island, N.Y., 1970; Walter Brueggemann, "Scripture and an Ecumenical Life-Style: A Study in Wisdom Theology," in *Interpretation,* Vol. XXIV, No. 1 (Jan. 1970), pp. 3-19; Stanley J. Chesnut, *The Old Testament Understanding of God,* Westminster Press, Philadelphia, 1968; Christian D. Ginsburg, *The Song of Songs and Coheleth,* Ktav Publishing House, Inc., N.Y., 1970; Robert Gordis, *Koheleth—The Man and His World,* Bloch Publishing Co., 1955; Norman B. Johnson, "Prayer in the Apocrypha and Pseudepigrapha: A Study in the Jewish Concept of God," in *Journal of Biblical Literature,* Monograph Series, II, 1948; Roland Murphy, O. Carm., "Ecclesiastes (Qoheleth)," in *The Jerome Biblical Commentary,* Vol. I, pp. 534-40; Roland Murphy, O. Carm., *Seven Books of Wisdom,* The Bruce Publishing Co., Milwaukee, 1960; O.S. Rankin, *Israel's Wisdom Literature: Its Bearing on Theology and the History of Religion,* T. and T. Clark, Edinburgh, 1954; R.B.Y. Scott, *Proverbs, Ecclesiastes* in *The Anchor Bible,* Doubleday and Co., Inc., Garden City, New York, 1965; R.B.Y. Scott, "The Study of the Wisdom Literature," in *Interpretation,* Vol. XXIV, No. 1 (Jan. 1970), pp. 20-45; Walther Zimmerli, "The Place and Limit of Wisdom in the Framework of Old Testament Theology," in *Scottish Journal of Theology,* Vol. XVII (1964), pp. 146-58.

2. English translations of the extant materials can be found in Pritchard's *Ancient New Eastern Texts,* Part VI, Didactic and Wisdom Literature, Princeton University Press, 1955, pp. 403 ff.

3. Rhys Davids, p. 742.

4. Pritchard, pp. 412–13.

5. *Ibid.,* p. 434.

6. The one exception seems to have been sortilege or casting lots. Urim and Thummim were used by the temple priests to divine the will of Yahweh (Ex 28:30; Lev 8:8; Num 27:21; Dt 33:8; 1 Sam 28:6; Ez 2:63; Neh 7:65). The Apostles continued a variant of this practice in the New Testament to obtain an unbiased choice to replace Judas and retain the number twelve to symbolize the twelve tribes of Israel (Acts 1:21–26).

7. For example, the Book of Ecclesiastes contains Persian words in 2:15 and 8:11. This is one of the important clues for saying that this piece of wisdom cannot have been written in its present form before 500 B.C. at the very earliest since Jewish contact with Persia only began in 538 B.C.

8. Robert Gordis, *Koheleth—The Man and His World: A Study of Ecclesiastes,* Schocken Books, N.Y., 1973, p. 85.

9. At this point in history, the sage is certainly only hinting at the possibility of distinction within God. A formal revelation of the Trinity does not even exist in the New Testament, let alone in The Wisdom of Solomon.

10. Here we take for granted that the sage has put his own sentiments into the mouth of Solomon who had become a kind of "patron saint of wisdom."

11. Pope St. Gregory the Great gave these instructions to St. Augustine of Canterbury when he sent him to evangelize the British Isles in the late sixth century. In the seventeenth century, St. Francis Xavier was very sensitive to the indigenous cultural values in Asia and the Far East.

12. Walter M. Abbott, S.J. (ed.), "Pastoral Constitution on the Church in the Modern World," par. 10, *The Documents of Vatican II,* p. 208.

13. *Ibid.*

14. *Ibid.,* par. 44., pp. 246–47.

15. Chapters I and II of the same document develop these themes. See pp. 210–31.

16. "Declaration on the Relationship of the Church to Non-Christian Religions," Par. 2 in *ibid.,* p. 662.

17. Thomas Aquinas, *Summa Theologica,* II-II q. 166, a. 2, Reply Obj. 1.

18. J. Neuner, S.J. and J. Dupuis, S.J. (eds.), *The Christian Faith in the Doctrinal Documents of the Catholic Church,* #709, pp. 196–97.

19. According to R.C. Fuller, the New Testament never cites the deutero-canonical books of the Old Testament but has numerous traces of them showing that the New Testament Church read and respected them as Scripture: Mt 6:14/Sir 28:2; Mt 27:39/Wis 2:12–15; Rom 1:20/Wis 13:13; Heb 11:35–39/2 Mac 6:18—7:42; Jas 1:19/Sir 5:11–13; 1 Pet 1:6/Wis 3:3ff. See R.C. Fuller, "The Old Testament Canon," in *A New Catholic Commentary on Holy Scripture,* Nelson, London, 1969, p. 25.

20. J.C. Turro, "Bible, III," in *New Catholic Encyclopedia,* Vol. 2, pp. 389ff. For an interesting and thorough Protestant explanation, see Bruce M. Metzger, "The Apocrypha of the Old Testament," in *The Oxford Annotated Bible with the Apocrypha* (RSV), Oxford University Press, 1965, pp. vii–xxii.

21. Neuner, #211, p. 70.

22. "Decree on Ecumenism," par. 4, in *The Documents of Vatican II,* p. 349.

Chapter VI

The Gospel and Catholic Teaching on the Trinity, Christ, and Mary

"God has made both Lord and Messiah this Jesus whom you have crucified."
—*Acts 1:36*

The Risen Lord Jesus Lives Among Us

How did the first Jewish Christians come to believe in the resurrection of Christ?

According to the most ancient apostolic testimony, Christ "died, was buried, and rose" all "in accordance with the Scriptures." Then he was "seen" by Cephas (Peter), the Twelve, the five hundred, and finally by Paul. This "seeing" of the risen Lord had been an inward spiritual seeing in faith. Thus St. Paul, the first of the New Testament authors, described a religious experience of conversion to Christ as "seeing him" (cf. 1 Cor 15, written ca. 56 A.D.).

This biblical quote above is from St. Peter's address to the bystanders at the first Pentecost. As such, it recalls the oldest public testimony of the Church to the central content of Christian faith: the crucified Jesus of Nazareth is the risen Messiah. Behind this written testimony stands the older oral tradition of Christian faith. This is called the kerygma or proclamation of the *evangelion*, the good news, the Gospel.

133

This oral kerygma constitutes the heart of the New Testament and pre-dates the written kerygma in the Epistles and the Gospels. Thus Peter's Pentecost address to the representatives of "all the nations under heaven" was given its final written form by St. Luke ca. 85 A.D.[1]

Those who "had seen" the risen Jesus with the interior eyes of faith "proclaimed" him as "good news" for anyone who would listen to them. The first Christians came to faith by *seeing* and *hearing*. That is why St. Paul could so confidently teach, "Faith, then, comes through hearing . . ." (Rom 10:17). Because the risen Lord Jesus himself was prompting them to speak—was, in a sense, speaking through them—the Apostles could say that through "the word of faith that we preach . . . what is heard is the word of Christ" (Rom 10:8, 17).[2]

Before we decide to believe in Jesus as the Lord, is there any evidence that he even existed as an historical man?

Yes. The probable date of the historical crucifixion of Jesus is Passover week of 33 A.D. There are some complex historical problems for determining the exact day, but no reason to doubt the historicity of Jesus' death on the cross. The existence of the Jewish temple establishment (Annas, Caiaphas, and the Sanhedrin) is confirmed by non-biblical sources. Pompey had conquered Jerusalem in 63 B.C. and the Romans had replaced the Greeks as the military oppressors of the Jews. The historicity of Pontius Pilate as *praefectus* of Judaea is archeologically verified by the discovery at Caesarea of a stone inscription bearing his name.[3] The New Testament account of Jesus' passion and death by crucifixion has received further corroboration by recent scientific studies on the Shroud of Turin. Current research tends to authenticate it as the burial sheet for Jesus' body mentioned in John 19:40 and 20:7.[4]

The Twelve had known Jesus in his historical ministry. That historical nearness had not brought them any closer to faith. It took the overwhelming religious experiences of the post-resurrection appearances of Christ and the communal religious experience of the Holy Spirit at Pentecost before the Twelve could *see* with the new eyes of resurrection *faith*.

According to the Gospels, what happened the first Easter when God raised Jesus from the dead?

No one saw Jesus' body leave the tomb. The first witnesses to his resurrection recognized the disappearance of his body as the first sign that he had been raised. The Gospels then say that Jesus appeared and disappeared during a forty-day period. Sometimes people could touch him and recognize him. At other times he disguised himself. In some appearances he brought certain laity to faith—like the disciples on the road to Emmaus (Lk 24:13ff) or Mary Magdalene (Jn 20:11–18). At other times he appeared to the Eleven giving them the apostolic commission to preach, teach, baptize, preside over the breaking of the bread, forgive sin, and recognize Peter as the first in apostolic authority (Mt 28:20; Lk 24:36–49; Jn 20:19–29; 21:15–19). After this initial forty-day period, Jesus ascended into heaven (Acts 1:9) where he has continued to "sit at the right hand of God" (Acts 2:34) until he comes again "like a thief in the night" (1 Thes 4:13—5.2).

What false impressions might we get about Christ's resurrection by just summarizing the data in the four Gospels as we did above?

While each element of this synthetic portrait of the risen Jesus is profoundly true, not every element should be read as an historical fact. The value of the composite picture is that it provides images for human minds to contemplate. That is probably why God inspired the Evangelists to include such visual aids in their Gospels. The human person could not be evangelized in a completely abstract manner. On the other hand even inspired images of the risen Jesus involved a profound risk for the development of Christian faith. Such images incapsulated the risen Messiah and had to ignore the truth that, *as risen*, Jesus is "the fullness of him who fills the universe in all its parts" (Eph 1:23). The risen Jesus is too immense to be painted and too glorious to be photographed. Every portrait of the risen Jesus runs the risk of "shrinking" the Lord to the manageable proportions of human imagination. When this happens, the resurrection of Jesus is misperceived as just one more historical memory, the most outstanding miracle which culminated the earthly career of Jesus, and thus something which can be debated as a confirmation of his divinity.[5]

The second problem with this superficial faith portrait of Jesus' resurrection is that it portrays the risen Jesus as living again in his glorified body *only* in Palestine and *only* two thousand years ago. After forty days the risen Jesus ascended into heaven where he now lives. Understood in this way, the risen Jesus is long ago and far away. The resurrection story understood in this manner may be true, but it certainly reveals nothing radically different about God nor functions as the good news of salvation for later generations. If we remember that Luke depicts Jesus as "ascending" both on Easter night (Lk 24:51) *and* forty days later (Acts 1:3, 9), "ascension" does not reveal the absence of the risen Christ, but his *presence* to the Father while remaining present among us in Word and Spirit. The power of the Scriptures to convert the hearts of those who hear must thus be recovered.

How can we recover the power of the word to come to faith as the first Christians did?

One way to do that is to show how the portraits of the risen Jesus developed in the four Gospels between 33 A.D. and 100 A.D.

The oldest book of the New Testament is St. Paul's First Letter to the Thessalonians (ca. 50–52 A.D.).[6] The oldest written testimony to the resurrection of Jesus is found in 1 Corinthians 15 (ca. 56 A.D.).[7] Here no picture of the risen Jesus is presented. Instead Paul recalls a series of apostolic faith affirmations about "Christ." These teachings were "handed over" to Paul from Christ himself and the other apostles. They therefore carry the weight of apostolic authority and not later embellishment. It is interesting to note that Paul does not use the name "Jesus" in this solemn teaching context. Paul was not recalling a human prophet who had died; rather Paul was recalling the faith proclamation of a Christ who is living still. "Christ" is the Greek translation of the Hebrew "Messiah." In Hebrew it meant "anointed" with oil and thus given the divine charisma to reign as king of Israel. *The* "anointed" prophesied by Isaiah would bring to Israel the "everlasting peace" (Is 9:6) for which the community longed. Since a Jewish "Messiah" sounded culturally and politically alien to potential Gentile converts, the early Church preached the risen *Christ.* They explained that as *Lord* Christ's power to save was not territorially limited to Palestine.[8] Only in Matthew 1:1 did "Christ" evolve fully into a last name and become Jesus Christ (ca. 85 A.D. in Antioch).[9] Matthew opens with a "family record of Jesus Christ."

Using this background, we begin to see how the first Christians preached Jesus by using special titles drawn from their resurrection faith that he was still alive as "Messiah, Christ, Lord, and Son of God." Historically Jesus had never called himself any of these things. These titles were written back into the Gospels and put on the lips of Jesus by the post-Easter Church. On Easter morning, the first believers had only the Jewish Scriptures, one another, and their new faith that the risen Lord was powerfully at work beyond the grave in some invisible manner. Our situation today is really quite similar except that we have the full New Testament and Catholic teaching to help us.

If there were so few proofs that Jesus had risen, what convinced others to join the first Christians?

Luke says that it was the Lord or his Holy Spirit who daily "added to their number" by giving them new hearts that were "exultant and sincere." This interior transformation was a pure gift from God himself. The new life-style of the first Christians also provided a confirmation that there was real substance behind their claims that Jesus had risen. They shared all things in common. They prayed together every day in the temple area. They broke bread in their homes. Some found new boldness to preach; others were gifted with the power to work miraculous healings. A new energy was obviously stirring among them—explain it how you will (cf. Acts 2:42–47). A "new way" of being Jewish had begun; to be reverently God-centered meant to "love one another" as God had loved them "in Christ" (cf. 1 Jn 2).

Can we still know the risen Lord as the first Christians did?

In faith, yes. Jesus stands at the door of every heart waiting to be welcomed personally as its King, its highest value commitment in love, its only Lord (Rev 3:20). We, like them, can turn within and surrender our hearts to the risen Jesus who lives everywhere in the universe simultaneously. Our language, our images, our style of devotion, and our witness of life will, however, all be conditioned by the fact that we are living in the modern world. We will not become first century Jews, but rather seek out fellow Christians for support, sharing, instruction, and the witness of public worship. In that way, not only can we still know the risen Lord, but we can also help others come to experience the joy of new life in Christ too.

Jesus Crucified Reveals the Father's Love for Us

If faith proclaims that Christ lives, why did the Apostles also preach Christ crucified?

To surrender one's heart to the risen glorious light of Christ involved having his crucified love for God and for every other human person. Only in this way could self-centeredness be overthrown and Christ-centeredness be authentically initiated. Thus St. Paul wrote in Galatians, "May I never boast of anything but the cross of our Lord Jesus Christ! Through it, the world has been crucified to me and I to the world" (Gal 6:14).

This faith in a crucified Lord Jesus who should be worshiped as God (Jn 20:28) was a whole new experience of paradox for the first generations of the Church. Whether Jew or Gentile, no one had ever dared to imagine a "crucified God." The fiery God of Moses, the Holy One of Israel, the Creator of the universe had "poured himself out" through the blood of Christ on the cross. No wonder Jesus had taught his disciples to call God "Father" and to remind them that the greatest love is to lay down one's life for one's friends (Jn 15:13). In Jesus crucified, the Father has given us all he has and all he is. He has chosen to give us the infinity of his inexhaustible love.

How did the New Testament Church members explain Christ's death as revealing the Father's love for us?

They used four principal methods: (1) they looked back into their Jewish Scriptures to find new insights into the meaning of Jesus' death; (2) they composed inspired hymns extolling the humility of Jesus; (3) they interpreted their own sufferings as privileged opportunities to share in Christ's outpouring of divine love; (4) they saw the Eucharist as their way of sharing in the self-sacrificial love of Christ for all.

The Jewish Scriptures Reveal
the Father's Love
Poured Out Through Christ

Where do we find examples in the New Testament of using the Old Testament to explain the meaning of Christ's crucifixion?

Almost all of the original preaching borrowed images and concepts from the "Old" Testament to explain Christian faith.

Matthew thought of the Church as a "wise scribe" searching its storehouse of inspired Jewish Scriptures and "taking out" something "old" to reveal something "new" (Mt 13:52). Very early in the life of the Church Isaiah 52:13—53:12 struck a powerful chord of sympathy in the hearts of the believers. The Isaiah passage had been written by an anonymous prophet in Babylon over five hundred years earlier. It spoke of some unnamed "servant of Yahweh" who would be "pierced" for our offenses and led like "a lamb to the slaughter," taking upon himself "the guilt of our sins" and a "chastisement that makes us whole." Yet he will "see the light in the fullness of days."

The image of God's "pierced servant" certainly coincided with what Christians remembered of the crucified Jesus on Calvary. Thus Paul could write: "For our sakes God made him who did not know sin to be sin, so that in him we might become the very holiness of God" (2 Cor 5:21). As a "sin offering" Jesus freed us from the guilt of our sins. This servant was God's "lamb"—gentle, obedient, sinless, uncomplaining and messianically victorious over his persecutors (Acts 8:32, 1 Pet 1:10, Rev 7:9–17) It was therefore "sin" that had killed the crucified Christ. No other explanation could account for this hatred of God. And in the resurrection, had not Christ "seen the light in the fullness of days"? Had not the final age begun? Were not the sins of many to be justified "through the sufferings" of Jesus? Yes, the awaited military Messiah had shocked the world by "conquering" it through pouring himself out as its servant. For the Jews this "poured out" Messiah was a "stumbling block" (*skandalon*) which kept the majority of them from believing in Jesus as the Messiah. For the Greeks, wise in their own eyes with the subtle conceits of philosophy, there could be no wisdom in believing in a crucified God. The whole notion was quite "stupid" (*morian*). But precisely here, according to St. Paul, was revealed in Christ "for those who are called the power of God and the wisdom of God" (1 Cor 1:20–25).

In a similar way the early Church meditated on Psalms 22 and 110 to find in Jesus crucified the revelation of a love that had the messianic power to be celebrated as a victory. Not only had the Father poured himself out in Christ, but all would gather in an assembly for the victory of the just when the crucified Messiah would return.

Inspired Hymns Revealed the Humility of Jesus Crucified

Where do we find examples of early Christian hymns in the New Testament?

St. Paul has preserved for us one of the most ancient hymns of the early Church which mentions that Jesus did not deem "equality with God something to be grasped at" (Phil 2:6). Was Jesus interpreted here as the eternal "person of Wisdom" which had been revealed in the mature period of late Judaism? Scholarship debates just what concept of the eternal Christ was presumed in this hymn. No one debates, however, that the hymn praises the "self-emtpying" or "kenosis" of Christ: "Though he was in the form of God ... he took the form of a slave ... accepting even death on a cross" (cf. Phil 2:6–11).

The opening praise of Christ in Ephesians extols the immeasurable generosity of "God" by which we are "filled with love" through "the blood of Christ" (Eph 1:4, 7–8; 2:5). If part of the "mystery" or secret of "God's plan" is that *we* have been redeemed, the deeper revelation is the "immeasurable scope" of *God's* generosity to us in Christ "his beloved" (Eph 1:6, 9, 19). The Hebrew Scriptures had spoken repeatedly of God's *hesed*—merciful love. Within the holy of holies, God had deigned to be present on his "seat of mercy." But this new penetration of our hearts and deepest hungers by the "blood and Spirit" of God's Christ exceeded the wildest expectations of the Jewish community of faith. The important "secret" was not the "hour" when Jesus would return, but the new insight into the inexhaustibility of the Father's love for all (Eph 2:11–22).

Perhaps the hymn in Colossians says it most bluntly: "It pleased God to make absolute fullness reside in him and, by means of him, to reconcile everything in his person, both on earth and in the heavens, making peace through the blood of his cross" (Col 1:19–20). In Jesus the "fullness" of the Godhead was poured out. The Father has drenched the entire universe with divine love made physical in Christ. That good news defies logical understanding, but alone satisfies our insatiable longings for love.

Our Suffering as Sharing in Crucified Love for the World

How was suffering interpreted as sharing in God's crucified love?

The Gospel faith of the first Christians did not deny or block out the reality of human suffering. Rather their faith brought the interior conviction that nothing human or super-human could separate them from the crucified love that God had poured into their hearts through baptism. Thus Paul could write that neither trial nor danger nor the sword, nei-ther time nor space nor anything that exists, "will be able to separate us from the love of God that comes to us in Christ Jesus our Lord" (Rom 8:31–39).

The cross was not only an historical fact. Because of the risen presence of Jesus, it was a continuing "mystery." The sufferings of the Christians were not meaningless torments to be stoically endured or speedily fled. They were "filling up" in one's "own flesh" what "is lacking in the sufferings of Christ for the sake of his body, the Church" (Col 1:24). There was a new sense of purpose, a sense of participation in God's grand scheme of bringing all things together as one in Christ. One's personal suffering never needed to be wasted if used to build up the members of the Church as servants of all.

Not only did the revelation of the Father's crucified love nurture faith and hope in the experience of human suffering, but it gave new motivation to live by love in return. "Christ suffered in the flesh; therefore, arm yourselves with his same mentality" (1 Pet 4:1). That mentality would reject sin and find the inner security to remain calm amid even the most terrible crises. Thus Peter could exhort the Church to be "constant" in love for one another (1 Pet 4:8).

The Eucharist as Sharing in God's Crucified Love

If the Eucharist is communion with the glorified flesh of the risen Christ, in what sense does it share in his outpoured love?

Jesus asked the Twelve to remember what he had said and done in his last "passover" supper (1 Cor 11:25). Given the association between Jesus' celebration of passover and its climax in his death on the cross, Paul could write, "Christ our passover has been sacrificed" (1 Cor 6:7).

Furthermore the early celebrations of the Eucharist seem to have been conscious of this divine outpouring of love expressed in the gestures of "breaking bread" and "drinking the cup" while giving thanks (*eucharistein*) (1 Cor 11:23–25). This Christian Eucharist had ultimately nothing in common with pagan rites which may have looked similar; according to St. Paul, in the Lord's Supper God is still present pouring himself out in love. "Is not the cup of blessing we bless a sharing in the blood of Christ? And is not the bread we break a sharing in the body of Christ?" (1 Cor 10:16–17). Because the Eucharist too revealed and communicated God's outpouring of love, to participate in the Eucharist was "to proclaim the death of the Lord until he comes" (1 Cor 11:26).

Liturgical custom in the communities which gave birth to the Gospels further reinforced the sign of the Eucharist as a revelation of God's outpouring love. According to Mark, at the Last Supper Jesus said, "This is my blood of the covenant, which is poured out for many" (Mk 14:24). Matthew's formula emphasized the redemptive consequences of God's passover outpouring of love, "Drink of it, all of you, for this is my blood of the covenant, which is poured out for many for the forgiveness of sins" (Mt 26:28). John's Gospel revealed Jesus as the "passover lamb" who "washed the feet" of the disciples during his final passover with them (Jn 1:29; 13:5ff; 19:14).

Did thinking about the cross make the first Christians sad?

No. Their sense of being overwhelmed by the Father's love "cast out all fear" (1 Jn 4:10, 18). The purifying reality of divine love "justified" them and gave them hearts "enlarged, consoled, and strengthened" (Acts 20:32; 2 Thes 2:16). Their prayer was transformed from an "obligation" into an experience of joyful "gratitude" (Col 3:16). When they gazed within themselves, they were awed to find that they were being transformed into the "image of the Son" (Rom 8:29). Each day could be a deeper experience of "gazing on the Lord's glory with unveiled faces," so that through their new faith in the Father's outpoured love, they found themselves being transformed "from glory to glory into his very image by the Lord who is Spirit" (2 Cor 3:18). The whole experience was so real, so wonderful, so awesome, so joyful, that even in the midst of suffering the first Christians felt interiorly impelled to share with others the crucified-glorious divine-human love they had received. The cross was good news.

What should we call this transformation worked within us by the Father's love for us in Christ?

The New Testament Christians eventually came to label their experience of this transformation as the beginning of a new "age" (Mt 24:3). In this new age God's merciful love exceeded anything he had done since the time of Abraham. Even the covenant of Moses and the gift of the torah seemed like shadows compared with this new substance of sharing in the Father's love. Therefore the new age was also called a "new covenant" in the blood of Christ (Heb 8:13). This transformation was so deep, personal, and total that there was nothing left for God to give. For those who shared in it, it was like a foretaste of heaven on earth. When Jesus returns, he will universalize this transformation in a cosmic revolution—giving birth to a new heaven and a new earth (cf. Rev 21). That will be the final age or "the end of time." In Greek, the word for end time is *eschaton.*

With Christ's resurrection, the final or eschatological transformation had begun in the baptized. This transformation thus began the life of the Church with whom Jesus, the risen Son of Man, promised to remain "until the end of the world" (Mt 28:20). This new age of the Church led to writing down its new "witness" to what God had done in Christ. "Witness" in Latin is *testamentum.* Therefore, as the eschatological transformation gave birth to the Church, the Church gave birth to the written witness of the New Testament and labeled the Jewish Scriptures the "Old" Testament.

The Gospel Becomes the New Testament

When was the New Testament written?

The oral tradition of proclaiming the Gospel lasted from ca. 33 to ca. 50 A.D. Because the Church expected Jesus to return soon, there seems to have been little concern to write down the witness to faith in his victory. As mentioned above, St. Paul was the first to write any part of the New Testament in the form we now have it. Because some Christians had died before Christ's return in glory, the church in Thessalonica had begun to have questions of faith about the meaning of their baptism. If the new age had begun, how could the baptized die? Paul had to explain that the baptized could share in Christ's returning victory even from the grave (cf. 1 Thes 4:13ff). This was written in 51 or 52 A.D.

Responding to various questions of faith, authority, or pastoral needs for guidance, correction, and encouragement the remainder of the New Testament kept being written until ca. 150 A.D. 2 Peter is usually considered to be the most recent book in the New Testament, reflecting, as it does, a rather developed sense of Church and daily Christian living. The twenty-seven books of the New Testament are ordinarily classified as: the four Gospels (Matthew, Mark, Luke, and John), the Epistles of Paul, the Pastoral Epistles (1 Timothy, 2 Timothy, Titus), the Catholic Epistles (James, Peter, Jude, John) and two special books, Acts of the Apostles, and Revelation (or Apocalypse). The authorship of several of the Epistles traditionally attributed to St. Paul is today heavily debated (especially Ephesians and Colossians). No one would now hold that Paul wrote Hebrews. Revelation was written to pastor the Church through the persecution of Domitian in 96 A.D. Luke wrote the Book of Acts to show how Mary's "yes" to being the Mother of Jesus (Lk 1—2) led in an unfolding history of salvation to the birth of the Church at Pentecost (Acts 2). From Peter's first witness to Christ in Jerusalem, Paul had carried the good news to Rome (Acts 28:11ff). Historically Peter and Paul had been martyred there by Nero ca. 64 A.D. Jerusalem had been destroyed by the Romans in 70 A.D. Luke, writing his Gospel and Acts ca. 85 A.D., was trying to show how the visible center of God's saving acts had shifted from Jerusalem to Rome.

Some books like the Shepherd of Hermas and the Didache were thought to be inspired and were used as readings during the liturgy in the second century after Christ. Gradually they fell into disuse. Thus when the persecuted Church was legalized by Constantine in 313 A.D., the Spirit seems to have led the local churches to a marvelous unity of faith in accepting the same twenty-seven books of the New Testament. When the Catholic bishops met at Hippo in 393 A.D. and in Carthage in 397 A.D., the official list or canon of the New Testament was closed.

When were the four Gospels written?

Today Mark is generally considered to be the oldest Gospel and is believed to have been written before the fall of

Jerusalem between 64 and 69 A.D. Since Matthew and Luke are so similar to Mark, and contain sayings of Jesus not in Mark, these three Gospels are called the Synoptic Gospels. They look at Jesus with "one eye" or a similar viewpoint.

Matthew and Luke are both dated ca. 85 A.D. and may have been written in part because about that time Christians were expelled from the synagogue by the Jewish rabbis. The Pharisee party, working under Rabbi Johanan ben Zakkai, had finally decided that the purity of Jewish faith was being undermined by those who adored Jesus as the risen Messiah. As the split between synagogue and Church grew, the Fourth Gospel was written. John is usually dated between 90 and 100 A.D.

Did Matthew and Luke use any other written source besides Mark to write their Gospels?

Yes. The sayings of Jesus found in Luke 9—18 are not in Mark, but are quoted almost verbatim by Matthew. Since careful study shows that Matthew and Luke never read each other's Gospels, we can detect that they both had access to some other earlier document which had listed the sayings of Jesus. In the nineteenth century a German Protestant scholar, Friedrich Schliermacher, named this hypothetical document the "Q" Source. It was probably written during the 40's. It contains the most typically Jewish kinds of sayings of Jesus. Matthew arranged the Q source in his Gospel into five sermons by Jesus, beginning with the Sermon on the Mount (Mt 5—7).

Why is the Gospel of John so different from the Synoptic Gospels?

John used another source which is called today the "signs" source. He included only seven miracles of Jesus and wanted the reader to see them as signs of the divine "glory" that was hidden in the flesh of Jesus while he lived on earth in the "flesh" (cf. Jn 2:11). John wanted to reveal the divinity of

Jesus as sharing in that of the Father, so he put inspired homilies back into the mouth of the historical Jesus. Thus Jesus keeps saying "I am," implying that he is Yahweh, "I am who am" (Ex 3:14).

Since the oral tradition had stressed the crucifixion-resurrection of Jesus, did the written Gospels in a sense grow backward?

Yes. Remembering Jesus' experience of being "Son" at his baptism allowed the infant Church to use Psalm 2:7 to make his baptism also a proclamation of good news.[10] Furthermore Psalm 110:3 had said: "Before the daystar like the dew I have begotten you." Therefore the Jewish Christians could begin to see that the risen Jesus had not started being God's Son only when he was baptized. He had always been God's Son. This is why Matthew and Luke open their Gospels with accounts of the birth of the Son of God (Mt 1:22–23; Lk 1:35).

Very early in the Johannine church a hymn to the eternal Word proclaimed the same faith: the Father had poured himself out in love in his Word, and his Word had poured himself out in love as human flesh, the Son. When he was on earth in the flesh, we had seen "the glory of an only Son coming from the Father, filled with enduring love." We have all had a share of his fullness, "love following upon love" (cf. Jn 1:1–16).[11]

A more technical way of saying how the Gospels were written backward would be to say that Jewish apocalyptic gradually became incarnational faith. We have seen the characteristics of Jewish apocalyptic in Chapter IV. Applied to Jesus, it meant that he was expected to return soon as Son of Man. When it became evident that those expectations were too limited, then the Gospels could explain that Jesus is still with us as risen, giving us the strength even to die for him, if need be, as martyrs. As the "incarnation" of God, Jesus had not ceased to be God while on earth, although neither he nor anyone else ever called him that historically.[12]

If the oral Gospel had not stressed the discovery of Christ's empty tomb, why was it included in the written Gospels?

First, all four Gospels imply that later generations should not long nostalgically to have "been right there on Easter morning." No one saw Jesus rise from the grave. The eschatological transformation could never be portrayed in pictures; only its effects could be described. Accordingly the empty tomb was not an adequate testimony in history to bring people to faith. A missing body could have been "stolen" as well as have "risen" (Mt 27:64). Asserting that the body had been stolen was certainly more "sensible" than claiming it had been completely "glorified by God." The only way an eyewitness of the empty tomb could *ordinarily* conclude from the "evidence" that Jesus had "risen" was through the supernatural testimony of one or more angels. The Synoptic Gospels are unanimous on this point (Mk 16:5; Mt 28:5; Lk 24:4).[13]

Why do the women keep silent about the resurrection of Jesus in Mark 16:8? Is this history or an inspired theology of Mark?

Mark's Gospel originally ended with three women at the empty tomb. They believed in the resurrection but "they said nothing to anyone, for they were afraid" (Mk 16:8). Jesus never appeared as risen in this oldest of the written Gospels. Mark cannot be recalling history when he asserts that the women kept silent. The parallels in all the other Gospels say that Mary Magdalene testified to the resurrection as the first Evangelist of the good news. Therefore Mark must certainly be adapting historical memories to fit a pastoral need in his local church. If Mark was written between 64 and 69 A.D. in Rome, one possible interpretation of Mark 16:8 would be that the women represent a local church terrified into silence. Peter and Paul were martyred in Rome ca. 64 A.D. Mark may be reassuring the local church that to keep silent about its faith through fear of persecution is not a betrayal of its Lord. He has reminded the people that the way Jesus had died on the cross was enough to bring a Roman soldier to faith (Mk 15:39). The way Christians were dying as martyrs in Rome would continue the same process of testimony. One did not have to throw oneself to the lions in some reckless fashion, however. A silent Church could testify to the faith and live in fidelity to the cross in a way that did not demand a suicidal rashness.

If the first Christians really came to faith in the risen Jesus without seeing him physically, why do the Gospels of Matthew and Luke portray the risen Christ as "touchable"?

Matthew and Luke developed the first human looking portraits of the risen Jesus about 85 A.D. For Matthew, Jesus' feet are touchable (Mt 28:9). This may be a new literary form through which Matthew was teaching his local church in Antioch to avoid the errors of heretical docetism. Followers of this heresy were so overwhelmed by pseudo-mystical experiences of divine light that they claimed Jesus was a heavenly Redeemer who had never really been a man. Matthew may be reminding the laity that the risen Christ had had "feet of clay" just like the rest of men.

Heretical Eucharists celebrated by such splinter groups were so prevalent in the early Church that a generation later St. Ignatius, the second bishop of Antioch (d. ca. 115 A.D.), had to order that Catholic Christian Eucharists could only be held with the explicit permission of the bishop, so that a visible unity in truth would be signified in the worship.[14]

Matthew did not give this same tangible quality to the risen Christ when he described the appearance of Jesus to the Eleven on the mountain. They "worshiped" him as the women had done, but some of them "doubted" (Mt 28:16). This is an eschatological appearance of Christ in which the "inward seeing" brings them to apostolic faith. It is in their mixture of faith and doubt that the risen Jesus commissions them to "make disciples of all nations" and to "baptize them."

Luke's account of the post-resurrection appearance on the way to Emmaus explicitly teaches that the risen Jesus can only be "seen" with the eyes of faith (Lk 24:24). Hearing the Jewish Scriptures preached as they applied to Christ inflamed the hearts of the two searchers and gave them a hunger to commune with the risen Jesus in the "breaking of the bread." "Stay with us," they prayed. But when the Communion meal was finished, the risen Jesus could not be seen or touched (Lk 24:31).

In Luke's version of the appearance of Jesus to the Eleven which occurred in Jerusalem, Jesus ate a piece of broiled fish (Lk 24:42). This may be Luke's way of showing how the Apostles (fishers of men) presented their "catch" of "transformed believers" to the risen Jesus. Thus in the eucharistic meal, the believers were not "eating Jesus"; rather, they were being engulfed in the immensity of the risen Christ.

What does John intend to teach in his portrait of the risen Jesus?

John, the "beloved disciple," is the one person mentioned in canonical Scripture who comes to faith only by peering into the darkness of the empty tomb (Jn 20:8). While this may recall the way John the Evangelist personally came to faith, the "beloved disciple" also represents all of the more contemplatively favored Christian mystics who outrun "Peter" and the rest of the community in the quickness by which they "see." Like the "beloved disciple" such believers must learn to wait on the others and not isolate themselves, which would be to risk pseudo-Christian mystical fantasies.

In John, Mary Magdalene only comes to faith by active search in the midst of the most painful personal grief. She learns to let go of Jesus as her human teacher and listen in solitude to the risen Lord call her by name. John presents the risen Christ as fully tangible, but no one ever touches him physically. Rather Christ touches their hearts spiritually. Then Mary Magdalene and Thomas believe, testify and adore Christ as Lord and God (Jn 20:17–18, 27–28). Since John's Gospel continually tries to reveal how Jesus was always the "flesh" of God, John may be teaching through the risen "flesh" of Christ that the same incarnational God of crucified love is present in the "glorified" Christ.

Whether or not the risen Christ appeared one or more times in a tangible form can well be debated from the scriptural data. This author doubts that Jesus ever chose to manifest himself in such a bodily form. It would have made the risen Lord seem like another Lazarus come back from the dead. People could see Lazarus and get angry (Jn 12:17–19). Only eschatological faith could recognize Jesus through the interior testimony of the Father and the Spirit as the outpouring of crucified incarnate divine love for all the nations under heaven (Acts 2:5).

The Relation of the Gospel to Catholic Faith

If Catholic dogmas are really rooted in the Gospel, why did it take three hundred years for them to start being formulated?

Several historical circumstances explain why. The first fervor of Christian conversion saw the totality of saving truth in the mystery of the servant Christ in a very holistic, undifferentiated way. The community had been consoled and strengthened in what it had been given by the Holy Spirit. It preferred to savor the interior joy and to live by the servant love rather than to analyze what it already understood to be humanly incomprehensible. Secondly, the apocalyptic atmosphere of first century Palestine led the first Christians to expect Jesus to return very soon. Any nagging questions about this or that point of Gospel faith would be seen answered on the day of the Lord. This made any theological questions seem unimportant. It would all be clear when Jesus returned. The important thing was to preach the good news of salvation and invite as many as possible to prepare for the Lord's return in the Church of the baptized.

The third force which kept the early church from reflecting on the kerygma was frequent persecution. From 33 A.D. until the edict of Constantine which made Christianity the state religion of Rome in 313 A.D., frequent efforts to suppress the spread of the new religion led to the history of the early martyrs (Acts 7). On the one hand the Jews tried to stop the spread of the "new way" as a "heresy" against the faith of Moses. Without the horizon of Christian faith, they were surely correct in their perceptions. On the other hand the Romans scattered the Jews in 70 A.D. and continued persecuting the Christians until Constantine. The Romans seem to have feared that the new religion would undermine the absolute authority of the state. They too were not entirely incorrect in their understanding. For a Christian "the God and Father of our Lord Jesus Christ" could be the only absolute. Burning incense to the emperor was completely out of the question.

Finally the early history of the Catholic bishops reveals an unmitigated conservatism. They understood their authority to be to "hand on" the teachings of the twelve apostles. They were interested in fidelilty to the kerygma and suspicious of novelty.[15]

Where did the first doctrinal questions develop historically outside the New Testament?

While the early Church was still in intermittent hiding from persecution, two centers of catechetical learning grew in importance for the handing on of the New Testament faith. *Catechesis* meant "to echo." Located in Alexandria, Egypt and Antioch, Syria, these groups of learned and devout Catholic Christians tried to be "a living echo" of the Gospel and the teaching of the New Testament in these centers: How could there be only one God and yet Jesus and the Father were also distinct beings? How could Jesus be God and man at the same

time? Was not this some kind of impossible contradiction?
Had Mary given birth to Jesus only as man or to Jesus as the
man-God?

How did the Catholic dogma of the Trinity develop (there is one God in three divine "persons")?

The Alexandrian school began to explain that the New
Testament had revealed that the one God is *God the Father*.[16]
The Son and Spirit share with him his divine life. While this
approach was profoundly biblical, it could make the Son and
the Spirit seem to be lesser expressions of God the Father, not
his equals in divinity. Arius, an Alexandrian, developed this
line of thinking even further. He began preaching that the
"eternal Word" of John 1 was not God, but an "instrument"
God had created in order to create the world. To the ears of his
Catholic listeners, this did not sound like a faithful echo of the
apostolic kerygma. The people were disturbed, the bishops
were disturbed, and the Roman Emperor was disturbed. To
heal the squabbles between Catholics and Arians, Emperor
Constantine convoked the First Ecumenical (General) Council
of the Church which met at Nicea from June 16 to August 25,
325. Three hundred and eighteen bishops attended. Pope Syl-
vester sent his personal representative from Rome.

If the challenge of Arius had been the only unfaithful
echo of biblical revelation, matters would have been somewhat
simple. In fact, however, an opposite error had earlier sprung
up in Antioch. Sabellius had insisted so strongly that God is
one that he denied any reality to the eternal Son or Spirit.
They were different "hats" God wore, but nothing one could
really be baptized into.

After a variety of presentations, Eusebius, the bishop of
Caesarea, won the hearing of the Council Fathers. He stated
that in Caesarea, Palestine, they had always baptized people
"in the name of the Father, and of the Son, and of the Holy
Spirit" (Mt 28:9). The Catholic Church must in fact believe in
the divinity of each of the persons of the Trinity since it had
always prayed in this way. In this manner the principle of *lex*

orandi, lex credendi (the law of prayer is the law of belief) also came to be accepted as a key method by which the Church would be able to articulate its own lived faith. The way the Church prayed revealed to itself what it believed in ways which formal reflection on the kerygma had never made explicit.

Using this "law of prayer," the Catholic bishops solemnly taught one new word: *homoousios* or "one in being." Christ is *one in being* with God the Father. Their authority to define more precisely the truth of the kerygma had come from the apostolic letter to the churches in Acts 15:28: "It is the decision of the Holy Spirit and ours too. . . ." This technical formula in Scripture revealed that the Holy Spirit guided pastoral teaching authority when gathered in solemn Councils.

Why do Catholics venerate Mary as the mother of God and not just remember her as the mother of Jesus?

A crisis broke out when Anastasius began preachiing that Mary was only the mother of the human Christ (*Kristotokos*). For some time Catholic Christians had been praying to Mary as *theotokos* (Mother of God). When Anastasius told them that their piety was misinformed, his denial of their faith sounded blasphemous. Anastasius had based his concept of Mary on the idea of Christ taught by Nestorius. In Jesus, the divine Word lived in his body as a "guest" in a temple. Therefore when the human Jesus touched us we were not really being touched by God.

To resolve this latest crisis in which feelings ran extremely high, Emperor Theodosius II convoked the Council of Ephesus which began June 22, 431 A.D. The legates of Pope Celestine I had not yet arrived when Cyril of Alexandria opened the meeting. At best, Cyril would have to be judged fanatically overzealous for orthodoxy. At worst, one suspects that he was troubled by terrible ecclesiastical rivalries. The Alexandrians had had their hands slapped by their brother bishops for Arianism. Now it was time to give the Antiochenes a dressing down for Nestorianism. Cyril got the Council Fathers to approve a letter he had written to Nestorius explaining the two natures of Christ: a marvelous "union" of humanity and divinity which nevertheless remained "distinct" and not some "confused" blob.[17]

If Cyril's strategies and motives were at times questionable, one has to admit that his insistence on the unity of Christ is a faithful echo of New Testament revelation: "The Father and I are one" (Jn 10:30).

As for the preaching of Anastasius, the Council of Ephesus judged the faith instincts of the people to be more trustworthy than those of the priest who had chided them. Thus the bishops taught that the divine Word really had entered the womb of Mary to become incarnate. God did not later take up special residence in Jesus. The God of the kerygma lowered himself to be born as a child. Mary did not create God; she gave birth to "the divine Word made flesh" (Jn 1:14). "Thus (the holy Fathers) have unhesitatingly called the holy virgin "mother of God" (*theotokos*).[18]

Why did the Council of Chalcedon teach that Christ is a divine person with not only a divine nature, but a human nature?

Excessive zeal for the divinity of Christ had led Bishop Dioscorus, patriarch of Constantinople, and Eutyches, a monk of Constantinople, to say that Christ had not really become a man. Christ had had only one nature—the divine. They were called the "monophysis" party (one-nature) or Monophysites. For them, the union of Christ's natures had been swallowed up in the splendid glory of his divinity. Eutyches was condemned at a synod in 448 A.D. in Constantinople. He appealed his case to Pope Leo in Rome.

Pope Leo wrote a beautiful letter summarizing the faith of the Gospels in Jesus who was human like us in all things but sin (cf. Heb 4:15). Jesus knows our experience of weakness, temptation, hunger, pain, and death. Leo wisely explained that our hope of salvation resides in the reality of God becoming man in Christ; we could not overcome the author of sin and death unless Jesus "took on our nature and made it his. . . ."[19]

When this letter of Pope Leo was read at the Council of Chalcedon in 451 A.D., the bishops exclaimed, "Peter has spoken through the mouth of Leo." They then set about to uphold the divinity of Christ affirmed at Nicea and to reject the Monophysitism that denied his humanity.[20]

Conclusion

How can we live by faith in the Gospel today?

1. *Turn within.* Romans 5:5 teaches us to behold the Spirit within our hearts pouring out the crucified love of the Father for us in Jesus. Jesus wants to descend into our personal hells and change them into gardens of new life and hope. He has already been through it all. He really knows. He really cares.

2. *Enflesh.* As the Word was made flesh in Christ (Jn 1:14), so it will not rest until it is made flesh in us. We fully enflesh the Word by living as unique members of one another in Christ's body on earth, the Church. The body enfleshes the Word fully only by pouring itself out for the world to heal its hurts through the blood of Christ, its head.

3. *Bend the knee.* Philippians 2:10 proclaims that every knee will bend before Christ. Our minds can humble themselves before the awesome mystery of God becoming man through the Virgin Mary. We can never grasp it fully—only savor its substance prayerfully. Our bodies can bend the knee before Jesus God, our Brother in the Eucharist. He deserves our adoration, love, and gratitude for humbling himself to "tent among us" in all the "tabernacles" of the world.

Notes

1. For the redactional features typical of the speeches in Acts, see Eduard Schweizer, "Concerning the Speeches in Acts," in Lean-

der E. Keck and J. Louis Martyn, *Studies in Luke–Acts,* Abingdon Press, N.Y., 1966, pp. 280ff. For a general orientation to the Gospel, see A.M. Ramsey, *The Gospel and the Catholic Church,* Longmans, Green and Co., N.Y., 1936.

2. Rudolf Bultmann has probably done more than anyone in twentieth century New Testament studies to bring Christians to a sense of the existential importance of the Word. For a readable explanation of how word and faith are related in the theology of Bultmann, see Walter Schmitals, *An Introduction to the Theology of Bultmann,* Augsburg Publishing House, Minneapolis, 1968, pp. 174–90. For a Catholic analysis of the strengths and weaknesses of Bultmann's form-critical method of New Testament exegesis, see Pierre Benoit, "Reflections on *Formgeschichtliche Methode*" in *Jesus and the Gospel,* Herder and Herder, N.Y., 1973, Vol. I, pp. 11–45.

3. Keith N. Schoville, *Biblical Archeology in Focus,* Baker Book House, Grand Rapids, 1978, p. 340. For other recent work on the historical context of Jesus' life and ministry, see Howard Clark Kee, *Jesus in History: An Approach to the Study of the Gospels,* Harcourt Brace Jovanovich, N.Y., 1977.

4. Ian Wilson, *The Shroud of Turin,* Doubleday, N.Y., 1979, pp. 245–52.

5. For a fuller explanation of the centrality of the resurrection of Jesus to the formation of the New Testament kerygma, see Joseph Schmitt, "Resurrection," part B, "Biblical Synthesis," in Karl Rahner *et al.* (eds.), *Sacramentum Mundi: An Encyclopedia of Theology,* Vol. 5, pp. 324–28. In the subsequent article Werner Bulst explains in what sense the resurrection of Jesus is central to contemporary Catholic apologetics; see pp. 328–29 in *ibid.*

6. Robert A. Spivey and D. Moody Smith, Jr., *Anatomy of the New Testament: A Guide to Its Structure and Meaning,* Macmillan, N.Y., 1982, pp. 322–23.

7. *Ibid.,* pp. 317–18, 331–32.

8. In Hellenistic culture, "lord" conveyed the idea that the bearer of this title had the power to dispose of a person or an object. For more, see "Lord," in John L. McKenzie, S.J., *Dictionary of the Bible,* pp. 517–18.

9. While Matthew 1:1 depends on Mark 1:1 for the wording "Jesus Christ," only Matthew makes this title the introduction to a genealogy—thus stressing its character as a proper name. See David Hill, *The Gospel of Matthew,* Attic Press, Inc., Greenwood, S.C., 1978,

p. 75. Historically Jesus would have been called *Jeshua ben Yosef* (Jesus, son of Joseph).

10. The view sketched above is open to the eschatological prophet Christology espoused by Schillebeeckx as the first stage of post-Easter faith. However I am not personally convinced that too much weight should be given to the omission of the crucifixion narrative from Q. Paul is preaching the centrality of the cross quite early. See Edward Schillebeeckx, *Jesus: An Experiment in Christology,* The Seabury Press, N.Y., 1979, pp. 274–282.

11. This translation comes from Raymond E. Brown, *The Gospel According to John: The Anchor Bible,* Doubleday, 1970.

12. For a fuller treatment of the title "God" for Jesus, see Joseph A. Fitzmyer, S.J., *A Christological Catechism: New Testament Answers,* Paulist Press, N.Y., 1982, pp. 84–91.

13. For a more detailed explanation of how the short formula of visions developed into the Gospel portraits of the post-resurrection appearances, see Raymond E. Brown, *The Virginal Conception and Bodily Resurrection of Jesus,* Paulist Press, N.Y., 1973, pp. 78ff.

14. Ignatius writes, "Be zealous, then, in the observance of one Eucharist. For there is one flesh of our Lord Jesus Christ, and one chalice that brings union in his blood. There is one altar, as there is one bishop with the priests and deacons, who are my fellow workers." See St. Ignatius of Antioch, "Epistle to the Philadelphians," par. 4. For evidence that docetism was the reason that Ignatius insisted that Jesus' post-resurrection appearances were tangible, see "Epistle to the Smyrnaeans," par. 2–5. Both passes are found in *The Fathers of the Church—A New Translation, The Apostolic Fathers,* Christian Heritage, N.Y., 1948, pp. 114, 119–120. The position I develop in this chapter contradicts Ignatius on the point of the tangibility of the post-resurrection appearances of Jesus, but my position is not docetist because it holds Jesus really suffered in his human body and that his resurrection from the tomb involved a bodily transformation or glorification of his human flesh.

15. Writing in 96 A.D., Pope St. Clement of Rome said, "The Apostles received the Gospel for us from the Lord Jesus Christ; Jesus Christ was sent from God. Christ, therefore, is from God and the Apostles are from Christ. . . . Preaching, accordingly, throughout the country and the cities they appointed their first-fruits, after testing them by the Spirit, to be bishops and deacons of those who should believe. *And this they did without innovation,* since many years ago

things had been written concerning bishops and deacons. Thus, the Scripture says in one place (Is 60:17), 'I will establish their bishops in justice and their deacons in faith.' " Quoted from "The Letter to the Corinthians," ch. 42, p. 42 in *ibid.* (italics mine).

16. See Hubert Jedin, *Ecumenical Councils of the Catholic Church: An Historical Outline,* Herder and Herder, 1960, pp. 13–18. For a definitive treatment, see Right Rev. Charles Joseph Hefele, D.D., Bishop of Rottenburg, *A History of the Christian Councils from the Original Documents,* trans. by William R. Clark, T. & T. Clark, Edinburgh, 1894, reprinted by AMS Press, N.Y., 1972, Vol. 1, pp. 231ff. Also see Jedin, pp. 24–27.

17. J. Neuner, S.J. and J. Dupuis, S.J. (eds.), *The Christian Faith in the Doctrinal Documents of the Catholic Church,* Christian Classics, Westminster, Md., 1975, #604, p. 141.

18. Jedin, pp. 33–35.

19. Quoted from Neuner, #609, 611, 612, pp. 145–46.

20. *Ibid.,* #614, p. 147.

Chapter VII

The Kingdom of God
and Catholic Teaching on
Personal Holiness and Social Justice

"Your kingdom come,
your will be done on earth . . ."
—Mt 6:10

The Historical Context in Which
Jesus Preached the Kingdom

Why did the Church of the risen Christ want to remember the historical teachings of Jesus?

Living the new life in Christ only made the infant Church more eager to remember what Jesus had said and done in his historical ministry in Palestine. The way he had historically incarnated the Father's love could teach the Church how to continue his mission on earth in very different historical contexts.[1]

What did John the Baptist and Jesus mean by the Kingdom of God?

In the Old Testament, the covenant relationship between Yahweh God and the people was imaged as making God their

"King." He was their highest value in faith and justice. God was the living presence around whose will Israelite society was to be organized. The heart of his will had been revealed in the torah of Moses. Later Judaism began to talk about the accomplishment of God's will on earth as the "establishment of his Reign or Kingdom" (cf. Ps 47:8; Dn 7:27). Thus when John the Baptist and Jesus invited the Jews to repent and prepare for the Kingdom, they were acting like the Old Testament prophets. They wanted their fellow Jews to live in that reverent fear of God which does justice to one's neighbor. In the spirit of Isaiah, Jeremiah, and the Deuteronomist, they wanted the people to rediscover the inner meaning of the Torah as "mercy, justice, and love."

Because the majority of the people were being oppressed both by their Roman conquerors and by their own priests, kings, and teachers, John and Jesus hungered for a real change in the social-political-economic situation too. With the majority of the poor, they expected the "day of the Lord" to come quickly and right these wrongs. The poor would then rejoice in being rescued from unjust suffering and the rich would stop their cynical laughter. Because John and Jesus shared in the Jewish apocalyptic sense of urgency, their invitations to repent and prepare for the Kingdom were urgent and threatened "wrath" and "fire" for the "brood of vipers" who rejected their warnings (Lk 3:7–9).[2]

Who were the main Jewish sects or parties addressed by John the Baptist and Jesus?

There were four main groups: (1) the Essenes, (2) the Pharisees, (3) the Sadducees, and (4) the Zealots.

Who were the Essenes?

Although historians still debate what caused the Essenes to form a separate sect of Jews, the Dead Sea Scrolls refer to the terrible deed of a wicked high priest. Alcimus, Jonathan

Maccabeus, and Simon Maccabeus (cf. 1 Mac 9) are the most likely candidates for this "wicked high priest."[3] At any rate at some point in the 160's B.C., the Essene Jews became so scandalized with the priestly administration of the temple that they refused to enter it and formed their own separatist communities. They were expectantly waiting for two messiahs to restore the Kingdom of God: a heavenly son of Man (Dn 7) and a military liberator from foreign domination (Is 9). In 66 A.D. the Essenes took arms with the rest of the Jews against the Romans and were exterminated.

John the Baptist may have had contact with the Essene monastery at Qumran on the shore of the Dead Sea just south of the Jordan River. Certainly his apocalyptic sense of urgency is similar to theirs. While the Essenes very conveniently styled themselves as the "sons of light," and labeled all other peoples "the sons of darkness,"[4] John the Baptist allowed no such "exemptions" from his general call to repentance. In this sense, John's views departed from those of the Essenes. He was renewing the classical prophetic emphasis on transformation of the heart. To be a Jew was to live by the covenant justice which Moses had revealed. The life of justice is what truly acknowledged the God of Israel as King. The Essenes by contrast were obsessed with maintaining torah purity and practicing ritual cleansing.[5]

Who were the Pharisees?

While Ezra had given birth to the impulse of torah piety some five hundred years earlier, by the first century the Pharisees had developed into a distinct party and represented the masses of the people. They looked down on the illiterate poor ('am hā'āres) as incapable of living the law.[6] They were teaching the Jews to believe in the general resurrection of the dead at the end of history—even though this doctrine was not revealed in the Hebrew Sacred Scriptures. The Pharisees developed the theory that there had been oral tradition from the time of Moses which had taught the doctrine of the general

resurrection on the day of the Lord.[7] Economically the Pharisees seem to have been middle class; politically they were
moderates. They hoped for the arrival of the liberator Messiah, but tolerated foreign dominance as long as it did not
interfere with temple liturgy or faithful observance of the
torah.[8]

Who were the Sadducees?

Since the time of Jonathan Maccabeus in 153 B.C., the
aristocratic priestly families had developed into the Sadducees
which generally dominated the temple council of the Sanhedrin. Economically they were the wealthy of first century
Jerusalem. Politically they were collaborationist. They found
the status quo tolerable and preferred co-existence with foreign invaders to any form of popular uprising to restore God's
Kingdom in Israel. Doctrinally the Sadducees were the tradi-
tionalists of first century Judaism. They rejected the pharisa-
ical belief in the general resurrection because it was not in the
Scriptures of Moses.

The political status of the Sadducees was intricately tied
to the ruling authority of the Hasmonean family line which
had developed through the Maccabean family and was solemnly legitimized on September 13, 140 B.C. "In a great assembly
of priests, people, rulers of the nation, and elders of the country," the following proclamation was made: Simon Maccabeus
and his sons would be the high priests with secular royal
authority to govern the people "until a true prophet" would
arise (cf. 1 Mac 14:41–48).[9]

Given the fact that the power elite of Israel was only
legitimized until a "true prophet" should rise up, it is quite
understandable that the Sadducees went scurrying down from
Jerusalem to the Jordan shore to "discern" whether or not
John the Baptist was to be the prophet who would disempower
them. The Sadducees, however, were not the only ones who
went to hear the Baptist. "All" the people of Judea and Jerusalem came (Mk 1:5). They had high hopes that the new
prophet would usher in a new age of freedom from oppression,

and the beginning of God's universal justice. John the Baptist was telling them to repent and prepare for the world-shattering event.

Who were the Zealots?

Among the disciples of John the Baptist and Jesus were members of another Jewish party, the Zealots. St. Peter and Judas had probably belonged to this group.[10] Peter was still playing the violent Zealot nationalist when he tried to prevent the arrest of Jesus in the Garden of Olives by cutting off the ear of Caiphas' servant Malchus (Mk 14:17; Jn 18:10). Peter appears to have broken with the Zealot value structure only when humbled by the realization that he himself was just as much an impediment to the coming of God's Reign as any of the Romans occupying his homeland. When it dawned on Peter that he had just denied knowing Jesus three times, "the Lord looked at Peter . . . and he went out and wept bitterly" (Lk 22:61–62). Judas may have betrayed Jesus because all of Jesus' talk about the need for the Son of Man to suffer and be persecuted was only slowing down the national liberation which would establish the Kingdom of God in Jerusalem.[11]

The Zealot party had formed just about the time that John the Baptist and Jesus had been born. When Herod the Great died, Caesar Augustus was taking a census of the whole world to squeeze as much tax revenue as possible out of subjugated peoples. Judea was becoming just "one more Roman province" centered in Caesarea. That plus the imposition of new taxes led to a popular rebellion headed by Judas the Galilean. "Zeal" for God's Kingdom inspired these guerrilla activities (cf. 1 Mac 2:24–30). The Romans named them the *sicarii* (dagger carriers) and watched from the Fortress Antonia on the north side of the Jerusalem temple to make sure they did not stir up nationalist uprisings, especially during the pilgrimages on high liturgical feasts. Josephus reports that the Zealots wanted the restoration of the old charismatic Israel where God alone was King, but would reign from his temple through his priests.[12]

What was the political context in which John the Baptist and Jesus preached?

The formal political context in which John the Baptist and Jesus preached was that of imperial Rome. In 63 B.C. General Pompey had used the occasion of a squabble between two pretenders to the high priestly office to march on Jerusalem and gain firm control. Thus Judah became "Palestine" (land of the Philistines) and was incorporated into the Roman province of Syria. This form of political oppression began to be modified in 47 B.C. when Antipater, the majordomo of the priestly court of John Hyrcanus II, got Caesar to name his two sons, Herod and Faesel, as military protectors of Judea and Galilee.

Seven years later the political life of Palestine changed significantly. By using flattery in Rome, Herod "the Great" managed to get the Roman senate to pass a bill which named him king of Judea. Herod agreed to protect his section of the Roman empire militarily. In turn he would report directly to Caesar in Rome and no longer be part of the province of Syria.

Thus from 40 B.C. on Herod began an extensive building program and developed the seacoast city of Caesarea on the Mediterranean shore. To appease the people and give his cruel reign some veneer of Jewish piety, he began an extensive refurbishing of the second temple. In this way he "bought off" the Sadducees by reaffirming the centrality of the temple to Jewish life.[13] Herod died ca. 4 B.C. and was mentioned in the Gospels (Lk 1:15; Mt 2). For this reason the birth of Jesus must be reckoned between 3 and 6 B.C.

When Herod the Great died, Judea became a Roman province again, this time governed by a proconsul headquartered in Caesarea. Galilee continued being a semi-autonomous tetrarchy under Herod's son, Herod Antipas.

Why did the Jews and first Christians mistakenly believe that the world was going to end so soon?

The difficult political and economic conditions had led the Jews to try to figure out God's "plan" for rescuing the just since the time of Daniel (ca. 167 B.C.). Some envisioned God's Kingdom as a golden age here on earth; others saw it as an eternal Kingdom in heaven. Some predicted that the Kingdom would be established by the direct intervention of God;[14] others taught that a Messiah would intervene.[15] Underneath the variety of predictions was the common expectation that God was shortly to establish his reign over the entire earth.[16]

What did most of the lower class Jews think was God's "plan" for the end of the world?

Perhaps the most influential apocalypse at the time was the Book of Enoch. Even inspired New Testament authors refer to Enoch or his scriptures with approval (Heb 11:5; Jude 14). Historically Enoch *the man* is lost in pre-Abrahamic legend as the seventh son of the seventh son of Adam who lived three hundred and sixty-five years. He was thus a "solar man" who had transcended death and had "walked with God, and he was no longer here, for God took him" (Gen 5:18–24).

This strange passage in Genesis led to the formation of the Book of Enoch centuries later. It was the product of multiple authorship probably written in the last two hundred years before Christ. The authors wrote as if they were living in the primeval age and predicting something about God's plan for the final age. One section of the book, "The Apocalypse of Weeks," provided a succinct summary of all of Israel's history and God's secret plan for its future. Historical-critical analysis suggests that this "vision of Enoch" was written during the Maccabean period. It alluded to all of the great moments of the past without naming the characters and then predicted how the Messiah would end all suffering and treachery (see accompanying chart). The Gospels reveal that both John the Baptist and Jesus had strong apocalyptic expectations that the Kingdom of God was quite near.

GOD'S HISTORICAL PLAN OF SALVATION ACCORDING TO THE BOOK OF ENOCH IN THE APOCALYPSE OF WEEKS[17]

First Week (undatable)	Enoch's birth and vision of God's plan for every age.
Second Week (undatable)	The great wickedness, the flood, and the divine rescue of Noah.
Third Week (at the end) (ca. 1850 B.C.)	Election of Abraham as the plant of just judgment.
Fourth Week (at the end) (ca. 1285 B.C.)	Revelation to Moses of a law for all generations and the building of an ark for the law.
Fifth Week (ca. 960 B.C.)	Solomon builds the glorious temple in Jerusalem.
Sixth Week (ca. 929–587 B.C.).	The sin of Jeroboam, the ascension of Elijah, and the Babylonian captivity.
Seventh Week (165 B.C.ff)	Post-exilic Judaism, an apostate generation (the Greeks and the Maccabees?), at the close of which will be "the election of the eternal plant of justice" (the Messiah.)

N.B. The seventh week was the age of sacred "jubilees" when debts were to be justly settled, the inequalities of slave and free were to be overcome, and people would live for a year off the previous fruits of their labor re-establishing the bonds of family and community under the Kingship of Yahweh (Lev 25). Many in the audience of John the Baptist and Jesus would have believed themselves to be living in this seventh week. Thus they were eagerly looking for "the election of the plant of justice" (the Messiah.)

Eighth Week (after the Messiah is elected)	Deliverance from oppressors. The building of a house for the great Messiah King in Jerusalem. All mankind will look to the path of justice.
Ninth Week (after Jerusalem becomes the capital of the world)	The time of general judgment for the earth. The wicked will vanish from the earth. The world will be written down for destruction.
Tenth Week (after the collapse of the universe)	The great eternal judgment. The Messiah will execute judgment among the angels. A new heaven will appear.

"And after that there will be many weeks without number forever. And all shall be in goodness and righteousness, and sin shall be no more mentioned forever." (xciii, xci. 12–17.)

What would have been the practical consequences of living by the repentance which John the Baptist preached?

In this highly charged political religious atmosphere John the Baptist dared to quote Malachi 3:1 and Isaiah 40:3. If we may be permitted a modern paraphrase, the effect would have been something like this: "Repent," he cried to the various parties of Jews sizing up this desert ascetic standing in an animal skin. "God is going to create a new just world order in which the valleys will be raised up and the hills flattened. A whole new power structure will result." (Cf. Mk 1:1–3 and Lk 3:4–6.) "Repent and be wheat, a positive nurturing element in the society that recognizes God as its King; the chaff will be burned as useless." (Cf. Mt 3:7–12; Lk 3:7–18.)

What happened to John the Baptist?

John the Baptist had the same kind of courage to call royal society to repentance that had characterized Elijah's struggle with Ahab and Jezebel. Firmly convinced that even legitimate authority could never justly put itself above the will of God the King, John called upon Herod Antipas to repent of his illicit marriage to his brother's wife, Herodias. And like Jeremiah, John the Baptist was jailed for prophesying God's will to the power elite (Lk 3:19). Such flagrant disregard for divine truth and lived justice seems to have signaled to Jesus that it was time for him "to go public." Jesus knew he had a special mission from his Father at the time of his own baptism at the hands of John.[18] It is historically likely that Jesus had spent some time in the Jordan area after his baptism (Jn 4:22; 10:40) and that he had gotten close to John and his disciples. But it was only in the silencing of John's prophetic voice that Jesus himself came to the fore and cried out, "The time is fulfilled, and the Kingdom of God is at hand. Repent and believe . . . " (Mk 1:15; Mt 4:17).

And yet to John the Baptist, rotting in his prison cell at Machaerus, the new age of God's reign of justice did not seem to be evident. "Now when John heard in prison about the deeds of the Christ, he sent word by his disciples and said to him, 'Are you he who is to come, or shall we look for another?' " (Mt 11:2–3; Lk 7:18–19). Jesus answered John by quoting a string of verses from Isaiah referring to the redemptive works of the servant: the blind see, the deaf hear, the lepers are cleansed, the lame walk, the dead are raised up, and the poor have good news preached to them (Is 29:18–19; 35:5–6; 61:1).

Was this scriptural answer enough to convince John? The Baptist had never dared to think of himself as Elijah returned (Mal 3:23–24; Jn 1:19–22). He thought of himself only as "a voice in the desert," a lonely voice. Jesus assured the first century Jews: "If you are willing to accept it, he [John] is Elijah who is to come" (Mt 11:14). Were the servant signs of the Kingdom of God cited by Jesus for John enough to console him in his martyrdom? Or did John die utterly desolate as the greatest of the martyrs of the Old Testament? The Gospels never tell us.

How was the preaching of Jesus different from that of John the Baptist?

John and Jesus were alike in wanting people to know the genuine freedom which comes from living out the Kingship of God. Their whole pastoral approach, however, was quite different. By his life of desert asceticism, John revealed the holy otherness of God. He made God his King as his sole "possession." If God was that consumingly important to allow John to forego legitimate human enjoyments, maybe other people could really come to believe that God could be that important in their lives, too.

By contrast Jesus revealed the inexhaustible mercy of God as Father by consorting with every strata of Palestinian society. If he befriended everyone, maybe all could believe that God really wanted to befriend them too. There was no one unworthy; there was no obstacle too great not to be dissolved by the Father's mercy. Measured in terms of human success, neither "pastoral strategy" had a widespread impact. This experience seems to have frustrated Jesus considerably:

> For John came neither eating nor drinking, and they say, "He had a demon"; the Son of Man came eating and drinking, and they say, "Behold, a glutton and a drunkard, a friend of tax collectors and sinners" (Mt 11:18–19).

John the Baptist was written off by many as an insane religious fanatic, and Jesus was easily dismissed as appallingly "loose" in his choice of personal companions.

Did John the Baptist recognize Jesus when he baptized him in the Jordan River?

When Jesus surrendered himself to John's baptism of repentance, only Matthew says that John recognized Jesus as the Messiah (Mt 3:13–15). John's Gospel explicitly denies this

(Jn 1:13). It says that the Baptist only recognized Jesus in faith when the Father spoke his word of interior revelation during the night following the baptism (Jn 1:31–36). The Gospels are equally divergent about what Jesus himself experienced in his baptism: Did he have an apocalyptic vision that he was the Messiah (Mk 1:10)? Or did everyone see a dove land on Jesus (Lk 3:22; Jn 1:32)? Did Jesus alone hear God speak (Mk 1:11; Lk 3:22)? Or did everyone hear the divine proclamation (Mt 3:17)? History and theology are so intertwined in these narratives that we can never know exactly what happened during the baptism of Jesus. We can be certain, however, that after his baptism by John, Jesus was convinced that he was the Messiah who would be instrumental in ushering in the new age of the Kingdom of God on earth.[19]

How did Jesus respond to the historical context of first century Palestine?

Mark, Matthew, and Luke agree that Jesus mingled with all economic classes and all the parties of Judaism (except the Essenes, who are never mentioned in the New Testament). He even befriended Romans, Samaritans and other Gentiles. If, however, he was present to all, Jesus is presented in the Gospels as "party to none." While his prophetic preaching was similar to that of John the Baptist, he formed a group of disciples separate from that of John (Jn 4:1–2, 13). While Jesus knew the torah well enough to debate it (Mk 12:28–34) and loved the torah enough to observe it reverently (Mt 5:17–18), he loathed the legalism of the Pharisees. External observances should never replace reverent fear of the Lord (Mt 15:11). Economic maintenance of the temple should never justify a cruel economic neglect of one's family (Mt 15:1–9). Therefore, just as Jesus was not a "baptizer," he was not a Pharisee.

The Gospels present Jesus as astonishingly wise (Mk 6:20), but not relying on ancient authorities for his wisdom like the scribes (Mk 1:21–22). While Jesus is presented in the

Gospels as a regular participant in synagogue and temple liturgy (Lk 4:16), he is Lord of the sabbath and not a cultic official (Jn 5:18; Mk 2:23–28). He gladly raised from the dead the daughter of the rich Jairus (Mt 9:18–23), but warned all the rich of the spiritual danger of being economically comfortable (Mt 19:23–24; Mk 16:6; Lk 6:24–26). He loved the people of Jerusalem enough to lament their failure to repent (Mt 3:37–39; Lk 13:34–35), but horrified Jerusalem's temple priests by prophesying that God would destroy their beautiful, freshly redecorated liturgical building (Mk 13:1–4; Jn 2:19; Mk 14:58).

With respect to governmental sectors, Jesus called Herod "a fox" preying on the people (Mk 8:15; Lk 13:32) and refused to speak to him during his sham trial (Lk 23:7ff). Like the Zealots, Jesus could be violent in his protests (Mk 11:15–19; Mt 21:12–13; Lk 19:45–48; Jn 2:13–17). Unlike the Zealots, he thought it just to pay taxes to the Romans, yet, unlike the Romans, he could not put loyalty to the government above loyalty to God (Mk 12:13–17; Mt 22:15–22; Lk 20:20–26).

From the Gospels a picture emerges of a Jesus very much involved with the socio-political or religious currents of his day. He seems to have supported each group when it fostered covenant justice. When some other value besides God became the reigning value and self-interest replaced the commitment to justice, Jesus denounced the same groups as corrupt and self-serving.

Jesus, however, did not confine himself to prophetic critique. He had a vision of God's Kingdom on earth and sought to inaugurate it. He called people into a community of faith and sharing which recognized him as its head. He taught that the apocalyptic Son of Man would soon return in the cosmic victory of God's justice (Mk 13:26; 14:25; Lk 22:16–18). He used parables to explain the meaning of the Kingdom and to teach the disciples how to be prepared for the impending crisis (Lk 12:35–38, 42–46; 19:11–27; Mt 24:43–51). His miracles were signs that the new Reign of God was already breaking forth in the earthly ministry of Jesus.

Why did Jesus show a preference for the economically poor?

Because sinful society (the kingdom of Satan—Lk 4:5-6) so "naturally" exploited the poor that God's Kingdom on earth had to redress the imbalance. Thus Jesus told the rich man who wanted to do everything for God that he must sell what he had, give it to the poor, and follow Jesus (Mk 10:21; Mt 19:21; Lk 18:22). Those who extorted money from the poor—even with a "pretense of long prayers"—would receive greater condemnation (Mk 12:40). To give out of one's abundance counted for nothing; to give from one's need was to make God one's King (Mk 12:41-44). To invite the poor into one's banquet was to be blessed by God, "because they cannot repay you" (Lk 14:13). When Zacchaeus followed Jesus, he gave "half of his wealth to the poor" and "repaid four times over" anyone he had defrauded (Lk 19:8). One could not serve God as King and money as one's chief value simultaneously (Mt 6:24; Lk 16:13). The rich man, who could daily starve the poor beggar at his gate, would rot in hell (Lk 16:19-31). The poor were given the Kingdom of God on earth not because they were more moral, but because they would benefit from God's justice more than all the rest of society (Lk 6:20).[20]

The Christian Path into the Kingdom of God

Where do the Gospels teach us how to follow Jesus and live by the will of God in his Kingdom on earth?

Jesus' teachings on the Kingdom have been arranged by St. Matthew into the Sermon on the Mount (Mt 5—7). Luke puts the same basic material into the Sermon on the Plain.

Why have Christians preferred Matthew's Sermon on the Mount to Luke's Sermon on the Plain for learning about the Kingdom?

Matthew's account is fuller, and a bit more organized for easy learning. It leaves out the negative "woes" to the rich and stresses the blessedness of interior humility. Where Luke quoted Jesus as saying, "Blessed are you who are poor" (Lk 6:20), Matthew has "Blessed are the poor in spirit" (Mt 5:3). The fact that Matthew developed the "Blessed" statements or "Beatitudes" into a beautiful summary of the new law of living by perfect mercy made Matthew's text very useful in religious education. It has been called the "Gospel within the Gospel."

In what sense do the Beatitudes in Matthew 5 reveal a new wisdom for how to live in the Kingdom of God?

Matthew's version of the Beatitudes takes random sayings of Jesus on the happiness of the kingdom and organizes them into a new wisdom synthesis.[21] He portrays Jesus seated on the mountain in Galilee revealing the inner meaning of the law of Moses (Mt 5:1–2). The Beatitudes thus presume the covenant of Moses and transform it into a wise path of Christian spirituality. This path consists of eight attitudes and eight consequences. In the history of exegesis there is a debate as to whether each Beatitude promises happiness only in heaven (St. Ambrose), only on earth (St. Augustine), or both on earth and in heaven (St. Thomas Aquinas). Furthermore, both the attitudes taught and the rewards promised are interrelated. This is what Augustine and Aquinas called the "ascending order" of the Beatitudes.[22]

Accordingly, in Matthew's arrangement the first four Beatitudes counsel openness to God's perfect love. The last four counsel human response to divine initiative. "Blessed" (*makarioi*, Greek) originally would have been "Oh how happy" (*ashre*, Aramaic). Thus a spontaneous human exclamation of joy has become a churchy-sounding adjective in the process of translation.

What is poverty of spirit and why does it make us happy?

"Oh how happy the poor in spirit for theirs is the Kingdom of heaven" (Mt 5:3).[23] The disciple of Jesus begins to enter into the reign of God with "poverty of spirit." Poverty *of spirit* is an interior attitude required of all, not an economic condition. To be inwardly *poor* is to sense one's need for God. To be inwardly rich is to be filled with self and think one has no real need for God. Being economically poor does not guarantee that one will be poor in spirit. One can become filled with bitterness very easily. Being economically poor does make it easier for one to feel the truth of one's littleness before God. Once the interior emptiness is acknowledged, God fills the person with a sense of profound reverence for God. And God manifests interiorly to the person that he indwells and that he cares. Thus God becomes accepted as one's chief value, one's *King*. The joy of finding one's emptiness filled, of sensing oneself unconditionally loved—this is to enter "the Kingdom of heaven" on earth.[24] Oh, how happy, when one tries to give up playing king and surrenders to the only eternal King of the universe—God.

How can mourning make us happy?

"Oh how happy are those who mourn, for they shall be comforted" (Mt 5:7).[25] This second paradoxical wisdom statement follows from the experience of "being in heaven on earth," of sensing oneself to be unconditionally loved. Such a judgment of truth about one's situation before God brings with it an inner security which allows one to drop the facade of being "OK" and to experience the new interior freedom to grieve without fear of personal disintegration. One grieves for the sins and imperfections which previously could not be admitted. One grieves for the hurts suffered which had been too painful to acknowledge. One grieves for the losses of human love suffered through social dislocation or death. One grieves for a society which is so brutally unjust.

The ability to mourn carries within it the new freedom to be consoled. This consolation comes interiorly through the comforting action of the Holy Spirit. The Spirit frees one of personal resentments, assures one of divine pardon and strengthens one to live in trust with the paradoxes of human life. God's comfort is also manifested humanly by those people who give one permission to mourn in their presence and pour their love into the depths of one's obvious human frailty. "Oh how happy those who mourn," now that they know themselves to be loved in those parts of themselves they had thought were totally unlovable.

How can meekness accomplish anything?

"Oh how happy the meek, for they shall inherit the earth" (Mt 5:5).[26] Underneath hurt there lurks anger. "Why? Why me? Why does God allow so much suffering?" Unbridled anger leads to murder, death and destruction. Meekness is not weakness; it is anger bridled or channeled into repeated acts of forgiving those who abuse or ignore one. Meekness is not discouragement, fatalism or cowardice. It is paradoxically dynamic. Meekness chooses to convert one's enemies rather than to kill them. Thus, gradually or suddenly, meekness inherits a communion of new friends. These "friends" may include plants and animals who are instinctively attracted to gentle spirits. All healthy living beings flee the threat of being wounded and respond positively to the offer of affection insofar as they can understand it. In this way a tiny part of the original harmony of creation—weakened through sin—is restored. The circle of God's Kingship is expanded as one begins to live in an ever wider circle of forgiving relationships with those who had been one's "enemies."

With so much injustice in the world, how can our thirst for justice be satisfied?

"Oh how happy are those who hunger and thirst for justice for they shall be satisfied" (Mt 5:6).[27] The circle of mutually forgiving personal relationships is always small in contrast to the immensity of the human family. Such a circle of gentle friends can become very inwardly turned. When this becomes excessive, group intimacy becomes the functional god and happiness is lost. Thus Jesus counsels the disciple who has begun to "inherit the earth" that now is the time to turn outward to the unfinished character of the Kingdom of heaven on earth. The disciple must open anew to the painful cries of those suffering injustice and make those cries one's own. Prayer and action on behalf of justice will always "be satisfied" in the sense that God sides with the just. This is not self-righteousness, but the certitude in faith that one's struggles to correct injustice are worth the pain and the exhaustion they entail. This certitude comes from believing that God himself is struggling to bring the victory of the just. In this sense the disciple can exclaim, "Oh how happy" even in the midst of the external failures to achieve a more just world.

How do the first four Beatitudes differ from the last four?

In the first four Beatitudes the disciple is "formed" into a Christian through the interior action of grace. The grace to begin a process of moral conversion and the decision to make God one's King initiated the transformation. The grace to seek healing and forgiveness continued the process. The grace to forgive one's enemies furthered the transformation, and the grace to be vulnerable to the sufferings of others completed the first phase of finding new happiness in the Kingdom of God on earth. This fourfold interior transformation gives the disciple a new sense of being personally empowered. The last four Beatitudes counsel the disciple how to use this new personal power in service of others rather than in service of self.

Why is it foolish to hate those who hate you?

"Oh how happy the merciful, for they shall obtain mercy" (Mt 5:7)[28] The satisfying struggle to create a just world usually leads to a clear recognition of mutually opposed groups. The "just" develop tactics to challenge the "unjust." Such knowledge can trap the disciple in hatred or mere tolerance of the oppressive groups. In this Beatitude, Jesus reminds the disciple that the universal reign of God even reaches to oppressive groups. Oppressors live in a prison of fear that they will lose their money and their power. Acts of aggression will only reinforce their fears. Acts of overwhelming merciful love have the chance of liberating them from their fear and leading them into a life of mercy. Receiving genuine kindness from a group that by rights should hate you is utterly disarming. A new wider circle of mercy is born where before there was only inter-group hatred.

Why waste time in prayer?

"Oh how happy the pure in heart for they shall see God" (Mt 5:8).[29] The power to convert hearts through mercy can be distorted into a human engineering of a new society where human plans replace the need for God. At just that point where one could be tempted to abandon prayer as socially useless, Jesus calls his disciples into a deeper contemplative life. So that unbridled social activism does not become idolatrous, the mercy of God must be recentered in the God of mercy. To be "pure of heart" is to be single-minded or to have one primary love which centers and integrates all other loves. Now the disciple is invited to let his relationship with God descend from the will into the depths of the self. Moral choice had put God first as King; the depths of personal affectivity can discover in God the King, God the Lover. To fall in love with God opens the interior eyes of faith to be more receptive. The disciple experiences in contemplative prayer the beauty and splendor of God in ways that had far exceeded his prior expectations. The God one "sees" is overwhelming because God is love. Thus the disciple comes to the intimate knowledge that the God of love is in love with the disciple. The intensity of such happiness makes every other human enjoyment appear pale by contrast.

Why stop praying when it feels so good?

"Oh how happy the peacemakers for they shall be called sons of God" (Mt 5:9).[30] At just that point when the disciple would like to be hidden in the bosom of God for all eternity, Jesus, the voice of God, invites the disciple to abandon the contemplative delights of God in order to embrace the will of

God. The divine Lover sends the disciple back into society with the mission to extend God's peace on earth which had been personally experienced in contemplative prayer. The peace-maker works actively to be an agent of authentic reconcilia-tion among others. One's personal vocation determines the sphere in which this peacemaking is actualized: the home, the parish, the extended family, one's religious community, the neighborhood, the nation or the planet. To have the wisdom to guide the human family in the process of peace leads one to be recognized as "a son of God." In the Old Testament the sons of God were the anointed kings of Israel. The disciple is thus recognized as a leader with the wisdom and the charisma to extend God's reign of peace in a given sphere of influence. The disciple knows that any success that he or she has as a peace-maker comes from being "adopted" or protected by God so that the enemies of peace do not win a victory for violence, oppression or exploitation.

Why die rather than "sell out" for the best offer?

"Oh how happy are those persecuted for the sake of jus-tice, for theirs is the Kingdom of heaven" (Mt 5:10).[31] The sin in each person and in society at large hates the peace of God. When offered, divine peace is always met with resistance. The new freedom from fear and vested self-interests offered by the peacemaker threatens whatever "hates the light." When peacemakers find themselves hated, not for their own stupid-ities, but for their Gospel values, the temptation would be to use their influence to get the upper hand and to exploit their enemies. The one who battles oppression most directly is al-ways the one most tempted to become an oppressor "for the sake of justice." Should that happen, one has become an agent in the kingdom of Satan. In the Kingdom of God one chooses martyrdom over murder. Only personal integrity can beget the just society over which God reigns as loving Father of all. The martyr for the Kingdom of God wins a personal eternal victory in heaven. On earth, the blood of martyrs serves as the "seed" of the Church. In this way the martyr's death helps spread the Kingdom of God on earth for which Jesus taught us to pray (Mt 6:10).

The Relation of Jesus' Preaching the Kingdom to Catholic Faith

New Testament revelation on the Kingdom of God is developed in the Catholic Church in two principal ways: pastoral exhortations to personal holiness according to the duties of one's personal vocation and magisterial teachings on social justice. The demands of living the Beatitudes are so total that only rarely are they perfectly accomplished in the ordinary lives of most Christians. If the Beatitudes are seen as a process of growth in personal holiness and living the demands of the Kingdom of justice, individual discouragement with personal failures can be avoided.

How does the official prayer life of the Catholic Church encourage its members to live the Beatitudes?

All of the Church's prayers which recognize the primacy of God and prayers for persons and nations to have abiding justice and peace encourage living the Beatitudes. One Catholic custom in particular is most noteworthy. The official evening prayer or vespers of the Church each night always includes the Canticle of Mary in Luke 1:46–52. It is both an historical memory of Mary's exultant joy at becoming pregnant with Israel's peacemaker and an artfully crafted hymn used in the early Church. From its translation into Latin, most Catholics know it as Mary's "Magnificat." This hymn is filled with Old Testament references to the heroines who had the courage to do God's will on earth.[32] As such, it is a nightly meditation for praying Catholics on the possibility of doing something concrete to live the Beatitudes in holiness and justice.

How does Mary's Magnificat encourage action against oppressors?

In Exodus 15 Miriam, the sister of Moses, had led the Israelites in a canticle of victory when the bodies of the Egyptian soldiers were discovered floating in the Red Sea. Like the ancient people of Exodus, Mary exults in God. She "jumps for joy" at the power of the Lord to reshape the currents of history in order to rescue Israel from foreign dominance. Like Miriam's victory taunt (Ex 15:12) Mary's canticle celebrates the "putting down the mighty from their thrones." The conception of her baby portends a messianic challenge to the current balance of power (Lk 1:52).

How does Mary's Magnificat motivate the "little people" to act on behalf of justice?

In Judges 5 Deborah had burst into a canticle of exultation when God had helped the woman Jabin give victory to the Israelites by driving a tent peg through the enemy general's head. So Mary, like Deborah (Jgs 5:24–31), exults that a "mere" woman is being used to foil God's enemies. Mary's pregnancy is a new sign of the "strength of God's arm" (Lk 1:51). The birth of her Son will initiate a new victory for God's Kingdom on earth. The example of Mary's motherhood encourages powerless persons to rethink their potential for doing "great things."

How does Mary's Magnificat hint that our efforts on behalf of justice will be "fruitful"?

In 1 Samuel 1 Hannah is mercilessly taunted by her rival wife, Penninah. Hannah is heartbroken because she is sterile and cannot bear children by Elkanah. In their annual pilgrimage to Shiloh she sobs so profusely in the sanctuary that Eli the priest thinks she is drunk. Rejected and rebuked, her prayer is answered, and the next time she has sexual intercourse with Elkanah, she becomes pregnant with the prophet Samuel. Like Hannah, Mary rejoices that her pregnancy is a "mighty act of God." This time the healing of sterility is surpassed by the miracle of virginal conception. In Hannah (1 Sam 2:8) and in Mary (Lk 1:52–53) the rich are made poor and the poor are made rich. Because God hears the cry of the brokenhearted, Mary's Son was born and reborn in resurrection. God wants Mary's experience of new life to be shared with all.

How does Mary's Magnificat reveal that she herself lived by God's will and knew the joy of the Beatitudes?

Like Judith who used her feminine beauty to assassinate the enemy general Holofernes (Jdt 13:4–9), Mary's Jewish cunning is a threat to all unjust aggressors. Like Judith who exclaimed, "Woe to the nations that rise against my people" (Jdt 16:7), Mary cries out that God "has scattered the proud in the imagination of their hearts" (Lk 1:51). Mary, like Judith, knew the inner strength and joy of personal victory that comes from holiness of life.

For Mary's singular contribution to the victory of God's Kingdom on earth, the people will say of her what they said of Judith, "You are the glory of Jerusalem, the surpassing joy of Israel; you are the splendid boast of our people" (Jdt 15:9–10). Mary's canticle thus prophesied that "all ages to come" would call her "blessed" (Lk 1:48). Therefore the Catholic liturgy can burst forth, "Oh how happy are you, O Virgin Mary! From you has been born the Sun of Justice, Christ our God." That light of justice and servant love was born not only from Mary's womb, but from her heart. She followed Jesus to the cross (Jn 19:26) and participated in the first novena of prayer awaiting the grace of Pentecost (Acts 1:14). As she saw a universal Church of all races and nations being born of the Holy Spirit, she glimpsed the first fulfillment of her prophetic canticle. How happy indeed she must have been. For Catholics, Mary is thus the fullest embodiment of personal holiness and the greatest sign of hope for the victory of God's justice in all human hearts who live by the teachings of Jesus. Thus we proclaim her in the Litany of Loretto, "Mirror of Justice" and "Cause of Our Joy."

What do Catholics believe about social justice?

The social teachings of the Catholic Church are too vast and complex to be adequately summarized here. They have gradually evolved over the past century since Pope Leo XIII wrote *Rerum Novarum* in 1891. Six abiding themes do keep being developed with greater precision: (1) the inviolable dignity and social nature of the individual human person; (2) the primacy of freedom in decision making; (3) the constitutive nature of social justice to living the Gospel; (4) the necessity of pluralism in fostering the Kingdom on earth today; (5) the moral obligation of the Church to serve the economically poorest of peoples; (6) the necessity of personal action.

How do Catholics understand the idea of human dignity?

With all secular humanists, Catholics understand the human race as "the center and crown" of everything on earth. From Scripture, Catholics believe that the human race was created in the "image of God" (Gen 1:27), so that we have the human potential to know and love God and to use all the rest of creation to glorify God (Ps 8:5–6). Because God created us as "male and female," we know that the innermost nature of each person is *social*. We cannot develop ourselves without relating to others.[33]

What do Catholics believe about freedom of religion?

In Catholic teaching "authentic freedom is an exceptional sign of the divine image within man. For God has willed that man be left 'in the hand of his own counsel' " (Sir 15:14). The same paragraph of Vatican II's "Pastoral Constitution on the Church in the Modern World" teaches that authentic freedom does not result from "blind internal impulse nor from mere external pressure." Freedom has communion with God as its goal and needs the assistance of divine grace to overcome the malice of sin.[34] Thus human dignity demands that people are to be free in religious matters and in the pursuit of truth.[35]

Why do Catholics see social justice as essential to living the Gospel?

The Gospel is ultimately the proclamation of God's work on earth in Jesus. Jesus declared that his earthly mission was to bring good news to the poor, liberty to captives, sight to the blind, release to prisoners, and the redistribution of land in the "year of jubilee" (Lv 25:8ff; Lk 4:18–19). Because Christians have tended to reduce "salvation" to its interior dimension only, in 1971 the Catholic bishops taught in their third Synod at Rome that "action on behalf of justice and participation in the transformation of the world fully appear to us as a constitutive dimension of preaching . . . the Gospel." In this way Christians continue to live as Jesus did—as God's good news for the world today.[36]

Can Catholics take "grass roots" initiatives or must they wait for specific orders from Rome?

In 1971 Pope Paul VI wrote an encyclical, *Octogesima Adveniens,* to commemorate the eightieth anniversary of *Rerum Novarum.* There he taught the necessity of Christian pluralism to give more concrete specificity to the universal principles of social justice. Each local Christian community should discern the options and commitments it should assume to accomplish the social, political, and economic transformations that are needed in each case. This local level of discernment should be pursued with the help of the Holy Spirit, in communion with respective bishops, fellow Christians of other churches and all men of good will.[37]

This pluralism allows Christians to be more prophetic in criticizing local level injustices and preserves the Catholic Church from any temptation to create a new world empire under the Pope. Instead, local level initiatives create endless pluriformity among those who work for justice. Collaboration with local pastors ensures that the unity of the Church is preserved.

Why does Catholic social action always favor the economically poor?

Catholic social teaching favors the poor because Jesus and his work for the Kingdom on earth favored the poor. Scripture teaches that God hears the cry of the poor (Prv 21:13; 22:22–23). To be godly, the Church must hear the cry of the poor too. Pope Paul VI stated this in *Populorum Progressio* and it was reiterated very strongly by the Latin American bishops in 1979 in their third general conference at Puebla.[38] One of the implications of the preferential option for the poor is the morality of expropriating private property when the excessive wealth of the few impedes the legitimate economic development of the many. Both Popes Paul VI and John Paul II have taught this.[39]

Why do Catholics believe that every individual is obliged to act on behalf of social justice?

Secular humanists are obliged to act because they know themselves to be part of the human family. Even the savage beasts care about the members of their own species. Christians are obliged to work for social justice or else they are hypocrites who cry "Lord, Lord" but will be excluded from the Kingdom if they do not do the will of God (Mt 7:21).[40]

Conclusion

How can we live today the teachings of Jesus on the Kingdom?

1. *Get the big picture.* Jesus spoke of the "Kingdom of God" being resisted by the "kingdom of Satan." To focus this conflict today, we can ask, "Who is suffering? Who is making decisions that cause suffering? Who owns too much of *God's* land and capital? Who are the defenders and the oppressors of

human dignity? What economic and political structures are making the rich richer and the poor poorer?" Reliable, up-to-date information is difficult to get, but not impossible. A disciplined hunger for truth seeks information from many sources and many viewpoints—especially those views which cause us to re-evaluate our own prejudices.

2. *Listen to the "little people."* Those of us with education, power, money, and reputation have a disproportionate influence on society and a dangerous tendency to excessive self-confidence. We can get a whole new picture of human suffering and hope in God by listening to all those whom society tries to hide or deny. We need to hear their story to be liberated from the illusion of being "in control" ourselves. To do that well requires a genuine empathy with people very different from ourselves.

3. *Act—consistently, wisely, and courageously.* To act consistently is to avoid hypocrisy, to make our lived values the same as our stated values. To act wisely is to work and pray for the coming of the Kingdom in the way Jesus taught us in the Beatitudes. To act courageously is only possible when we value the gift of God's Kingdom within us more than we fear insult and injury from outside. Reflection on Mary and the lives of the saints can inspire us to heroism.

Notes

1. This conservative tendency is clear in the way St. Paul used the word "tradition" (in Greek, *paradosis*). Taken from the rabbinical practice of "handing on" from one generation to another, the early Church "handed on" what Jesus had said and done. See 1 Cor 11:2, 23; 15:3ff; 2 Thes 2:15; 3:6; Col 2:8. Outside of Paul, see 2 Pet 2:2 and Jude 3. In what follows we reject Bultmann's excessive skepticism about the historical trustworthiness of the Gospels and follow the more moderate school of form-criticism initiated by O. Cullmann. In our view the best single book on Jesus still remains that of Gunther Bornkamm, *Jesus of Nazareth,* Harper and Row, N.Y., 1960. On faith and history in the Gospels, see especially pp. 20–26.

2. I refer here to the "Q-Source"—those verses of Scripture

common to Matthew and Luke. For an interesting contemporary explanation of Q, see Chapter 3 of Howard Clark Kee, *Jesus in History: An Approach to the Study of the Gospels,* Harcourt Brace Jovanovich, 1977, pp. 76ff.

3. "Zadokite Document," III, 12-IV, 6, p. 65 and "Commentary on the Book of Habakkuk," II, 7–8, p. 253 in Theodore H. Gaster, *The Dead Sea Scrolls,* Doubleday, N.Y., 1956. For a discussion of the identity of the wicked priest, see Millar Burrows, *The Dead Sea Scrolls,* Viking Press, N.Y., 1956, p. 298 and pp. 160–186. For an extremely cautious view of identifying the Qumran community, see Gaster, pp. 24–28.

4. "The War of the Sons of Light and the Sons of Darkness," 1, 1–17, in Gaster, *Dead Sea,* p. 281.

5. "The Zadokite Document," X, 10-XII, 22 in Gaster, *Dead Sea,* pp. 77–80.

6. William Barclay, *Commentary on Matthew,* The Westminster Press, Philadelphia, 1975, Vol. II, pp. 244–245.

7. For a good overview of the parties of Judaism, see Robert A. Spivey and D. Moody Smith, Jr., *Anatomy of the New Testament; A Guide to Its Structure and Meaning,* Macmillan, 1974, pp. 15–27.

8. In what follows I rely on the analysis by Jorge Pixley of the economic structures and class conflicts in first century Palestine. See his *Reino de Dios,* Asociación Editorial La Aurora, Argentina, 1977, pp. 63–67.

9. Josephus, *Antiquities of the Jews,* Bk. XII, ch. VI.

10. See Oscar Cullmann, *Jesus and the Revolutionaries,* Harper and Row, N.Y., 1970, pp. 39ff and 73ff.

11. Such historical conjecture need not contradict the Gospel explanations of Jesus' betrayal by Judas (Mk 14:49; Jn 12:6).

12. Josephus, *Wars of the Jews,* Bk. IV, ch. 3.

13. Pixley, *Reino,* pp. 63–66.

14. "Assumption of Moses," 10.1.

15. "Apocalypse of Baruch," 73.

16. For a balanced article on the Kingdom, see O.E. Evans, "Kingdom of God," *Interpreter's Dictionary of the Bible,* Vol. K-Q, pp. 17–26. Evans is especially helpful in the treatment of Old Testament background, rabbinic teaching, and apocalyptic currents. His section on the Kingdom in the New Testament lacks some of the precisions more recently offered by redaction criticism and the sociology of Palestine.

17. "Book of Enoch," XCIII, XCI.12–17 in Charles, *Apocrypha,* pp. 262–65.

18. For an excellent treatment of Jesus' self-understanding, see Jacques Guillet, S.J., *The Consciousness of Jesus,* trans. by Edmond Bonin, Newman Press, 1972.

19. Here we sidestep the form-critical problem of the "Son of Man" sayings in the Synoptic Gospels. What the phrase meant to a first century Jew is still highly debated. See Ernest Todt, *The Son of Man in the Synoptic Tradition* for a highly apocalyptic interpretation. See Geza Vermes, *Jesus the Jew* for a denial that Son of Man is titular. For Vermes, it is a Jewish circumlocution. Only when that problem is settled can Jesus' historical use of the title be reconstructed form-critically with some major consensus among New Testament exegetes. To date such a consensus has not been achieved.

20. Segundo Galilea has a very clarifying discussion of this point when he explains the relationship between Luke 6:20–21 and the preferential option for the poor taken by the Latin American bishops at Puebla in 1979. See S. Galilea, *Espiritualidad de la evangelización: Según las bienaventuranzas,* CLAR, Bogotá, 1981, pp. 19–22.

21. For a much fuller account of the *Sitz im Leben* of this pericope see the wealth of data amassed by W.D. Davies, *The Setting of the Sermon on the Mount,* Cambridge, 1964. In general Matthew is showing how life in God's Kingdom (the Church) differs both from that of the torah observance in the synagogue and from the antinomian Gnostics who felt themselves enlightened beyond the need for any external moral norms.

22. See Thomas Aquinas, *Summa Theologica,* Part I–II, q. 69, a. 2 and a. 4, reply to obj.

23. The interconnecting logic in the Beatitudes can be appreciated by focusing on the connotations of each of the key terms in the eight attitudes and eight consequences. In the Old Testament "poor" denoted the "anawim Yahweh" who were the economically poor—the widows, orphans, and aliens. This physical poverty is frequently a condition for learning experientially one's dependence on God. In the period of the exile and the Maccabean crisis, the poor were frequently the persecuted and then the "pious ones." Luke 6:1 offers probably the more historical words of Jesus, "Oh how happy, you poor."

24. In later Judaism targumic authors substituted "Kingdom of heaven" for "Kingdom of God" to avoid the possible inference that God himself would appear on earth. Matthew seems to be in this line

of Jewish redaction of the prophetic tradition. See O.A. Evans, "Kingdom of God," in *Interpreter's Dictionary of the Bible,* Vol. K–Q, p. 18.

25. *Ashre* in Aramaic is an interjection (Oh how happy); *makarioi* in Greek is an adjective. In the Greek, it is *penthountes,* the mourning ones. In the Hebrew mindset, the sadness of mourning is related to the mystery of sin—either personal or the sins of one's fathers (social sin) or the inherited guilt and interior disorder from the "sin of Adam." *Paraklethesontai* is "shall be comforted." In Johannine theology, the Holy Spirit is called the "Paraclete," the one who brings comfort to Israel.

26. Psalm 22 was the final prayer of Jesus on the cross. Verse 27 speaks of the messianic victory of the poor "who will eat their fill," and verse 22 says that "all the ends of the earth shall remember and turn to the Lord." Paul speaks of Christ as meek, of himself as meek, and asks the Corinthian church to live in meekness with one another (cf. 2 Cor 10:1).

27. In Greek "justice" is *dikaisune.* Some Bibles translate it "righteousness," but this translation tends to focus only on the vertical God-self dimension of justice and to lose the relational aspect with one's neighbor. In Matthew's Gospel only God, Jesus and St. Joseph are called *dikaios* (cf. Mt 1:19; 5:45; 27:19, 24).

28. *Eleemon* in Greek indicates "being moved to pity and compassion by the tragedy and includes the fear that this could happen to me." See Fritz Rienecker, *A Linguistic Key to the Greek New Testament,* Zondervan, Grand Rapids, Mich., 1976, Vol. 1, p. 12.

29. A "clean" heart comes from right living in the external order (Acts 20:26). A "clean" heart gives rise to faith (1 Tim 3:9) and to charity (1 Tim 1:5). It involves purity in sexual relationship (1 Pet 1:22). The life-giving water of baptism is also "clean," making one a citizen of heaven with the angels who are "clean" (Rev 15:6). Thus Paul writes, "All of us, gazing on the Lord's glory with unveiled faces, are being transformed from glory to glory into his very image by the Lord who is the Spirit" (1 Cor 3:18).

30. See Ps 2:7. God adopts the king during the ceremony of royal coronation. Peace is also associated with the offering of blood sacrifice to God to seal the covenant between him as the king and the people as agreeing to live as chosen for service (Ex 24:6; Lev 3:1; Jos 8:31; 1 Sam 10:8; Ez 46:2, 12). In the Matthean context the sacrifice is to turn from "seeing God in prayer" to "serving the need of God's people for reconciliation" (cf. Rom 5:10; 2 Cor 5:18–19).

31. In Greek the perfect passive participle (*diogmenoi*) indicates

that the group referred to are those already tortured or already dead. Matthew associates being persecuted with preaching the word (Mt 13:21). That word challenges all the personal idols and all the demonic powers and all of the self-serving power structures in society. *Uranos* (heaven) is not the Kingship of God over one's life on earth, but is now the vision of God in glory (Rev 5:9–13).

32. See Raymond E. Brown, *The Birth of the Messiah,* Doubleday, N.Y., 1977.

33. "Pastoral Constitution on the Church in the Modern World," par. 12, in Walter Abbott, S.J., *The Documents of Vatican II,* America Press, N.Y., 1966, pp. 210–211.

34. *Ibid.,* par. 17, p. 214.

35. "Declaration on Religious Freedom," par. 2 and 3, in *ibid.,* pp. 678–81.

36. For a clarifying explication of the implications of "constitutive," see Charles M. Murphy, "Action for Justice as Constitutive of the Preaching of the Gospel: What Did the 1971 Synod Mean?" in *Theological Studies,* June 1983, Vol. 44, No. 2, pp. 298–311.

37. Pope Paul VI, "Octogesima Adveniens," par. 4 in *The Pope Speaks,* Vol. 16, No. 2 (1971), p. 139.

38. Pope Paul VI, "Populorum Progressio, 1968, par. 47 in Claudia Carlen, I.H.M., *The Papal Encyclicals 1958–1981,* MacGrath, 1981, Volume 5, pp. 191–92.

39. Pope John Paul II, "Address to the Indians of Oaxaca and Chiapas": "The Church defends the right of private property . . . but there is always a social mortgage on all private property so that goods may serve the general assignment that God has given them, and if the common good demands it, there is no need to hesitate at expropriation itself done in the right way" (p. 24). Quoted in John Engleson and Philip Scharper (eds.), *Puebla and Beyond,* Orbis Books, Maryknoll, N.Y., 1979, p. 82.

40. Pope Paul VI, "Octogesima Adveniens," par. 48–49, p. 162.

Chapter VIII

The Apostolic Church
and Catholic Teaching on
Authority and Sacramentality

*"Every time . . . you eat this bread
and drink this cup,
you proclaim the death of the Lord
until he comes."*
—1 Cor 11:26

From Pentecost (ca. 33 A.D.) to the Death
of Peter and Paul (ca. 64 A.D.)

***What can we really prove about the
trustworthiness of the history of the Church
reported in the New Testament?***

Six historical dates in the apostolic period can be corroborated from non-biblical sources and are thus used by historians to reconstruct the probable dates for other events in the early Church. The famine predicted by the Christian prophet Agabus (Acts 11:28) occurred in 46 A.D. The edict of Claudius ordering all Jews to leave Rome (Acts 18:2) was issued in 50 A.D. The Roman proconsul Gallio, before whom St. Paul appeared (Acts 18:12), took office in Corinth in the summer of 51 A.D. Porcius Festus, the Roman governor of Caesarea who left Paul in prison (Acts 24:27), took office in the summer of 59

A.D. During the persecution of Christians instigated by Emperor Nero, Peter and Paul were martyred in 64 A.D. In 70 A.D. during the reign of Emperor Vespasian, Titus marched on Jerusalem and destroyed the temple. With less certainty the Council of Jerusalem is dated in 49 or 50 A.D. (Acts 15; Gal 2:9–10).

What kinds of Jews began following the "new way" of being Jewish by praying in the name of Jesus?

The primitive Church in Palestine seems to have had converts from six different varieties of Judaism: (1) the Hebrew party, (2) the Hellenist party, (3) the Essenes, (4) the Galileans, (5) the Samaritans, (6) the Baptist sects.[1]

What was the Hebrew party?

Because its importance disappeared after the fall of Jerusalem in 70 A.D., St. Luke largely ignored the importance of the Hebrew party in his history of the Church in the Book of Acts. Luke focused on Hellenist and Essene sources which had more relevance for his Gentile Christian audience. Careful investigation into the Book of Acts, using the archeological find of the Dead Sea Scrolls, has recently pointed toward the Hebrew party as the dominant group in the mother church at Jerusalem. As followers of "the new way" they basically understood themselves as a sect within Judaism, yet open to accepting Gentile members (Acts 10:47).

The hierarchical organization of the members shows their dependence on the synagogue and Qumran. Peter, the leader of the Twelve, seems to have appointed James, the brother of the Lord, to be in charge of the local church at Jerusalem. According to the first Church historian, Bishop Eusebius of Caesarea (ca. 260–340 A.D.), James, the brother of the Lord (Gal 1:19), was called "the Just" because of his great personal holiness.

Eusebius also asserts that this James was a blood brother of Jesus and the "son of Joseph." James lived by the nazirite vow through which he would have consecrated himself to God, abstained from strong drink, and let his hair grow—as a sign of separation from the softness of society (cf. Num 6:2ff). He was reputed to have spent such long hours in prayer in the Jerusalem temple asking God to forgive the sins of the people that his knees resembled those of a camel. Paul called James one of the "acknowledged pillars," along with Cephas (Peter) and John, at the Council of Jerusalem in 49–50 A.D. (Gal 1:19). Eusebius reports that James, "as the records tell us," was the first "to be elected to the episcopal throne of the Jerusalem church."[2] According to the Jewish historian, Josephus, James was executed in Jerusalem in 62 A.D.[3]

How was authority organized in the mother church at Jerusalem?

Peter is always mentioned first in every list of the Twelve in the New Testament. Peter spoke first at Pentecost to interpret the action of the Holy Spirit (Acts 2:14ff). Peter, therefore, must have ordained James as the Jerusalem bishop. James in turn governed the local church through a kind of group of elders (presbyters) following the hierarchical structure of the synagogue. The original group seem to have been called "the brothers of the Lord" (Acts 12:17).[4]

Were James the Just and the other "brothers of the Lord" the sons of Joseph and Mary as Eusebius thought?

Eusebius was probably identifying James the Just with the James mentioned as one of the "brothers and sisters" of Jesus in Mark 6:3. Since Mark 15:40 calls one of the women at the foot of the cross "Mary the mother of James," and does *not* identify her as the mother of Jesus, Mark may have used the word "brother" in Mark 6:3 in a more extended sense than understood by Eusebius. The Greek word (*adelphos*) was used in Scripture in the broad sense of a "neighbor" (cf. Mt 5:22–24), a "step-brother" (Mk 6:17–18), or a "relative" (Gen 29:12; 24:48). Thus Jesus, James, and the "brothers and sisters" of Jesus could well have had different mothers. The growing tradition that Mary remained perpetually a virgin could be historical without Eusebius' having attended to it.[5] Belief in the perpetual virginity of Mary grew in the second and third century and became universally accepted in the fourth century.

How did the Hebrew party interact with the other groups of converts in the early Church?

Since the twelve Apostles all belonged to the Hebrew party, it had the prestige of founding authority among the other groups of Christian converts. Since the majority of the first Jewish Christians spoke Aramaic, the first century derivative of Hebrew, the Hebrew party was also *culturally* dominant. This led to neglect of the Greek-speaking widows of the Hellenist Jews living in Jerusalem (Acts 6:1). To compensate for this pastoral insensitivity, the Twelve created the office of "deacon" or "servant" under the leadership of Stephen. Thus very early the Church became operatively bilingual-bicultural in its organization.

While the Book of Acts makes it clear that the Hebrews lived in visible communion with the Hellenists, the exact identity of the Hellenist party is debated by historians. Were they blood Jews who had grown up in the diaspora or were they proselyte Jewish converts who had been associated with the synagogue of the freedmen (Acts 6:9)? What is most important is that the Hebrew party was pro-temple and pro-torah while the Hellenist party of Christians was anti-temple. Thus the Jewish Pharisees favored the Hebrew party of Christians (Acts 5:33–41) and persecuted the Hellenist party of Christians. Stephen the deacon was martyred and the other Hellenists were exiled from Jerusalem in 36 A.D. This caused the Hellenist Christians to become missionaries through Caesarea, Joppa, and Gaza. Philip the deacon evangelized this territory. According to Daniélou, the fact that Peter followed up on Philip's work "seems a proof of the control that the Twelve felt obliged to exercise over the Church as a whole."[6]

Who were the Galilean Christians?

Galilee was the hot spot of Zealot revolutionary efforts to free the Jews from Roman oppression. It would have consisted of mostly farmers and fishermen. Historically the Galileans simply disappear with almost no trace in the early Church. Perhaps Daniélou is right when he suggests that the Galileans disappeared because they identified too closely with the Jewish Zealots who were crushed by the Romans in 70 A.D.[7]

Who were the Samaritan Christians?

Since 721 B.C. the Samaritan region of Palestine had come under the pagan influence of Assyrian religion. Since the refounding of the temple by Ezra, the Jews had been forbidden to intermarry with the Samaritans (ca. 538 B.C.). At the time of Peter, Simon Magus was trying to create a blend of Judaism, magic, and the Christian gift of miracles. Peter and John administered the anointing of the Holy Spirit to the recently baptized Samaritans, but refused to administer the rite to Simon Magus (Acts 8:20). The Jewish Christian sect of Simon Magus was at least one of the sources of the first Christian heresy of Gnosticism from 70 A.D. on.[8]

Who were the Baptizers?

Several different sects of Jews practiced the ritual of repeated baptisms of purification. They were influenced by the apocalyptic mysticism of the Noah tradition. This recalled the purifying flood in Genesis and added the belief that the River Jordan was sacred. The followers of John the Baptist who refused to become Christians found similar groups across the Jordan River who had sanctuaries to the Old Testament Gentile saints: Lot, Job, and Melchizedek. From them the Church certainly learned about baptism. However, since Christian baptism was God's action by which the person "died and rose" with Christ (Rom 6:1–4), Christian baptism could not be repeated. The baptizer sects developed into the Mandaeans and Ebionite sects in the second century. The Baptizers called themselves Nazoreans (observers) and were hostile to the offering of sacrifice.[9]

How did the Church spread throughout Asia?

The missionary journeys of Paul occurred between ca. 47 and 60. At first he and Barnabas traveled together and then parted in disagreement. Damascus and Antioch in Syria became the first leading centers of the Gentile Church. The authority to govern these Gentile churches seems to have been entrusted to "prophets and doctors" (cf. Acts 11:27; 13:1; 1 Cor 12:28). These prophets and doctors had more than personal charisms. Daniélou suggests that they were missionary ministers under the authority of Barnabas. Thus Barnabas was to the "prophets and doctors" in Antioch what James the Just was to the "brothers of the Lord" in Jerusalem. The sharp disagreement between Barnabas and Paul may well have been motivated by a dispute over who had legitimate authority to decide whether or not John Mark had the strength required to endure the life of a missionary (cf. Acts 15:36–40).[10]

How did the Church get to Rome?

Herod Antipas died in 44 A.D.; therefore, his beheading of James the Great must have occurred in 43 (Acts 12:1). At that time, after miraculously escaping from prison, Peter left Jerusalem "for another place" (Acts 12:17). Peter then disappears from the New Testament until the Council of Jerusalem in 50 A.D. Eusebius, however, reports that Peter came to Rome in about 44 at the beginning of the reign of Emperor Claudius. This report is trustworthy because the Roman pagan historian, Suetonius, says that Claudius expelled the Jews from Rome in 50 since they were becoming agitated at "the prompting of Chrestos." The confused report of Suetonius certainly recalls heated controversies between the Jews and Jewish Christians living in Rome between 44 and 49. In 51 Paul met some converted Jews who had been driven from Rome to Ephesus: Aquila and Priscilla (Acts 18:2, 26; 1 Cor 16:19). In 57 Paul addressed the community of Rome, already considered

important. In 60 he found communities established in Puteoli
and in Rome.[11]

Why did Nero begin the first Roman persecution of the Church in 64 A.D.?

Nero's reign was marred by scandalous self-indulgence,
murder, graft, economic ruin of the city, and filling government posts with the dregs of society. Tacitus and Suetonius
both report that Nero ordered a fire be set to Rome. Evidently
burning the city was the most "efficient" way to end over-
crowding and promote urban "revival." Thousands of people
died in the fire that devastated almost half of Rome. Nero's
unbelievable cruelty caused him to be called the "antichrist"
and the "beast" whose secret number was "666." In the Hebrew alphabet, each letter has a numerical value. The total of
N-E-R-O equals 666 (Rev 13:11–18). After Nero died first century Christians feared that he would rise from the dead and
continue his vicious oppression in some ghostly manner.

When the Roman nobility learned of Nero's order to burn
Rome, they were outraged. Nero tried to turn the blame on
the "Christiani" (adopted sons of Christ) (cf. Acts 11:26). Ru-
mors were already spreading that this new "sect" did wicked
things when they held their secret mystery rites. Since non-
baptized people were not allowed to stay at Eucharist after the
Scripture readings, it was easy for enemies of the Church to
assert that Christians were "eating the flesh" of babies, etc., in
their "abominable rites." Peter and Paul were martyred in
that persecution, so that later Christian tradition revered
Rome as the local church born of the blood of the two most
famous apostles of the primitive Church.[12]

The Church as the Fullness of God's Love

Did Jesus intend to found the Church?

Yes and no. A form-critical reading of the New Testament
shows that Jesus preached the Kingdom of God but probably
never spoke historically about the *Church* of God. Apparently

Jesus hoped to renew the covenant of Moses within the "assembly" of Israel for whose salvation he humanly wept (Lk 19:41). The post-Easter Christian community put the word "Church" on the lips of Jesus in the Gospels to show the continuity between his earthly mission of gathering together the Twelve and a community of disciples with the apostolic Church. The rejection of faith in Jesus by Israel and the expulsion of Christians from the synagogues ca. 85 A.D. led to the total split between synagogue and Church which God has promised to overcome mysteriously in the fullness of time. In the meantime, has God rejected his people Israel? St. Paul said, "Of course not" (Rom 11:1).

What does the word "Church" mean?

Most people today think of the Church as a building in which Christian worship is held or as a particular denomination to which people belong: Catholic, Lutheran, Baptist, etc. In the Greek New Testament the word for Church is *ekklesia.* This word occurs almost one hundred times in the Greek Old Testament. Seventy-two times it translates the Hebrew word *qahal,* "assembly." The Church in the New Testament is thus the assembly of God or the assembly of Christ (cf. Dt 23:1–3; Neh 13:1; Mt 10:18). Therefore Paul could write, "In legal observance I was a Pharisee and so zealous that I persecuted the Church" (Phil 3:6).

Where today Catholics would refer to a "diocese," the New Testament also spoke of the Church in a certain place—Jerusalem, Corinth, etc. (cf. Acts 8:1; 1 Cor 7:17). Finally the word "Church" was used in the New Testament the way Catholics today would use the word "parish." Thus Paul wrote in the oldest book of the New Testament that the Thessalonians "have been made like the churches of God in Judea which are in Christ Jesus" (1 Thes 2:14). The Apostles, therefore, thought of the one Church of God or Christ expressing itself in various local churches which kept in visible bonds of communion (*koinonia*) with one another through their pastoral leaders (cf. 3 Jn).

How is the Church of God the culmination of all the Scriptures?

The Greek word for Church is related to the verb *ek-kalein*, "to call someone out of." In this sense the Church is the result of God calling men and women apart from the values of the world in order to free the world for the worship of God (1 Cor 3:21ff; Jn 3:16; 12:47; Eph 1:22ff). Historically God's call to become Church is rooted in the vocation of Abraham to "leave your land" for a place "I will show you" (Gen 12:1). Aware of this saving history, the authors of 1 Peter and Hebrews thought of the Church as a pilgrim who is a stranger and foreigner walking through the sufferings of the present toward the heavenly city which God has prepared for his beloved (Heb 11:13–16; 1 Pet 2:11).

Like the "little poor ones" rescued by Yahweh from oppression and slavery in Egypt (Ex 15:1–18), the "world's lowborn and despised" have become the new "Israel of God" (Gal 6:16) by participation in the death and rising of Christ our "passover" through baptism (1 Cor 5:7; Rom 6:3). Like Judah after the exile, God made the Church the servant light of grace and peace for the world (Rom 6:16–18; Mt 5:14; 1 Cor 1:3; Jn 3:16–17). Like the Maccabean Jews, God made the Church the assembly of those who live in "festal harmony" with its members martyred for their faith in Jesus. Here we are nurtured at the "altar" of Jesus' flesh and blood—of which unbelievers are deprived (Heb 12:22–24; 13:10; Jn 6:53). Like the eternal splendor of Lady Wisdom (Prv 8:22ff; Wis 7:25ff) God created the Church "before all ages" (Eph 3:11) to be "the bride" of Christ (Eph 6:32) and the "mother" (Jn 19:27; Rev 12:2) of *many* sons and daughters (Rom 8:29). God calls it to live in "holiness" (Eph 2:21), on the "foundation of the Apostles and prophets" (Eph 2:20), sharing with "all its members" the spiritual wealth of Christ's "glorious heritage" until every "barrier of hostility" is broken down and by means of him everything is reconciled "in his person, both on earth and in the heavens, making peace through the blood of his cross" (Eph 1:20).

St. Paul's Love for the Mystery of the Church as the Body of Christ

What do we know historically about the life of St. Paul?

Based on the sketch of Church history given in the first section of this chapter and on internal clues in the Letters of Paul, we can assert the following. Paul was converted, baptized, lost his sight and recovered it ca. 36 A.D. (cf. Acts 9). Then he withdrew into the desert of Arabia—presumably to pray and receive infused contemplative knowledge of the mysteries of the risen Christ (Gal 1:17; 2 Cor 2:12; Eph 1:9; 2:10). Paul probably visited Jerusalem in 36 A.D., returning ten years later with money collected from the local churches to help victims of famine. His first missionary journey probably occurred in 47–48, after which he attended the Council of Jerusalem in 50 as an outspoken critic of the Judaizers. Subsequently Paul evangelized Corinth in 50 A.D. He left Corinth two years later to spend from the autumn of 53 to the summer of 56 in Ephesus. At the end of 56 he returned to Corinth. He spent Passover of 57 at Philippi and reached Jerusalem for Pentecost in 57. After two years in prison he appeared before Festus in the summer of 59 and eventually reached Rome in 60. He was released the first time and then subsequently arrested again and martyred in 64 A.D.[13]

Why is Paul called the "Apostle" to the Gentiles, since that would make him the thirteenth Apostle?

The risen Christ personally converted Paul from Judaism through a vision and the grace of repentance (Acts 9:1–9). After being baptized, Paul met Barnabas in Antioch who helped him meet Peter and James the Just in Jerusalem (Acts 9:26–30; Gal 1:19–20). They allowed him to continue his ministry of preaching in the Church—thus recognizing the legitimacy of the apostleship of their former persecutor.

Paul called himself an "apostle" who was "born out of due time" (1 Cor 15:8). Jesus had picked the Twelve to judge the twelve tribes of Israel (Mt 19:28; Lk 22:30). He had "sent them out" (*apostelein*) to proclaim the Kingdom (Mk 3:13ff; 6:7ff). As the founding authority of the Church under the headship of Christ (Eph 2:20), the twelve Apostles represented the *continuity* between the faith of Israel, the teaching of Jesus, and the faith of the Church in Jesus as its risen Lord (Eph 1:7–10).

By contrast, Paul's preaching to the Gentiles emphasized the *discontinuity* between the law of Moses and the Gospel of Jesus Christ. Paul begged the "Apostles" and "presbyters" (Acts 15:23) at the Council of Jerusalem not to "burden" the Gentile Christians with the Jewish disciplinary laws of circumcision and kosher foods (Acts 15). Having spent his life in countless sufferings to plant the Church throughout Asia and Rome, Paul well deserves the title "Apostle to the Gentiles" (cf. 1 Cor 4).

What did Paul teach about "justification by faith"?

Paul taught that personal faith in the efficacy of Christ's death on the cross allows us to live in the hope of sharing God's glory in heaven and thus avoid discouragement during the sufferings we endure in this life (Rom 5:1–2). Overcoming discouragement allows us to "persevere in virtue" and recognize that "the love of God has been poured out in our hearts through the Holy Spirit" in the "death" of Christ, God's Son (Rom 5:4–9). Because Christ is our sacrificial sin offering (2 Cor 5:21), our faith in the "reconciliation" Christ has achieved between us and God allows us to live in "peace with God" (Rom 5:1, 11).

What did Paul teach about "freedom from the law"?

As baptized in Christ "we have been released from the law." We are dead to the law which was revealed to overcome sin but only caused us to sin more because we could never live it perfectly. Thus we Christians serve "in the new spirit, not the antiquated letter" (Rom 7).

In Christ, each person receives personal manifestations of the Holy Spirit (1 Cor 12:7). Thus one's human spirit is not only dead to the law, but is actively prompted by the divine Spirit of God. There is then a direct communion with God in the grace of sonship which shapes the perception of the truths of faith which one believes and the concrete moral choices one makes. The immediacy of this human-divine communion is most obvious in charismatic manifestations like prophecy, speaking in tongues and miraculous healings. Such charisms or gifts from the Spirit were very common in the first two centuries of the Church, were abundant at Corinth, and are being renewed in the Church today.

What prompted Paul to write his First Letter to the Corinthians ca. 56 A.D.?

Nothing would appear more ideal than a local church filled with such manifestations of the divine presence and transforming power. The new life of the risen Christ was palpably flowing through his body on earth, the community of believers. The gifts of the Holy Spirit were quite evident. The beauty of this ideal, however, was severely tarnished in the sinful members of the church in Corinth. With everyone convinced of his or her personal communion with the Spirit and individual freedom from the law, the most appalling distortions of apostolic teaching soon began to undermine the lived integrity of the people's faith. This prompted members of Chloe's household to visit Paul in Ephesus and beg him to correct the abuses which had grown up in the six years since he had first proclaimed the Gospel in Corinth (1 Cor 1:11).

What was the underlying cause of all the immorality and rebellion against apostolic authority in the church in Corinth?

Msgr. Ronald Knox is correct, I believe, in suggesting that the theological confusion at the root of the Corinthian chaos was an "enthusiastic" rather than an "orthodox" concept of grace. What Knox called "enthusiasm" has resurfaced periodically in Church history and is generally called "revivalism" in America. Knox clarifies the two concepts of grace as follows:

> Our traditional doctrine is that grace perfects nature, elevates it to a higher pitch, so that it can bear its part in the music of eternity, but leaves it nature still. The assumption of the enthusiast is bolder and simpler; for him, grace has destroyed nature, and replaced it. The saved man has come out into a new order of being with a new set of faculties which are proper in his state ... he decries the use of human reason as a guide to any sort of religious truth ... a direct indication of the Divine will is communicated to him at every turn.... If no oracle from heaven is forthcoming, he will take refuge in sortilege, anything, to make sure he is leaving the decision in God's hands. That God speaks to us through the intellect is a notion which he may accept on paper, but fears, in practice, to apply.[14]

This concept of grace is coupled with other corollary beliefs typical of enthusiasm. An inward experience of peace and joy is both the assurance which the soul craves for and its characteristic prayer-attitude. This strengthens the faith of the enthusiast with a strong imaginative life in prayer. Ecstasy, tongues speaking, convulsions in the Spirit, and even rolling in the nude have all been used to act out this new freedom. Confident that God was at work in some powerful new way, and that Jesus would return soon, the enthusiasts were "ultrasupernatural." Each was inclined to give the absolute authority of God to most of his or her personal impulses—no matter how deviant or opposite they might be. Thus the apparently contradictory symptoms of sexual prudishness and unembarrassed sexual licentiousness could emerge from the same enthusiastic misperception of how grace works in the life of the Church.

What did Paul mean in his Letter by the "spiritual milk" he had already given the Corinthians and the "spiritual meat" he was going to give them?

Paul was extremely concerned that the Church had been fragmented into factions, each claiming a different authority: Paul, Apollos, Peter or Christ (chs. 1—4). The celebration of the Eucharist was a scandal (ch. 11), the new freedom of Christian morality was being distorted (chs. 5—8), and the exercise of the spiritual charisms was in serious disarray (chs. 12—14).

Faced with this disheartening array of pastoral problems, Paul wrote the super-spiritual Corinthians and called them "men of flesh" acting like "infants" (1 Cor 3:1). Paul hinted that he might have some of the responsibility for their deviations from the apostolic faith because he had given the Corinthians only the spiritual "milk" suitable for beginners. Presumably this metaphor of milk referred to the main themes of initial evangelization: the Father's plan of love to save all people; the possibility of being baptized into new life in the risen Christ; the freedom to live by the Gospel, not the law; the joy, peace, and transforming power that comes from new life in the Spirit. This spiritual milk had unfortunately been soured by asserting that one could have the interior light of Christ (as proved by the impressive charisms), and not live by love for Christ's body, the apostolic Church.

To correct these distortions, Paul had to give them spiritual "meat" even though they were not ready for it. The metaphor of meat seems to include the key elements by which the body of Christ on earth truly lives as Church: a visible unity among the members; active cooperation with apostolic authorities who have God-given power to govern; exercising new freedom in Christ for holiness, not sin; a reverence for the eucharistic body and blood of Christ which understands the sacred mysteries as a communion not only in risen power of Christ, but also in his crucified love for the poor; a recognition that the primary charism in the Church is love which harmonizes all the other charisms into a manifestation of divine truth and a sign of divine peace.

What did Paul intend to teach by calling the Church the body of Christ on earth?

Viktor Warnach is probably right in asserting that "body of Christ" is not just one more metaphor for Church in the Scriptures like "vine" or "flock." With the term "body" Paul moves from metaphor to analogy—or from picture language to substantive content.[15] He knew that the Corinthians needed a way to understand themselves as inter-related *members* of the Church. Their Greek understanding of their bodies as "houses of their souls" was causing them to act like competing, individualistic atoms.

In Hebrew there was no word for the human "body." Instead they thought of human breathing "clay" as *basar* or flesh. Humans *related to* one another and "all flesh" through the medium of their human flesh. Since the "flesh" was subject to death and sickness because of human sin, the flesh might achieve a communion with other flesh as *just,* in the line of Abel sacrificing its disordered urges to the higher holiness of God, or the flesh might achieve dominance over others by *wickedness* in the line of Cain the murderer. Thus, while morally ambiguous, human flesh was always a sacramental expression of one's interior values. The interiority of the person in Hebrew was called the *leb,* heart. The *leb* thought, evaluated, chose, and acted. The *nephesh* was the throat that hungered and thirsted for water, bread, and became spiritualized as one's soul longing to see the face of God. The *ruah* or breath was associated with one's vital energies received from the Holy Breath (Spirit) of God. Thus visceral urges and groanings had their source in *ruah.*[16]

When the Hebrew Old Testament was translated into Greek, *nephesh* was translated *psyche* (soul), *leb* was translated *kardia* (heart), and *ruah* was translated *pneuma* (spirit). *Basar* (flesh) was translated *soma* (body). In Greek philosophy a material body is a cause of individuation. The body closes off one with his or her own soul which does the thinking and choosing and remembering. This cultural difference threatened the whole communal sense of being Christian. Paul then used the Greek word *soma* in a deliberately *collective* sense, so that the Corinthian Christians could begin to reinterpret themselves as *inter-related* through Christ, *not* simply *self-enclosed* with the light of Christ.

What does "body of Christ" teach about authority and sacramentality in the Church?

In 1 Corinthians 10:16 "body" refers to the Eucharist. Paul asks: Do we not share in the body of Christ? In 1 Corinthians 10:17 Paul says: "We, many though we are, are one body, for we all partake of the one loaf." "Body" here means the Church. In chapter 12 Paul explains how the variety in the body of Christ as Church makes each member *unique* but organically related with *complementary* functions that contribute to the health of the whole (1 Cor 12:12–20). The poorest or the lowliest members are given the greatest honor just as we drape underwear over the weakest parts of our individual bodies (1 Cor 12:21–26). Then Paul explains that the body of Christ as Church has been set up by God with a hierarchical authority structure: "first Apostles, second prophets, third teachers, then miracle workers, healers, assistants, administrators, and those who speak in tongues" (1 Cor 12:28). Thus in the body of Christ the authority to hand on the faith of the Apostles as a teacher ranks above the personal charisms of miracle workers and speakers in tongues, etc.

What is the life principle of the body of Christ?

After explaining the unique role of each member of the Church, Paul culminates his explanation with his incomparable description of the primacy of love. The love that has no limit in its power to forgive the members of Christ's Church, the love poured into our hearts by the Holy Spirit who is love (1 Cor 13:4–13), gives the mysterious Godlife to the whole body so that it truly enfleshes the life of Christ in the world today.

That divine-human love is the only thing that will endure beyond death, so that all wisdom, knowledge, power, and personal charisma can be subordinated to mutual forgiveness, kindness, and generosity.

The New Testament Church After the Death of Peter and Paul

How was authority handed on in the New Testament Church by the Apostles to others?

In 1 Corinthians 4:1 Paul had explained that the Apostles were "servants of Christ" and "stewards of the mysteries of God." The *mysteries* were the various rites of baptism, Eucharist, laying on of hands for receiving the Holy Spirit, and being ordained to preside and teach. The *episcopos* (overseer) or bishop was designated the second generation "steward" of the mysteries. They were assisted by the *presbyteroi* (elders) and *diakoinoi* (servants) (Ti 1:5; Acts 6:1ff). 1 Timothy, 2 Timothy, and Titus repeatedly counsel that such men should be holy and blameless, patient with those who are weak or follow false doctrines, and steadfast in holding to the true doctrine taught by the apostles (cf. 1 Tim 1 and 3). Such men might not be very "exciting" but would be men of interior substance and practical wisdom in pastoring their brothers and sisters. Such "pillars of truth in the Church" could be married only once (1 Tim 3:15).

How did the Apostles and their successors regard Christians who formed splinter groups outside the visible communion of authority and unity of love in the Church of Christ?

Paul called the puffed up men who tried to deny his authority in Corinth the "false apostles" (2 Cor 11:13). Those who followed them were following a different Jesus than the one proclaimed by the Apostles (2 Cor 11:4). The schismatic

Diotrephes (3 Jn 9) is probably one of the "many antichrists" in 1 Jn 2:19. Such separatists were "false prophets" (1 Jn 4:4). They had taken the murderous "road of Cain" (Jude 11) and like Korah had sinfully rebelled against God's chosen leaders. Korah had said to Moses, "Enough from you! The whole community, all of them, are holy; the Lord is in their midst. Why then should you set yourselves over the Lord's congregation"? (Num. 16:3; Jude 11). Paul feared that such false teachers had been corrupted by the same serpent which had seduced Eve (2 Cor 11:3).

How did the New Testament Church await the return of Christ?

Bishop Eusebius informs us that in 40 A.D. the Roman emperor Caligula threatened to put his statue in the Jerusalem temple and rename it "Temple of Jupiter the Glorious, the Younger Gaius," in honor of himself.[17] A whole group of Christians took this threat as the final "sign" of the end and fled to Pella east of the Jordan River to escape the destruction of Jerusalem and prepare themselves to welcome Jesus as the heavenly Son of Man coming on the clouds of heaven. Caligula died and the temple was not subjected to Roman desecration until thirty years later when it was destroyed in 70 A.D. Contrary to popular expectation the return of Christ did not occur even then.

In fact, between 64 and 70 A.D. things had gotten worse. Peter and Paul had been killed in the general persecution of Christians under Nero in 64. Mark wrote his Gospel in the wake of that suffering between 64 and 69 A.D. Remembering the Pella fiasco of a generation earlier, Mark has Jesus say about the end, "But when you see the desolating sacrilege set up where it ought not to be (let the reader understand), then let those who are in Judea flee to the mountains" (Mk 13:14). The Christians were not to overreact to the current woes and see them as a sign of the end.

Writing about 85 A.D. fifteen years or so after the destruction of the temple, Matthew has Jesus insist that Christians should not believe anyone who tells them that the return of Christ is so imminent that they should change their lifestyle:

> So, if they say to you, "Lo, he is in the wilderness," do not go out; if they say, "Lo, he is in the inner rooms," do not believe it (Mt 24:26–27).

The return of Christ will involve such a cosmic systems collapse that it will be evident to all and not a point for conjecture or debate:

> For as the lightning comes from the east and shines as far as the west, so will be the coming of the Son of Man. Wherever the body is, there the eagles will be gathered together (Mt 24:27–28).

Thus when the universe is nothing but a dead carcass we will know that Christ has returned in glory.

What does Revelation 20:1–6 teach about the "millennium" or "Reign of Christ for a thousand years"?

The Book of Revelation was written ca. 96 during the persecution of the Church by the Roman emperor Domitian. The inspired author was encouraging fidelity to the apostolic Church in spite of the terrible sufferings being endured. In Revelation 20:1–6 four main truths are taught: (1) the return of Christ will restore paradise, (2) all things will be subjected to Christ as Messiah (cf. 1 Cor 15:20–28), (3) the martyrs and confessors of the faith will share in Christ's reign as judges (Rev 20:4), (4) Christians should be "watchful" in order to avoid the second death, hell (cf. Mk 14:33; Rev 20:6).

What is meant by Christ restoring paradise?

Jean Daniélou has found a Jewish apocryphal scripture which reads, "Adam died when he was seventy years old, before he reached a thousand years" (Jubilees 4:20). This proves that first century Jews thought of the number 1000 as the symbol of the *fullness of life*.[18] Thus when Revelation speaks of the "reign of Christ for a thousand years" it means that the return of Christ will end all suffering and death which sin has brought into the world (cf. Rev 21:4). As suffering and death end, the "garden of Eden" will be restored (Gen 2) so that we will again live in the innocent delight for which Yahweh created us.

Will this restoration of paradise occur on earth or in heaven?

The vision in Revelation 20:1–6 is a "court scene" in heaven. Scripture says nothing about what will happen on earth. The "first resurrection" (Rev 20:6) should be understood not in a carnal sense, but in a glorified sense: the prophets and martyrs "reigning in glory with Christ."[19] If we ask what kind of bodies will they and we have, St. Paul answers, "A nonsensical question" (1 Cor 15:36). We will each radiate that personal intensity of glory (1 Cor 15:37ff) according as our union with God is manifested in our works of mercy toward suffering people on earth (Mt 25:31ff). While the "restored garden of Eden" is thus not physical, it can be helpful to meditate on our future heavenly delights in order to endure virtuously the trials of this life. On the other hand, to persevere as a Christian merely to get "real estate" in the millennium would be both egotistical and intellectually childish.[20]

What does it mean to live in watchfulness?

It means to live in the "reverent fear" or humility which characterized the first Christians and expresses itself in the effort to be "found without stain or defilement, and at peace in [God's] sight" (2 Pet 3:14). To be watchful does not mean to keep looking for the "signs" of the end of the world. Jesus warned against "false prophets" and "false messiahs" (Mk 13:22) who manipulate the hopes of suffering humanity to their own personal gain. 2 Peter 3:17 warns against distorting

Scripture passages about the return of Christ which are "hard to understand." Those who have tried to predict the return of Christ have been wrong—whether they have been Catholic saints or Protestant fundamentalists.[21] As to the exact day or hour when Christ will return, "no one knows it ... not even the Son, but only the Father" (Mk 13:32).

The Relation of the New Testament Faith in the Apostolic Church to Catholic Teaching on Authority and Sacramentality

Where do Catholics find the scriptural justification for developing teaching about faith and morality beyond what is taught in the New Testament?

Catholics continue the practice begun at the Council of Jerusalem. Since the Holy Spirit abides in the Church (Acts 2), the Apostles and presbyters could add to the historical teachings of Jesus. Thus when they dispensed the Gentiles from observing the Jewish disciplinary laws, they wrote, "It is the decision of *the Holy Spirit and ours* too" (Acts 15:28). Thus Catholic faith believes that the Holy Spirit continues to work in the whole Church and guide the Pope and bishops in a special way when they gather in solemn Councils.[22]

How did the Catholic concept of authority in the Church develop beyond what is revealed in the New Testament?

The Catholic concept of Church authority involves three main aspects: (1) the tripartite hierarchy of deacons, presbyters (priests), and bishops, (2) the monarchical episcopate, and (3) the papacy as the continuation of the primacy of Peter.

The tripartite hierarchy was well established before the New Testament stopped being written (ca. 150 A.D.). Both synagogue and Essene influences helped furnish the Church with models of government. The earliest written evidence of the monarchical episcopate dates from the letters of St. Ignatius, the second bishop of Antioch (d. ca. 110 A.D.). Because some Christians were denying the humanity of Christ and others were having sex orgies during the eucharistic "love feasts," Ignatius ordered that the "universal" or "catholic" Christians could only celebrate the Eucharist with the permission of their bishop. This made the bishop the governing monarch in the local church.[23] The custom quickly spread.

On his way to die as a martyr, Ignatius wrote seven letters which were widely read in the early Church. In them he speaks of the Church as "a marvelous choir" which receives its fundamental note from God. The cooperation between the members generates a heavenly harmony with the angels. All, therefore, should respect their bishop, presbyters, and deacons as "of one mind with Christ" to the ends of the earth. To resist them would be proud, and "God resists the proud" (Prv 3:34). We have spoken sufficiently of the papacy in Chapter VI.[24]

Why do Catholics emphasize the sacraments so much, although the word does not occur in Scripture?

The word "sacrament" comes from the Latin for "oath," *sacramentum,* or *sacrare,* "to make sacred." The person of the minister, the act of consecration, and the person or object consecrated could all be the meaning of the term in various contexts. From the third century on, the Latin Church began using *sacramentum* instead of *mystery* (secret) which was used in the New Testament and is still used in the Greek Church. Since Church is the culmination of the Scriptures, and the sacramental mysteries are those moments in the life of the Church when the Church most fully lives as Christ's body, Catholics emphasize the sacraments to glorify God by sacramental sharing in the new life of Christ. The specific rites are in fact mentioned in the New Testament.

Baptism, the Eucharist, and the laying on of the hands to be sealed with the Holy Spirit are all mentioned in the Book of Acts and elsewhere. Catholics call these the "sacraments of

"initiation" into the passover mystery of Christ. Christ gave
the power to forgive sin to the Twelve in John 20:23. Paul
counseled Timothy not to use the "laying on of the hands" too
readily (1 Tim 5:22) and called the Apostles "stewards of the
mysteries" of Christ (1 Cor 4:1). James tells us to "confess [our]
sins to one another" and to "anoint one another" for healing
(Jas 5:13–16). Catholics call these the sacraments of "healing
and reconciliation" (2 Cor 5:18). The laying on of hands to
ordain is found in Acts 6:6. The Christian rite of marriage is
never explicitly mentioned in Scripture, but the centrality of
marriage in the life of the Church is (Eph 5:22–32).

Why do Catholics say there are seven and only seven sacraments, since the whole life of the Church is a sacramental sharing in the presence of Christ?

The Catholic Church simply lived the sacramental mystery of Christ in the various rites and liturgies of the Church
for a thousand years without ever numbering them. As theological reflection tried to distinguish between rites, sacramentals, and sacraments, various numbers were proposed. The
phrase "seven and only seven sacraments" was first used by
theologians in the twelfth century. At that time, the Latin and
Greek Churches were discussing the possibility of formal re-
union. When they compared their faith, both the Catholic and
Orthodox Churches said that they had always believed there
were seven sacraments. When the Protestant Reformers
claimed that there were only two or three sacraments, the
Council of Trent reaffirmed the traditional number.[25]

Thus, for Catholics "marriage" is a sacrament while the
rite of religious profession for brothers and nuns is a public act
of consecration of oneself to God. Marriage, priesthood, forgiveness of sin, and healing all serve the centrality of the
eucharistic mystery as the supreme sacrifice of praise which
Christ offers to the Father in his body on earth. By contrast, a
rite of Christian burial or a rite of profession of vows as a
religious is secondary to the very constitution of the Church.
Such rites witness to faith and promote holiness of life.

Is the Catholic use of sacramentals like relics or blessed candles rooted in the New Testament?

Yes. Luke mentions the use of sacramentals by Paul's local church in Ephesus. "When handkerchiefs or cloths which had touched [Paul's] skin were applied to the sick, their diseases were cured and evil spirits departed from them" (Acts 19:12).

How is the Catholic belief in the bodily assumption of the Virgin Mary into heaven rooted in Paul's concept of the Church as Christ's body on earth?

Catholic faith knows Mary to be "the woman" totally transformed by Christ's grace and thus the quintessence of the Church. The Book of Revelation speaks of the Church as "a woman clothed with the sun, with the moon under her feet, and on her head a crown of twelve stars" (Rev 12:2; cf. Jn 2:4; 20:26–27). Because the Immaculate Virgin Mary is the only member of the body ever greeted by God as "full of grace" (Lk 1:28), the Catholic Church believes that the grace of Christ transformed not only Mary's conception so that she was always free from original sin, but also her death. Christ transformed her experience of dying into a bodily assumption into heaven. Pope Pius XII solemnly defined this in 1950, after explaining how this dogma has been believed since the New Testament period and how he had been requested by almost all the bishops from all over the world to solemnly define it.[26]

In Mary's bodily assumption we contemplate the effects of Christ's return on both our own future bodily resurrection from the dead and the Church's ultimate victory over the satanic forces of history: lying, hatred, religious, economic and political persecution of the just. The physical reality of the victory of Christ's grace in Mary's body reminds us that the mission of the Church is to *enflesh* the glory of its Lord. Beholding her glorified body with the eyes of faith, we proclaim her "star of evangelization" as she continues to give birth to the Word in the hearts of all who believe in her Son.

Conclusion

How can we live today by faith in the apostolic Church?

1. *Consider*. Think of every Christian you know as one of the "living stones" in the holy temple of God's Church (1 Pet 2:5). Each member, in spite of external faults, contains "the glorious heritage" which is ours in Christ (Eph 1:18). Refuse to be judgmental of clerical and lay leaders in the Church. Let Christ be their judge, so that you can be awed at the interior beauty of their godliness received in baptism (1 Cor 3:10—4:5; Rev 22:13-17).

2. *Invite*. Invite *unbelievers* to see how the world needs the Church of Christ as a guardian of freeing truth (2 Tim 1:13-14) and a living presence of Christ's peace (Heb 13, esp. v. 20). Invite those who *claim to believe in Jesus and not need his Church* to recognize the spiritual danger of worshiping privately "another Jesus" than the one preached by the Apostles (2 Cor 1:3-6). Invite *inactive Catholics and unchurched* friends to become active Roman Catholics. In this way you will share with them the "fullness of the ordinary means of salvation" (Christian faith, the Scriptures, the Eucharist, the other sacraments, the apostolic teaching authority) which you have been given by the Spirit of Jesus. Not to share what you have been given would jeopardize your own salvation;[27] however, to coerce another's freedom of religion would be unfaithful to the Spirit of Jesus (Mk 10:20-23).[28]

3. *Restore*. Work and pray for the restoration of unity in God's Church between Catholic,[29] Orthodox, and Protestant Christians (Jn 17:21). Emphasize the points of faith we have in common. Note the hierarchy of truths in order to focus on what is most important: (a) God as our Father, (b) Christ as our Redeemer, (c) the Holy Spirit in the Church, (d) Mary as mother of God and of all humanity.[30] Refuse to fight about differences (Col 3:5-17). Stay open to Christ's love and be Church.

Notes

1. Jean Daniélou and Henri Marrou, *The Christian Centuries,* Vol. I: *The First Six Hundred Years,* Paulist Press, N.Y., 1978, pp. 6–12.

2. Eusebius, *The History of the Church from Christ to Constantine,* trans. by G.A. Williamson, N.Y. University Press, 1966, Bk. II, 2, p. 72; II, 23, p. 100.

3. J. Daniélou, *The Christian Centuries,* p. 9.

4. *Ibid.,* pp. 9–10.

5. For a fuller discussion of the "brothers and sisters of Jesus," see Joseph A. Fitzmyer, S.J., *A Christological Catechism: New Testament Answers,* Paulist Press, 1982, pp. 71–73.

6. J. Daniélou, *The Christian Centuries,* p. 21.

7. *Ibid.,* p. 22.

8. *Ibid.,* p. 19.

9. *Ibid.,* p. 20.

10. *Ibid.,* p. 27.

11. *Ibid.,* p. 28.

12. Karl Hoeber, "Nero," in *The Catholic Encyclopedia,* Vol. 10, pp. 752–54.

13. Here I have followed G.B. Caird, "Chronology of the New Testament," in *Interpreter's Dictionary of the Bible,* Vol. A–D, pp. 603–07. For a fuller and fascinating treatment of the chronological problems in Paul, see Robert Jewett, *A Chronology of Paul's Life,* Fortress Press, Philadelphia, 1979.

14. Msgr. Ronald Knox, *Enthusiasm: A Chapter in the History of Religion with Special Reference to the XVII and XVIII Centuries,* Oxford Univ. Press, 1961, p. 7.

15. Viktor Warnach, "Church," in J. B. Bauer (ed.), *Sacramentum Verbi: An Encyclopedia of Biblical Theology,* Vol. 1, p. 105.

16. Hans Walter Wolff, *Anthropology of the Old Testament,* Fortress Press, Philadelphia, 1974, *passim.*

17. Eusebius, Bk. II, 6.

18. Jean Daniélou, "Millennium," in *Sacramentum Verbi,* Vol. 2, p. 583.

19. Eduard Shick, *The Revelation of St. John,* Crossroad, N.Y., 1981, Vol. 2, p. 88.

20. St. Augustine, *The City of God,* Bk. XX, Ch. 7.

21. For the Catholic saints (and others), see Bernard McGinn,

Visions of the End: Apocalyptic Traditions in the Middle Ages, Columbia University Press, 1979. For the historical source of the anti-Catholic, pro-Jewish Zionist, dispensational theology of modern American fundamentalism, see Eric W. Gritsch, *Born Againism: Perspectives on a Movement,* Fortress Press, 1982, pp. 13–27.

22. For all the technical qualifications of just what constitutes a general or ecumenical council, see Right Rev. Charles Joseph Hefele, D.D., *A History of the Christian Councils,* AMS Press, 1972. St. Robert Bellarmine numbered the ecumenical councils in the sixteenth century. Using his numbering, Vatican II was the twenty-second Ecumenical Council of the Catholic Church (1960's).

23. St. Ignatius of Antioch, "Letter to the Smyrnaeans," #8, in *The Fathers of the Church: A New Translation: The Apostolic Fathers,* p. 121.

24. *Ibid.,* "Letter to the Ephesians," I, 5, p. 89.

25. J.R. Quinn, "Sacraments, Theology of," in *New Catholic Encyclopedia,* Vol. 12, p. 811.

26. Pope Pius XII, "Munificentissimus Deus," in *The Christian Faith in the Doctrinal Documents of the Catholic Church,* #715, p. 200.

27. Pope Paul VI reminded Roman Catholics that by God's mercy others can be saved without hearing the testimony of our faith. He asked us to meditate on whether we can be saved if we refuse to proclaim it. Cf. *Apostolic Exhortation Evangelii Nuntiandi, On Evangelization in the Modern World,* Dec. 8, 1975, par. 80.

28. Zeal for the Gospel and the Church should never degenerate into coercing the sacred freedom of conscience which God has given all. See "Declaration on Religious Liberty," par. 4, in *The Documents of Vatican II.*

29. "Decree on Ecumenism," *ibid.,* par. 11.

30. The hierarchy of truths in Catholic faith is listed as the four principal mysteries of faith in *Sharing the Light of Faith: National Catechetical Directory for Catholics of the United States,* #974, pp. 47–62.

Index of Biblical Texts

Note: The boldface references are chapter citations. The page numbers follow in lightface.

219

1 Samuel 1–2 85; 1:3–4, 21 85; * 2:8 182; 2:13 81; 2:15–16 86; 2:18 85; 2:19 85; 2:28 86; * 6:14 86; * 7:9 86; * 8, 12 75; 8:10–18 50; * 10:1 76; 10:8 86, 190; * 11:15 76; * 13:2–14 76; 13:9 86; * 15:4–35 76; * 16:14–23 76; * 17:55–58 76; * 19–31 50; 19:18–24 54; * 22:18 82, 85; * 23:6–9 82; * 28:6 131; * 30:7 82

2 Samuel 1:1–6 51; 1:3 52; * 2:1–4 13; * 5:1–5 13, 51; 5:13–14 82; * 6 51; 6:14, 20 85; 6:17f 86; 6:17–18 86; * 7 52, 60; 7:1–2 52; 7:5–7 52; 7:11–14 53; 7:15 53; * 8:17 82; * 14:2 112; * 15:24–29 81; * 17:15 82; * 19:12 82; * 20:16 113; 20:25 82; * 24:25 86

1 Kings 1:7–2:22 83; * 2:26–27 83; 2:35 83; * 3:4 86; 3:12 113; 3:15 86; * 4 84; * 8:10–13 118; * 9:25 86; * 18:38 86

2 Kings 2:9–12 80; * 11:9f 84; * 12:1–20 51; 12:8f 84; 12:10 84; * 16 60; 16:7–18 61; 16:10f 84; 16:13 86; * 19:2 84; * 22 54; * 22:4 84; 22:8–23:25 63; * 23:4 84; 23:8 85; 23:9 86; 23:28–30 64; * 24:8–17 65; * 25:13–17 66; 25:18 84

Isaiah 1–39 60; * 6:3 59; * 7:1–9 60; 7:4 60; 7:6 60; 7:6–9 61; 7:10–13 61; 7:14–17 61; * 8:2 84; 8:15 62; 8:16–20 62; * 9 163; 9:6 137; * 20:1–5 59; * 29:18–19 170; * 35:5–6 170; * 37:2 84; * 40–55 66; 40–65 60; 40:3 169; 40:8 19; 40:25 75; 40:25–29 67; * 42:1–4 68; * 49:1–7 68; * 50:4–11 68; * 52:13–53:12 140; * 53:12 73; * 55:11 118; * 61:1 170

Jeremiah 5:1–3 64; 5:4–5 64; 5:12 64; * 7 65; 7:11–15 65; 11:15–16 65; * 13:15–17 65; * 19:1 84; * 26 65; 26:11 65; * 29:24–29 84; * 31:31–34 41; * 34:10 64; * 38:14–24 66; * 52:24 84

Ezekiel 2:63 131; * 14:14, 20 93; * 28:3 93; * 29:3 94; * 31 93; * 32:2 94; * 37 48, 67; * 39:25–29 67; * 40–48 67; * 44:15–31 83; * 46:2, 12 190

Hosea 2:8–18 59

Amos 3:9–11 58; * 5:18 58; * 7:12–13 58; 7:12–25 57

Haggai 2:20–23 80

Zechariah 4:11–14 80; * 6:11 80; * 9:9–10 80

Malachi 2:1–9 87; * 3:1 169; * 3:23–24 80, 170

Psalms 2:7 148, 190; * 8:56 184; * 14 110; 14:1 110; * 22 140, 190; * 34:8–10 110; * 37:34–40 113; * 47:8 162; * 69:34–37 68; * 78:60 65; * 89:28 54; * 107:27 113; * 110 140; 110:1–3 53; 110:3 148; * 111:10 108; * 137 66

Job 4 114; * 7:12 94; * 9:13 94; * 26:12 94; * 42:1 116

Proverbs 1:7 110; * 3:18 118; 3:34 213; * 7:4 118; * 8:22ff 200; 8:22–36 117; 8:35 118; * 14:18 115; * 21:13 186; * 22:4 115; 22:22–23 186; * 30:2–3 116; 30:19 117; * 31:10–31 113

Subject Index